'Cult Wars' in Historical Perspective

'Cult Wars' in Historical Perspective provides a broad characterization of the shifting religious contours over the past several decades. Offering an assessment of several important topics in the study of new religions, this book explores developments in well-known groups such as the Unification movement, The Family International (Children of God), the International Society for Krishna Consciousness (ISKCON), and the Church of Scientology. Bringing together both insiders and outsiders from various academic disciplines and personal perspectives, this book takes account of the ways in which the cult question is defined and addressed in different countries. It offers a vivid depiction of how the cult wars or cult controversies of the late twentieth and early twenty-first centuries first took shape; the transformation of deeply entrenched positions on cults and sects as at least some members of new groups, cult watchers, and academics entered into serious and sustained conversations about topics of mutual concern; the shifting foci and concerns of the general public, law enforcement and the courts, and academics in various countries; and the complex histories of individual groups in which many dramatic transformations have occurred despite their comparatively short life spans.

Eugene V. Gallagher is the Rosemary Park Professor of Religious Studies Emeritus at Connecticut College in New London, Connecticut. He is the author of *Reading and Writing Scripture in New Religious Movements*, *The New Religious Movements Experience in America*, coauthor of *Why Waco?: Cults and the Battle for Religious Freedom in America*, coeditor of the five-volume *Introduction to New and Alternative Religions in the United States*, and author of many essays on new religious movements and religions in the ancient Mediterranean world. He is a co-general editor of *Nova Religio: The Journal of New and Alternative Religions* and associate editor of *Teaching Theology and Religion*.

Inform Series on Minority Religions and Spiritual Movements

Series Editor: Eileen Barker, London School of Economics (UK)

Inform is an independent charity that collects and disseminates accurate, balanced and up-to-date information about minority religious and spiritual movements.

The *Routledge Inform Series* addresses themes related to new religions, many of which have been the topics of Inform seminars. The series editorial board consists of internationally renowned scholars in the field.

Books in the series will attract both an academic and interested general readership, particularly in the areas of Religious Studies, and the Sociology of Religion and Theology.

For a full list of titles in this series, please visit www.routledge.com/religion/series/AINFORM.

Spiritual and Visionary Communities
Out to Save the World
Edited by Timothy Miller

Prophecy in the New Millennium
When Prophecies Persist
Edited by Suzanne Newcombe and Sarah Harvey

State Responses to Minority Religions
Edited by David M. Kirkham

Revisionism and Diversification in New Religious Movements
Edited by Eileen Barker

Global Religious Movements Across Borders
Sacred Service
Edited by Stephen M. Curry and Helen Rose Ebaugh

Minority Religions and Fraud
In Good Faith
Edited by Amanda van Eck Duymaer van Twist

Legal Cases, New Religious Movements, and Minority Faiths
Edited by James T. Richardson and François Bellanger

The Public Face of African New Religious Movements in Diaspora
Imagining the Religious Other
Edited by Afe Adogame

Visioning New and Minority Religious
Projecting the Future
Edited by Eugene V. Gallagher

'Cult Wars' in Historical Perspective
New and Minority Religions
Edited by Eugene V. Gallagher

New Religious Movements and Counselling
Academic, Professional and Personal Perspectives
Edited by Hamish Cameron and Sarah Harvey

Minority Religions and Uncertainty
Edited by Kim Knott and Matthew Francis

Minority Religions in Europe and the Middle East
Mapping and Monitoring
Edited by George D. Chryssides

Fiction, Invention, and Hyper-reality
From Popular Culture to Religion
Edited by Carole M. Cusack and Pavol Kosnáč

'Cult Wars' in Historical Perspective

New and minority religions

Edited by Eugene V. Gallagher

LONDON AND NEW YORK

First published 2017
by Routledge
2 Park Square, Milton Park, Abingdon, Oxon OX14 4RN

and by Routledge
711 Third Avenue, New York, NY 10017

Routledge is an imprint of the Taylor & Francis Group, an informa business

© 2017 selection and editorial matter, Eugene V. Gallagher; individual chapters, the contributors

The right of Eugene V. Gallagher to be identified as the author of the editorial material, and of the authors for their individual chapters, has been asserted in accordance with sections 77 and 78 of the Copyright, Designs and Patents Act 1988.

All rights reserved. No part of this book may be reprinted or reproduced or utilized in any form or by any electronic, mechanical, or other means, now known or hereafter invented, including photocopying and recording, or in any information storage or retrieval system, without permission in writing from the publishers.

Trademark notice: Product or corporate names may be trademarks or registered trademarks, and are used only for identification and explanation without intent to infringe.

British Library Cataloguing in Publication Data
A catalogue record for this book is available from the British Library.

Library of Congress Cataloging-in-Publication Data
A catalog record for this title has been requested.

ISBN: 978-1-472-45812-4 (hbk)
ISBN: 978-1-315-57522-3 (ebk)

Typeset in Bembo
by Apex CoVantage, LLC

Printed in the United Kingdom
by Henry Ling Limited

Contents

Contributors — vii

1 Introduction: "Cult wars" in the twentieth and twenty-first centuries — 1
EUGENE V. GALLAGHER

PART 1
Watching and studying new religious movements — 7

2 From cult wars to constructive cooperation – well, sometimes — 9
EILEEN BARKER

3 CESNUR: a short history — 23
MASSIMO INTROVIGNE

4 Are the cult wars over? And if so, who won? — 33
TIMOTHY MILLER

5 From deviance to devotion: the evolution of NRM studies — 43
GEORGE D. CHRYSSIDES

6 Writing on and researching new religious movements: a view from the American academy — 55
BENJAMIN E. ZELLER

7 The law, the courts, religious freedom, and the evolving pattern of jurisprudence in Western societies — 69
JAMES T. RICHARDSON

8 Is an anti-cult movement emerging in Croatia? 81
   DINKA MARINOVIĆ JEROLIMOV AND ANKICA MARINOVIĆ

PART 2
Developments in specific groups 93

9 From the radical to the routine: the history and future
   of The Family International (Children of God) 95
   ABI FREEMAN

10 The Family International: the emergence of a virtual new
   religious community 108
   CLAIRE BOROWIK

11 The Unification movement: key issues in historical
   perspective 121
   RICHARD BARLOW

12 The changing perception of ISKCON: ancient faith or
   dangerous cult? 134
   ANUTTAMA DASA

13 From the Church of Scientology to the Freezone 152
   TERRIL PARK

14 Scientology: from controversy to global expansion and
   recognition 165
   ERIC ROUX

   Index 177

Contributors

Eileen Barker, PhD, OBE, FBA is the founder of INFORM, the chair of INFORM's board of governors, and an honorary research fellow for INFORM. She is Professor Emeritus at the London School of Economics. A sociologist of religion, she has been researching minority religions and the responses to which they give rise since the early 1970s. Her study of conversion to the Unification Church (UC) for her PhD led to an interest in a wide variety of movements, and she has personally studied, to a greater or lesser degree, more than 150 different groups. As the first-generation movements aged, she became interested in the changes, particularly the arrival of second-generation members and those who leave the movements. For the past twelve years, she's been interested in differences between "cult-watching" groups and the dynamics within and between these groups and the religions. She has more than 300 publications, translated into twenty-seven languages. She travels extensively for research purposes, particularly in North America, Europe, and Japan, and, since the collapse of the Berlin Wall, in Eastern Europe and, more recently, China. She was the first non-American to be elected president of the Society for the Scientific Study of Religion.

Richard Barlow embarked on a quest while studying at University College, Rhodesia. He joined the Unification Church (UC) in London in the early 1970s. For two years he was a state director in America before being married by Rev. and Mrs. Moon in 1975. After a further period in Rhodesia/Zimbabwe as a missionary, he gave lectures in the United Kingdom on the UC's teaching, the *Divine Principle*. He and his wife then became missionaries to Trinidad (his wife's home nation), but in 1990 they returned to the United Kingdom to seek treatment for a daughter with leukemia. Increasingly disillusioned with the UC, Richard read for a degree in the study of religions at London University's School of Oriental & African Studies, before ill health forced him to give up in his final year. One of Professor Barker's original interviewees, during his long association with INFORM he gave talks at some of its seminars.

Claire Borowik is a communication consultant and grant writer for nonprofits. She is the co-director of the nonprofit Web-based Worldwide Religious News Service, providing religious news to the academic and legal communities, and has participated in numerous initiatives promoting religious diversity. She is currently a public relations consultant for The Family International. Claire served as the director of international public affairs for The Family International from 2006 to 2010, and previously managed legal and media affairs for the organization in South America for four years, and in North America for ten years. She has lived for twenty years in several countries of Central and South America directing mission centers, nonprofits, and schools.

George D. Chryssides is an honorary research fellow in contemporary religion at the University of Birmingham (UK). He was head of religious studies at the University of Wolverhampton until 2008, and has authored numerous books and articles on new religious movements, including the *Historical Dictionary of Jehovah's Witnesses* (2008), the *Historical Dictionary of New Religious Movements* (2nd edn., 2012) (Scarecrow Press), and *Jehovah's Witnesses: Continuity and Change*, (Ashgate, 2016).

Anuttama Dasa is the minister of communications for the International Society for Krishna Consciousness (ISKCON), a monotheistic Vaishnava Hindu tradition. He has served as a member of ISKCON's international Governing Body Commission (GBC) since 1999, and was the GBC chairman in 2014. Dasa also serves as trustee of Bhaktivedanta College, ISKCON's first accredited college, located in Belgium, and on the board of Religions for Peace USA. He is the convener of the annual Vaishnava–Christian and Vaishnava–Muslim Dialogues held in Washington, DC, and the Vaishnava–Christian Dialogue in India. In the context of this book, he has attended the International Cultic Studies Association (ICSA) annual meeting for nearly twenty years, and spoken on multiple ICSA panels.

Abi Freeman was formerly a member and spokesperson of The Family International (TFI), previously known as the Children of God. She joined the movement in her teenage years, subsequently living in TFI communities in England, Iran, Turkey, the Indian subcontinent, and various parts of Europe, including Eastern Europe, until 2007. Her involvement with TFI now is limited to writing articles for TFI's evangelical magazine. Trained and qualified as a teacher/lecturer, she writes and edits faith-based books, and volunteers with various health-related charities.

Eugene V. Gallagher is the Rosemary Park Professor of Religious Studies Emeritus at Connecticut College in New London, Connecticut. He is the author of *Reading and Writing Scripture in New Religious Movements: New Bibles and New Revelations*, *The New Religious Movements Experience in America*, coauthor of *Why Waco: Cults and the Battle for Religious Freedom in America*, coeditor of the five-volume *Introduction to New and Alternative Religions in the United States*, and author of many essays on new religious movements and religions in the ancient Mediterranean world. He is a co-general editor of *Nova Religio: The Journal of New and Alternative Religions* and associate editor of *Teaching Theology and Religion*.

Massimo Introvigne teaches sociology of religious movements at the Pontifical Salesian University in Torino, Italy, and is managing director of the Center for Studies on New Religions (CESNUR). In 2011, he served as representative of the Organization for Security and Co-operation in Europe) (OSCE) for combating racism, xenophobia, and religious intolerance and discrimination. Since 2012, he has served as the chairperson of the Observatory of Religious Liberty established by the Italian Ministry of Foreign Affairs. Dr. Introvigne is the author of some sixty books and more than 100 articles and chapters in the field of new religious movements, contemporary religious pluralism, and modern Western esotericism.

Dinka Marinović Jerolimov, PhD, graduated in sociology and pedagogy at the Faculty of Philosophy, University of Zagreb, where she also received her MA and PhD in the field of sociology of religion. She is a scientific advisor at the Institute for Social Research in Zagreb and a principal investigator of the International Social Survey Programme (ISSP) for Croatia. Her main fields of interest are traditional church religiosity, new religious movements, and youth religiosity. She is the coauthor of, among other published works, the book *Vjerske zajednice u Hrvatskoj (Religious Communities in Croatia)* with Ankica Marinović and the book chapter "Mutual Relations between the State and Minority Religious Communities: The Case of International Society for Krishna Consciousness (ISKCON) in Croatia, Poland and Slovenia" in Dorota Hall and Rafal Smoczinsky (eds.) *New Religious Movements and Conflict in Selected Countries of Central Europe*.

Ankica Marinović, PhD, graduated in sociology and comparative literature at the Faculty of Philosophy, University of Zagreb. She received her MA and PhD at the same faculty in the field of sociology of religion. She is a scientific advisor at the Institute for Social Research in Zagreb and teaches undergraduate courses on comparative religion at the University of Zagreb. Her main fields of interest are sociology of religion, particularly unchurched religiosity and religious experience, and sociology of media.

Timothy Miller is a professor of religious studies at the University of Kansas. He studies new religious movements in the United States, with a special focus on groups in the past and present that practice communal living. Among his books are *The Quest for Utopia in Twentieth-Century America*, *The 60s Communes*, and the edited volume *America's Alternative Religions*. His *Encyclopedic Guide to American Intentional Communities* was published in 2012, and his edited volume in the Ashgate series, *Spiritual and Visionary Communities: Out to Save the World*, was published in 2013.

Terril Park first became interested in Scientology around 1965. He became a NED (New Era Dianetics) auditor, which is his highest level of technical training, around 1979. He joined the staff of the London organization toward the end of this training and stayed there for three years. In that time he went to Flag to do the OEC (Org Executive Course) and FEBC (Flag Executive Briefing Course), which are the highest administrative training courses Scientology offers. Around 1991 he left the Church of Scientology, never to return. But he remained a Scientologist. Some seven or eight years later he undertook further training in Scientology in the Freezone/Independent area. He has been one of the most active promoters of the practice of Scientology outside of the Church of Scientology for many years and has formed two Yahoo! forums, one of which is the largest Yahoo! Freezone forum still.

James T. Richardson, JD, PhD, is a professor of sociology and judicial studies at the University of Nevada, Reno, where he directs the Grant Sawyer Center for Justice Studies, as well as the judicial studies graduate degree program for trial judges. He has done research for decades on various aspects of new religious movements, and has focused in recent years on social control of minority religions, including new religious movements, using legal and judicial systems. His recent books include *Regulating Religion: Case Studies from around the Globe* (Kluwer, 2004) and *Saints under Siege: The Texas State Raid on the Fundamentalist Latter Day Saints* (New York University Press, 2011, with Stuart Wright).

Eric Roux has occupied many functions in the Church of Scientology in France for more than twenty years, including lecturing on Scientology at many levels. He is currently the president of the Union of the Churches of Scientology in France. He has worked on the topic of religious freedom for many years at national and international levels. He has been a speaker on this subject at many events, including at OSCE, Council of Europe, the U.S. Capitol, and so forth, and he works in various interfaith platforms. He is a member of the Steering Committee of the European Interreligious Forum for Religious Freedom.

Benjamin E. Zeller is an associate professor of religion at Lake Forest College (USA). He researches religious currents that are new or alternative, including new religions, religious engagement with science, and the quasi-religious relationship people have with food. He is author of *Prophets and Protons: New Religious Movements and Science in Late Twentieth-Century America* (New York University Press, 2010), *Heaven's Gate: America's UFO Religion* (New York University Press, 2014), coeditor of *Religion, Food, and Eating in North America* (Columbia University Press, 2014), and co-general editor of *Nova Religio: The Journal of Alternative and Emergent Religions*.

1 Introduction

"Cult wars" in the twentieth and twenty-first centuries

Eugene V. Gallagher

Since the late 1960s and early 1970s, "cults," "sects," or new religious movements have been a controversial part of the religious landscape in Europe, North America, and beyond. Members and supporters of innovative groups have eagerly promoted the new truths that they have discovered at the same time that parents of members, ex-members, and their allies have sounded alarms about the damage that such groups do to their participants. While academics sought both to contextualize the apparent rise in new religions in various ways and to test empirically some of the more dramatic claims made by and about new religions, they, too, were often drawn into broader public controversies, sometimes labeled "cult apologists" and accused of turning a blind eye to the harm that new or alternative religious groups can do to their members.

Taken together, the essays in this volume provide a broad characterization of the shifting contours of the "cult wars" over the past several decades, an assessment of the current state of the question about several important topics in the study of new religions, and accounts of developments in specific, well-known groups such as the Unification movement, The Family International (Children of God), the International Society for Krishna Consciousness (ISKCON), and the Church of Scientology. In keeping with INFORM's practice for its conferences and seminars, this volume brings together both "insiders" and "outsiders" from various academic disciplines and personal perspectives. It also takes careful account of how the "cult question" is defined and addressed in different countries, at different times, and in different contexts.

The essays in this volume, with the exception of Anuttama Dasa's contribution on the International Society for Krishna Consciousness, were first presented at a conference marking the twenty-fifth anniversary of INFORM. Often in response to the conversations that they generated, the authors have refined their presentations for publication. This volume devotes particular attention to "cult-watching" groups, research organizations such as CESNUR (based in Italy) and INFORM (UK), and the legal situation of new religious movements in various Western countries. It also features an essay on the nascent anti-cult movement in Croatia. Several contributions examine the history of the treatment of new religions in both academic and more popular publications, particularly in the United Kingdom and the United States.

The essays on individual groups focus on their development over time, including their responses to the departures of members and the formation of schismatic perspectives or groups. They clearly show the dynamism of new religious groups, in response both to internal factors such as theological creativity or leadership transitions and external factors such as pressure from watchdog groups or legal challenges. In some cases, they show the potential for dialogue between cult-watching groups and the groups that they watch in which each side can deepen and complicate its understanding of the other and in which groups on either side can be led to take a hard look at their own practices.

As a whole, the essays in this volume provide a vivid depiction of how the "cult wars" or "cult controversies" of the late twentieth and early twenty-first centuries first took shape, the transformation of deeply entrenched positions on "cults" and "sects" as at least some members of new groups, cult watchers, and academics entered into serious and sustained conversations about topics of mutual concern, the shifting foci and concerns of the general public, law enforcement and the courts, and academics in various countries, and the complex histories of individual groups in which many dramatic transformations have occurred despite their comparatively short life spans.

The first part of this volume focuses on both cult-watching groups and the scholarly study of new or alternative religions. Eileen Barker chronicles the development of concerns about "cults" in the West and the crystallization of the cult awareness movement in response to the perceived dangers that new, minority, or alternative groups pose to the status quo. Alongside that, she traces the history of the scholarly interest in new religions from the 1960s to the present. Barker then maps in two stages the interactions between cult awareness groups, new religious groups themselves, and the scholars who study both of those groups, noting both the persistence of some entrenched positions and the halting steps toward cooperation that have the potential of diminishing the vitriol involved in the cult wars, if not totally eradicating it.

Massimo Introvigne charts the development of the Center for the Study of New Religions (CESNUR) as a research organization focused on new and minority religions. He mixes an autobiographical account of his own developing interest in the field with an organizational history of CESNUR. As CESNUR grew from its humble beginnings in an initial conference with three presentations and about a dozen attendees, it was drawn into cult controversies in several countries and those associated with CESNUR were branded "cult apologists." Over time, CESNUR also broadened its focus to include more "mainstream" religions as well, thus at least implicitly making the case that new religions are religions just like their longer-lived and more established brethren.

Despite his distaste for the bellicose metaphor, Timothy Miller poses the question of whether we can identify a winner in the general controversies about "cults." Miller observes that conflicts about new religions are endemic to human history and should not be viewed as the product of a single historical moment. To buttress his case, he provides a brief overview of the opposition to new religious movements in the United States through the nineteenth and twentieth centuries, which provides a context for the emergence of the contemporary anti-cult movement in the 1970s. Miller, however, finds the conflicts over new religions to have died down somewhat in the United States today. Among the reasons he proposes are that increased immigration has rendered religions with an Eastern flavor less strikingly different, that the excesses of the anti-cult movement (e.g., in deprogramming) have undermined its credibility, that the focus on abusive behaviors has shifted to more mainstream religious groups such as the Roman Catholic Church, that, as Barker also notes, the anti-cult movement itself has modulated both its rhetoric and its practices, that new threats have come to dominate the public consciousness, and that at least some scholars have effected a rapprochement with the anti-cult activists. While acknowledging that conflicts about cults seem to have died down in some areas, Miller observes that in other areas they may be heating up. Thus, he concludes, there is still work to do to ensure religious freedom for new and minority religions.

George Chryssides focuses on the academic study of new religions, beginning in the late eighteenth and early nineteenth centuries. He notes that until after the Second World War new religious movements were mostly treated as dangerous heresies and sometimes as simply nonsensical. In the postwar period, however, a number of substantial and influential studies began to set the study of new religions on much firmer academic ground. Chryssides studies important themes like the failure of prophecy and the process of conversion and treatments of individual groups such as the Unification Church, the group that eventually became known as Heaven's Gate, and the Jehovah's Witnesses. Chryssides also notes a change in the literature written against new religions in which theological judgments played a less significant role and the focus shifted to coercion and even "brainwashing." Chryssides identifies several trends in the contemporary study of new religions, including the diversification of methodological perspectives beyond the sociological and the contributions from scholarly insiders from new religious groups. Chryssides concludes by pointing to areas of research that need further attention, such as the influence of new religions on the arts in general, something that has recently been a focus of interest for CESNUR, and what he calls "old new religions," such as the Christadelphians and the Jehovah's Witnesses.

Benjamin Zeller also examines the contemporary scholarship on new religions, focusing on the shifting locations of new religions studies in colleges and universities in the United States. He notes how the study of new religions has only a precarious foothold in PhD-granting programs, with most of the prominent scholars of new religions in the United States not holding positions in graduate programs. Like Chryssides, Zeller notes the increasing methodological diversity as the study of new religions has moved away from being dominated by sociologists and has been taken up by a diverse array of scholars within the interdisciplinary field of religious studies, including historians of American religions and historians of religions. Zeller also chronicles the institutionalization of the study of new religions in such forms as a successful program unit that offers multiple sections of papers at the annual meeting of the American Academy of Religion and the journal *Nova Religio*, which appears quarterly and is devoted to the study of new, alternative, and emergent religions.

James Richardson provides an overview of significant recent cases concerning new religious movements in both Europe and the United States. He emphasizes the pronounced differences in the treatment of religious freedom from one country to another in Europe and notes the variability among the states formerly dominated by the Soviet Union. When he turns to the United States, Richardson focuses on how since the early 1990s, the legal tide has decisively turned against admitting the brainwashing thesis in the courts. Richardson also maps the recent legal and legislative moves concerning religious freedom in the United States. In conclusion, Richardson suggests that there is an identifiable pattern of increasing tolerance in both Europe and the United States.

Of course, there are also counter-currents to the picture that Richardson sketches. Dinka Marinović Jerolimov and Ankica Marinović show how anticult activities are increasing in Croatia at the same time that they are decreasing in other countries. Their contribution underlines how "cult wars" are decisively shaped by local contexts, even though they are not isolated from broader developments elsewhere.

Contributions to the second part of this book focus on the histories of individual groups or movements. Both Abi Freeman and Claire Borowik focus on The Family International, formerly known as the Children of God, and both address the dramatic consequences for the group of the 2010 "Reboot" which dramatically altered the terms of membership and did away with communal living, and whose continuing effects are still being felt in The Family. Drawing on her familiarity with members, Freeman provides a composite account of the challenges that the Reboot has posed to long-term members. Despite those difficulties, she does not see The Family returning to its communal roots any time in the near future. Borowik's essay takes more account of The Family's ongoing interactions with its opponents as an element of the context for the Reboot. She agrees that the move toward theological rapprochement with mainstream Protestantism and the abandonment of communal living make it difficult to determine just what The Family International constitutes today.

Richard Barlow's presentation at the INFORM conference drew on his years as a member of the Unification Church and his continuing familiarity with the movement after he left it. Sadly, he died before he could put the finishing touches on his essay. Professor Eileen Barker graciously worked with his wife and family to bring the essay into its current form. Barlow focuses on how, since Rev. Moon's death in 2012, information about his life, particularly his sexual adventures outside of marriage, has become public. Although he notes that such practices have deep roots in Korean shamanism, Barlow observes that such revelations about Moon undermine the image he cultivated of himself as the True Parent and moral exemplar. As Barlow notes, the tarnishing of Rev.

Moon's reputation in some quarters is directly related to the ongoing crisis of leadership within the Unification movement.

Anuttama Dasa writes from the perspective of a continuing member of the International Society for Krishna Consciousness (ISKCON). In addition to reviewing the status of ISKCON as a new religious movement with deep roots in Hindu history, he provides a vivid account of efforts to open conversations with dedicated opponents of his movement. Anuttama Dasa shows how he has both learned several things from anti-cult activists and attempted to change their minds about what he sees as misconceptions about ISKCON.

This volume closes with two essays on Scientology. Perhaps no new religious movement has been as prominent in the recent "cult wars," in multiple countries, as the Church of Scientology. Like other contributors to this section of this book, Terril Park focuses on the leadership transition in the Church of Scientology, specifically the accession to power of David Miscavige. Park focuses on former members of the Church of Scientology who have become convinced that Miscavige has led the Church away from the true teachings of its founder and "Source," L. Ron Hubbard. Many of them have not wanted to give up on the practice of Scientology as they know it and have migrated to what has become known as the "Freezone," where a variety of individuals strive to implement the fundamental teachings of Hubbard independent from the organizational structure of the Church of Scientology. Eric Roux takes a very different approach. From his perspective, the Church of Scientology has not only survived but has prospered, despite an often hostile environment. He sees the October 1993 recognition by the Internal Revenue Service of the United States that the Church of Scientology has tax-exempt status as a religion as a turning point in the Church's history. Roux cites David Miscavige's statement soon after the IRS decision that "the war is over" as signaling a period in which the Church of Scientology could turn all its energies to providing individuals all over the world with Scientology's spiritual technology. In his view, the Church of Scientology has come out of the "cult wars" a stronger and more vigorous organization, dedicated more fully and successfully than ever to the dissemination of L. Ron Hubbard's original teachings.

The contrasts between the final two contributions to this volume drive home again some of the key insights into the contemporary "cult wars" that this volume provides. Perspectives on individual groups are thoroughly shaped by personal commitments and local contexts. One person's thriving religious group can be another's erring organization that has completely lost its way. Generalized social concern about particular groups can attain a fever pitch in one context only to burn itself out there and flare up in another context. From that vantage point, despite what some of the contributors see as a general tendency toward greater recognition of religious freedom for new and minority religions, it seems that as long as there are religious groups that challenge the status quo in a given context, there will be those who oppose them even to the point of denying their right to exist. If that is the case, then the cult wars may very well be with us for quite some time.

Part 1
Watching and studying new religious movements

2 From cult wars to constructive cooperation – well, sometimes

Eileen Barker

No two people see a social phenomenon in the same way, and few are likely to evaluate it in the same way. However, systematic differences exist between individuals and these can, to some extent, account for different perceptions and different evaluations. Certain groups with certain interests are likely to share certain images that differ significantly from the images constructed by other groups with other interests. Thus it is that members of 'cults', 'sects' or new religious movements (NRMs) construct images of themselves and of the world that differ significantly from the images constructed of them, on one hand, by their opponents and, on the other hand, by the scholars who study them.

Such perceptual diversity is but one reason why, if one wants to understand a particular NRM, it is essential to look not merely at the movement, but also at the wider context within which it operates – that is, to attempt an understanding of the different sections of society that affect and are affected by the movement, and of the dynamics between the different players.

In this chapter the main, though not exclusive, focus will be on post–World War II NRMs in the West. Several, such as the Church of Scientology and the Unification Church, were founded in the 1950s or earlier, but most did not become visible to the general public until the late 1960s or early 1970s. It was then too that the other actors with which this chapter is concerned emerged as visible entities in the so-called cult scene.

Cult scene participants

Numerous individuals participate either directly or indirectly in any social phenomenon, and, so far as the cult scene is concerned, one could include a vast array of individuals and institutions. To varying degrees, the media, the social services, government policy-makers, civil servants, the police, lawyers, medical professionals, counsellors, traditional religions, relatives and friends of members, former members and other members of the general public have all been involved in one way or another. Here, however, I shall concentrate primarily on three categories: the movements themselves; the cult-awareness movement (CAM), which has frequently, and somewhat derogatorily, been termed the anti-cult movement (ACM); and scholars of religion.

The cults, sects or new religious movements (NRMs)

Many debates have arisen over definitions of the terms involved in the cult scene. Scholars have used the technical and non-judgemental concepts of 'cult' and 'sect' in opposition to 'church' or 'denomination' as 'ideal types' for comparative purposes (McGuire 2002), but by the early 1970s, 'cult' and 'sect' had acquired such pejorative overtones in popular parlance that scholars of religion preferred to use the more neutral label 'new religious movement' or, more simply, 'NRM'. This too has had its problems, but the term NRM will be used in this chapter to refer to contemporary religious movements which consist predominantly of a first-generation membership (Barker 2004).

By the end of the 1970s hundreds, if not thousands of NRMs had mushroomed throughout the West. Although the enormous range of beliefs and practices makes generalisations about the movements well-nigh impossible, they tended to share some characteristics, such as disproportionately attracting youth in their early twenties from the white middle classes; having founders who wielded charismatic authority over their followers; and, especially when they fell into Wallis's (1984) 'word-rejecting' category, drawing clear boundaries between themselves and the rest of society, not infrequently severing ties with relatives and erstwhile friends. Such characteristics, together with the fact that the movements were offering alternative beliefs and lifestyles to those the rest of society espoused, meant that they were liable to engender suspicion, fear and distrust. Furthermore, alarming stories started to hit the headlines.

One early atrocity was the murder of the pregnant Sharon Tate and others by the Manson Family in 1969; another was the kidnapping of Patty Hearst by the Symbionese Liberation Army in 1974, with a widely publicised photograph of her holding a gun during a bank raid. Then, in 1978, the world was horrified by reports of the suicides and murders of more than 900 members (including more than 200 children) of Jim Jones's Peoples Temple in the Guyana jungle (Kilduff and Javers 1978; Moore 2006).

Concerns for the NRMs from around the 1970s

From their early days, an overriding concern for NRMs was simply survival, and they felt their existence was threatened in several ways. The media, eager to get and keep readers, listeners or viewers, were always on the lookout for novel and sensational stories. One of the chief sources of such stories was the cult-awareness movement (CAM).

A persistent source of frustration for the movements was the use of labels such as 'destructive cult' applied to any NRM, with an indiscriminate generalising of the sins of the few visited upon them all, accompanied, after 1978, by frequent references to Jonestown. Being labelled a cult or sect might mean that members became unemployable, that their children were not accepted in schools, they could not rent places for worship and/or they found themselves in various other ways ostracised and discriminated against by society (Lheureux et al. 2000).

The NRMs also faced frequent difficulties in obtaining official recognition. Countries requiring registration for religions usually employ such criteria as a minimum number of national members and a minimum period of existence in the country, both of which could militate against a new religion. In some societies, becoming registered (or, in Britain, gaining charitable status) has been a method of obtaining certain financial privileges, but in other societies not being legally recognised can mean that a movement is denied the possibility of, for example, acquiring property, or even being allowed to exist.

So far as the law is concerned, some NRMs have felt that they have had to be aggressively litigious any time they have been attacked or, in their eyes, treated unfairly. An aphorism found in numerous Scientology publications, including a plaque at the movement's headquarters at Saint Hill, proclaims:

The price of freedom: Constant alertness, constant willingness to fight back. There is no other price.

NRMs have had to defend themselves in financially crippling court cases. In the early 1980s, in the *Robin George v. ISKCON* case, a jury awarded a young woman who had been 'rescued' from the International Society for Krishna Consciousness $32 million in a California court (Bromley and Shinn 1989). Although after seventeen years of appeals, the amount was greatly reduced, the drawn-out legal battles severely drained ISKCON's resources. The Robin George case involved claims for damages for false imprisonment, emotional distress, libel and invasion of privacy, but NRMs have faced or instituted trials that have covered numerous other issues, including apostasy; bigamy; blasphemy; blood transfusions; breaking up families; child abuse (physical, emotional, sexual); child custody; clothing; confiscation/restitution of property; conscientious objection; conservatorship; copyright violations; drugs; education; employment law; extortion; extremist literature; faith healing/alternative medicine; fraudulent sales; free speech; kidnapping/imprisonment; murder; peddling licences; polygamy; proselytizing; rape; registration; robbery/theft; saluting a flag and/or swearing allegiance; same-sex marriage; slander; tax (avoidance/exemption); terrorism; vehicle lights; violence; zoning violations – and more.

A further issue about which NRMs have frequently protested has been 'apostates bearing false witness'. This, they complain, has been particularly the case when former members have undergone deprogramming or exit counselling by the CAM (see later) and have been taught what trials they were subjected to whilst they were in the movement. Another galling concern for the NRMs is how they feel they have been misinterpreted. Not only are they accused of believing and doing things that they insist they do not believe or do, but when it is acknowledged that they have performed actions or proclaimed beliefs that would normally be recognised as 'good', these have been dismissed on the grounds that the movement was only doing or saying something good for public relations reasons.

The cult-awareness movement (CAM)

Just as NRMs have existed throughout history and throughout the world, individuals and organisations have always opposed them. Frequently such individuals and organisations have been representative of older religious groups complaining about the heretical beliefs NRMs hold. In the 1970s, however, much of the opposition was more concerned with what the movements purportedly *did* than with what they believed (Barker 2002).

Parents who had 'lost' their offspring to an NRM and did not know where they were or how to make contact were understandably frightened about what had happened to their (usually adult) children. But those who were still in touch were also bewildered and disturbed by the changes they observed in their sons' or daughters' behaviour.

In an attempt to understand what seemed to be the adoption of apparently incredible beliefs and inexplicable behaviour of young people who were prepared to sacrifice their families, careers, worldly goods and material comfort and, possibly, take part in an arranged marriage to a stranger who might not even speak the same language, there seemed only one possible explanation: that the convert had been subjected to some kind of irresistible mind control. Such an explanation could absolve from blame not only the convert, but also relatives, many of whom were desperately wondering where they might have gone wrong.

The post-World War II CAM can be traced to the early 1970s, when a group of concerned relatives formed an organisation called The Parents' Committee to Free Our Children from the Children of God (FREECOG), one of whose founders, Ted Patrick, introduced the practice of 'deprogramming' – that is, (illegally) kidnapping converts and holding them against their will until they managed either to escape or to convince their captors they had renounced their faith (Patrick 1976).

It was not long before a number of other groups emerged throughout the West with the aims of warning society in general, and potential recruits in particular, about the dangers of what they commonly referred to as 'destructive cults', and rescuing the 'victims', who, it was widely believed, were incapable of leaving of their own accord. The metaphor of brainwashing, justified by studies of prisoners of war (Lifton 1961; Schein 1956), proved a powerful tool in the hands of a growing number of deprogrammers who would tell anxious parents that their only hope of 'rescuing' their children was to kidnap them and hold them in a secure environment until they could be restored to their 'real, pre-cult selves'.

FREECOG and several other groups eventually merged into the Cult Awareness Network (CAN). Among other groups, one of the most influential was the American Family Foundation (AFF), whose membership overlapped with that of CAN, but who did not advocate deprogramming (Giambalvo et al. 2013). In England, a parents' support group, Family Action Information Rescue (FAIR), was founded in 1976; in continental Europe some governments and some traditional religions became more closely involved in anti-cult organisations (Beckford 1985). The Danish Dialogue Centre was founded in 1973 (Rothstein 2004) and, before long, had spawned several independent Centres in different parts of Europe. In France various local groups were co-ordinated in 1974 by the Union Nationale des Associations de Défense des Familles et de l'Individu (UNADFI). In West Germany, several groupings came under the umbrella organisation Aktion für Geistige und Psychische Freiheit (AGPF) in 1977. Further groups were formed in Belgium, Italy, Spain and Sweden, and frequent networking took place with yet more groups that arose further afield in, for example, Argentina, Australia, China, Czechoslovakia, Hungary, Israel, Japan, Poland and Russia (Richardson 2004; Shupe and Bromley 1994).

Issues for the CAM

The primary issues for the early CAM concerned the fate of converts and the breaking up of families. Soon it was collecting an ever-increasing list of concerns about the movements: stories emerged about exploitatively long hours of drudgery; about poor diet, unhygienic conditions and psychological abuse giving rise to physical and mental illnesses that received inappropriate, scant or no medical attention; about corrupt financial and political dealings; about leaders living in the lap of luxury while their followers lived in abject poverty; and about the ever-present fear of suicides, murders and other criminal activities. Then, with a second generation being born into the movements, came disturbing reports of physical, emotional and sexual child abuse.

The scholars of religion

Studies by scholars of religion of post-war movements in the West initially focussed to a large extent on the 'counter-culture' that was first visible in California, but spread across the Atlantic to parts of Europe in the 1960s and 1970s (Glock and Bellah 1976; Roszak 1970; Wuthnow 1976). Bryan Wilson's groundbreaking work on nineteenth-century sects (1961; 1970) inspired a number of his students and others to investigate contemporary movements (Wilson 1967). Early studies of NRMs included Lofland (1966) on the Unification Church, Needleman (1970) on movements of Eastern origin, Judah (1974) on ISKCON and Wallis (1976) on Scientology.

The scholars of religion whose work focussed on NRMs from around the 1970s were frequently sociologists, but others came from religious studies, theology, history, anthropology and social psychology, and a few from apparently unrelated disciplines such as medicine, politics and law. Among their number were Dick Anthony, James Beckford, David Bromley, Marc Galanter, Gordon Melton, James Richardson, Tom Robbins, Anson Shupe and myself. These scholars tended to use qualitative rather than quantitative methods, most of them visiting centres and conducting in-depth interviews with representatives of the NRMs; some stayed for varying periods with one or other movement.

Issues for the scholars

At the most general level, scholars of religion are interested in asking questions about who believes what, under what circumstances, with what consequences, and how this varies according to time and place. From the mid-1970s, however, some of those studying NRMs were expressing concern about human rights violations with, in particular, the growth of illegal deprogramming, and the occasional hospitalisation of converts on such grounds as 'delusion' – even when most doctors were unable to find anything clinically the matter with the 'patients' (Coleman 1985; Robbins and Anthony 1982). Several began to wonder how they might correct the ignorance and misinformation (emanating from the movements, their opponents and the media), which, some felt, could lead to inappropriate responses that exacerbated the situation.

Such concerns resulted in a few scholars becoming more proactive in disseminating the images they were constructing of the NRMs. Some found themselves mediating between converts and their parents, trying to explain to each why the other 'side' was thinking or behaving as it was. Several were interviewed on radio or television or wrote articles for popular magazines or newspapers. Some became expert witnesses, appearing in courts of law, giving evidence in child custody cases, or preparing reports for official bodies such as the government, the police or the social services.

A small number of scholars went on to found organisations that have been termed research-oriented groups (ROGs), devoted to disseminating information about minority religions that is as reliable and up to date as possible (Barker 2002). As early as 1967, Gordon Melton had founded the Institute for the Study of American Religion (ISAR), which built up one of the world's largest collections of books, articles and other manuscripts related to minority religions.[1] With the 'cult controversies' at their height, I myself established INFORM (the Information Network Focusing on Religious Movements) with the support of the British government and mainstream churches in January 1988.[2] Later that same year, Massimo Introvigne inaugurated the Center for Studies on Religious Movements (CESNUR) in Italy.[3] Several other ROGs have since been launched around the world in Canada, Denmark, Germany, Hungary, Japan, Lithuania, Poland, Slovakia, Sweden and Switzerland. These differ from each other in many ways, but they share the common goal of trying to provide information about the NRMs that is as balanced and objective as possible, based on the methods of the social sciences (Barker 1995).

The cult wars: stage one

The dynamics of the relationships between NRMs, the CAM and scholars between the 1970s and early 1990s might be caricatured along the following lines.

First the NRMs protested against society

NRMS as protest movements have been a regular occurrence throughout history. Following the Second World War, the antinuclear campaigns of the 1950s were among the first organised protest movements in the West. Some of these morphed into the 1960s' counter-culture and then the new age or human potential movements. Other arrivals on the scene were more community-based, world-rejecting movements (Wallis 1984) such as the early Unification Church, ISKCON and the Children of God. In one way or another, all these movements were offering something that significant numbers of (mostly) middle-class youth felt, or were encouraged to feel, was missing from and/or wrong with society.

Then the CAM protested against the NRMs

The initial concerns of converts' relatives through fear of the unknown and/or the incomprehensible became magnified as tales of atrocities hit the headlines. An increasing acceptance of the brainwashing hypothesis led to the spread of deprogramming which, NRMs commonly alleged, could involve rape and being held at gunpoint. This in turn led several NRMs to advise or order members not to visit relatives; parental requests to come home for Christmas or to visit a terminally ill grandmother were interpreted, sometimes quite accurately, as ploys to kidnap the member. Such reactions, especially when unjustified, resulted in reinforcing parents' fear and their susceptibility to deprogrammers' claims that drastic measures really were necessary (Barker 1983).

At a more public level, the flames of protest were fanned by the horror stories in the media adding fuel to CAM narratives of dangerous cults. Claims of brainwashing were presented in law courts throughout the world (Richardson 1996). Negative mainstream reactions were exacerbated by lumping all NRMs together under the single derogatory label of 'cult' (Subhananda 1978). Pressure from CAMs resulted in a number of governments commissioning reports on the movements, and while some of these stated that existing legislation provided sufficient protection from possible abuses, others insisted special laws ought to be introduced to control (or ban) the movements (Richardson 2006). Reports ordered by the French and Belgian governments contained lists of movements,[4] and, although these were accorded no official status, several NRMs found themselves discriminated against merely because they were 'on the list' (Lheureux 2000).

Then scholars protested against the CAM

The dissemination of what scholars considered methodologically flawed and inaccurate depictions of the NRMs by the CAM resulted in both individual scholars and professional organisations attempting to counter the CAM's near monopoly as a public information resource. This held true particularly with attempts to counter the widely accepted 'brainwashing thesis', which was leading to restrictions on religious freedoms through deprogramming, conservatorship cases in the courts and discriminatory laws focussing on NRMs. Academic studies revealed a widespread resistance to the movements' proselytising efforts and the high turnover rates among the membership, thereby severely undermining claims about NRMs' 'irresistible and irreversible' techniques (Barker 1984; Galanter 1989; Wright 1987). Scholars, standing as expert witnesses, challenged CAM experts and succeeded in persuading courts in the United States that 'brainwashing' was not a scientific term − an achievement that resulted in members of the CAM suing scholars for hundreds of thousands of dollars for loss of earnings (Anthony 1990; Richardson 1998: 7, 14). Scholars also became more proactive in supplying the media with alternative accounts of the NRMs, and a few were instrumental, to at least some degree, in influencing governmental policies (Kirkham 2013; Lindholm et al. 2004; Richardson 2004).

Then the CAM protested against the scholars

Members of the CAM reacted, in some cases quite fiercely, to the scholars' appearance on the cult scene. The very fact that the scholars, as part of their research, had direct contact with NRMs led members of the CAM to accuse the scholars of being deceived by and/or controlled by the movements. Condemned as 'cult apologists', scholars were accused on the one hand of being too 'close' to the NRMs and on the other hand of being too remote and not understanding the families' anguish. A further cause for suspicion arose when scholars accepted invitations to conferences organised by NRMs (Horowitz 1978). The media were fed stories that were frequently false and/or just plain silly; politicians were fed stories that occasionally resulted in their making pronouncements about scholars, who would have sued for libel were it not for 'parliamentary privilege'.

Then there were further moral panics involving 'deviance amplification'

In his study of the furore surrounding Mods and Rockers in the 1960s, the sociologist Stanley Cohen (1972) applied the concepts of 'moral panics' and 'deviance amplification' to processes where a deviant action reported in the media provoked an overreaction, which in turn provoked an even more deviant response, giving the other side 'permission' to react more precipitously, thereby inciting an ever-increasing spiral of deviance.

A similar pattern could be detected in the cult wars between the 1970s and mid-1990s, overreactions provoking what the other actors considered unacceptable responses. Progressively vitriolic allegations were made of ever-more unacceptable practices on all sides; deprogrammings mushroomed; court cases proliferated; and the media constantly reminded an increasingly concerned population of the dangers cults posed to both individuals and society.

This situation arguably culminated in the FBI's storming the Branch Davidians' compound at Waco, Texas, on 19 April 1993, an action that resulted in the deaths of more than seventy Davidians including twenty-three children (Noesner 2010; Stewart 2003). A further response, exactly two years later, was the bombing by Timothy McVeigh of a U.S. government office complex in Oklahoma City, claiming 168 lives, including nineteen children (Wright 2007).

But nothing ever stays the same.

The cult wars: stage two

Some NRMs denominationalised

It is not uncommon for the early enthusiasms and extremism of the beliefs and practices of NRMs to become tempered with the passage of time, and for cults and sects (in the technical sense) to become more like denominations – that is, less in tension with the wider society (McGuire 2002; Niebuhr 1929).

Towards the end of the 1990s, many of the NRMs that had been giving rise to alarm since the early 1970s had changed quite radically. A second generation had meant scarce resources such as time and money had to be devoted to the children, leaving less time for proselytising; charismatic leaders had died and been replaced by a more predictable and accountable leadership; first-generation converts were no longer as zealous and, perhaps, naïve as they once had been, having matured and, then, started to age (Barker 2012).

Disillusionment over the apparent failure of expected 'specialness' in their children (Van Eck 2015), and millenarian and other prophecies (Harvey and Newcombe 2013) frequently resulted not only in disappointment but also in an increased pragmatism. Furthermore, as the second generation grew older, there was no guarantee that they would be attracted by their parents' beliefs or lifestyle. It is not uncommon for members of NRMs initially to try to control their offspring with (sometimes literally) the stick, but when too many children abscond, sometimes supplying the CAM with stories of abuse, movements are likely to start to offer the proverbial carrot, accommodating and adjusting to more 'normal' and socially acceptable ways. Estranged parents can become reconciled grandparents. And, rather than stressing how distinctive they are, NRM members may start to insist that they are 'just like everyone else'.

However, by no means all NRMs denominationalise (Wilson 1970); some give rise to more extreme schisms; and, of course, *new* NRMs are always emerging.

Some of the CAM denominationalised

Just as NRMs are in a constant state of flux, the CAM has undergone substantial changes since its origins. Originally consisting primarily of concerned relatives, its membership was soon embracing deprogrammers and then former members, some of whom would join its ranks as the culmination of their deprogramming experience. Later there was an influx of second-generation members. Over time, many of the CAM groups became more professionalised, with counsellors, mental health specialists, lawyers, some politicians and a few academics playing a significant role. Furthermore, several of the former members (both converts and second-generation adults) acquired professional qualifications as counsellors, psychologists and academic researchers. This diversity led the CAM to become an increasingly 'broad church', with the emphasis shifting from 'rescue' and lobbying towards information, education, support and counselling.[5]

Although court cases involving NRMs and the CAM continued, they became less frequent, especially in the United States. This was partly because the 'brainwashing' defence had been declared inadmissible, and partly because NRMs were winning a number of cases. One of the most notable cases occurred in 1996 when the Cult Awareness Network (CAN) was bankrupted in a suit involving a deprogramming, and Scientology bought its name and telephone number, thereby controlling the 'New CAN' (Shupe and Darnell 2006).

The changing legal situation contributed to the almost total abandonment of the practice of forcible deprogramming in the West,[6] but it had also become more widely acknowledged within CAM circles that, quite apart from human rights and ethical considerations, the practice could exacerbate rather than ameliorate a situation. With the development of more nuanced models of counselling, interventions took the form of 'voluntary exit counselling', followed by 'Thought Reform Counselling', which followed a strict ethical code (Giambalvo et al. 2013), and then some practitioners began to focus on family reconciliation rather than trying to remove members from their movements.

Some scholars denominationalised

Facing generally false accusations that they did not speak to former members, and being rebuffed when they had attempted to approach the CAM during the early stages of their studies, a number of scholars had begun to collaborate with each other in the construction of images of the CAM that were reminiscent of the images they accused the CAM of constructing of NRMs, lumping them all together and generalising without conducting first-hand empirical investigation into what was actually happening (Barker 1995).[7]

In 1998, with considerable trepidation, I wrote to the AFF asking whether I and one of the INFORM researchers could attend its annual conference in Philadelphia. To my surprise, I received a warm response, saying we would be welcome. Although several participants were openly hostile, the president and the executive director went out of their way to be friendly. As our mutual fears decreased and our curiosity increased we arranged that four of 'them' would meet with four of 'us', and just before the 2002 Seattle conference we spent a day discussing our differing perspectives. While we certainly did not agree on everything, both 'sides' came away with a greater respect and understanding of the 'other'.

The twenty-first century has seen a gradual increase in exchanges between scholars and sections of the CAM. Individuals and groups from both camps have collaborated on certain 'cases', spoken at each other's conferences, written articles and chapters in each other's literature, held joint workshops to which NRMs have been invited to discuss a particular issue, and even visited some of the movements together – events practically inconceivable twenty years previously.

It has not, of course, always been a smooth path towards mutual understanding and co-operation, and plenty of people in the CAM remain strongly opposed to having any contact with academics, let alone with NRMs. But there can be no doubt that the virulent antagonisms of the past have become significantly less noticeable. Overlaps and the complementarity of certain interests have been recognised, as have misunderstandings that have arisen through different questions being asked with different concepts: 'What are the dangers of harmful cults?' as opposed to 'What are new religions like?'

Then there was a waning of moral panics

With the changes in the attitudes and pronouncements of the NRMs, the CAM and the scholars became less extreme and oppositional, and as more reliable information became available to other sections of society, 'the fear of cults' gradually diminished across the wider social scene in much of the West. Following the Waco tragedy, FBI agents consulted with the American Academy of Religion and a number of individual scholars; the British government, Scotland Yard and mainstream religions turned to INFORM for information concerning minority religions. The media became less prone to printing unsubstantiated, exaggerated or sensational stories about NRMs.

Then, following 9/11 in 2001, came a dramatic shift in public concern, with extremist Islamic groups perceived as a far more serious threat than NRMs. Around the same time, widespread publicity surrounding the sexual child abuse perpetrated by priests of the Catholic and other traditional religions contributed to the realisation that it was not only new religions that indulged in such criminal practices. Furthermore, some NRM practices, such as vegetarianism or sexual freedom, formerly considered 'unnatural', deviant or dangerous became more widely accepted or even viewed in a positive light.

But, to repeat, nothing ever stays the same. New NRMs are continually being spawned, and as older NRMs denominationalise, it is not uncommon for members to believe their movement has accommodated too far and schisms emerge exhibiting many of the more fundamentalist characteristics of first-generation movements. A similar process has occurred when CAMs' members perceive them as having become too cosy with scholars and/or NRMS, and have broken away to form more militant anti-cult groups. And new scholars appearing on the scene will, no doubt, succeed in disagreeing with both NRMs and their opponents, thereby engendering yet more potential antagonisms in the future.

Nonetheless, one can perceive a move away from the cult wars to constructive cooperation – well, sometimes.

Notes

1 www.cesnur.org/2008/london_melton.doc
2 www.Inform.ac.uk
3 www.cesnur.org
4 http://cftf.com/french/Les_Sectes_en_France/cults.html; http://users.skynet.be/wihogora/r-sectes.htm
5 In 1994, with increasing public disapproval of forcible deprogramming, FAIR (Family, Action, Information, Rescue) changed its 'R' to Resource.
6 Involuntary deprogramming continues in Japan (Fautré 2011).
7 Among the few scholars to write about the CAM were Arweck (2004), Beckford (1985) and Shupe and Bromley (1980).

References

Anthony, Dick 1990. Religious movements and brainwashing litigation: Evaluating key testimony, in: Thomas Robbins (ed.) *In Gods We Trust: New Patterns of Religious Pluralism in America* (2nd edition). New Brunswick, NJ: Transaction, pp. 295–344.

Arweck, Elisabeth 2004. *New Religious Movements in the West*. London: Routledge.

Barker, Eileen 1983. With enemies like that . . . Some functions of deprogramming as an aid to sectarian membership, in: David G. Bromley and James T. Richardson (eds.) *The Brainwashing/Deprogramming Debate: Sociological, Psychological, Legal and Historical Perspectives*. New York: Edwin Mellen Press, pp. 329–44.

——— 1984. *The Making of a Moonie: Brainwashing or Choice?* Oxford: Basil Blackwell.

——— 1995. The scientific study of religion? You must be joking! *Journal for the Scientific Study of Religion* 34(3), 287–310.

——— 2002. Watching for violence: A comparative analysis of the roles of five cult-watching groups, in: David G. Bromley and J. Gordon Melton (eds.) *Cults, Religion and Violence*. Cambridge: Cambridge University Press, pp. 123–48.

——— 2004. What are we studying? A sociological case for keeping the 'Nova'. *Nova Religio* 8(1), 88–102.

——— 2012. Ageing in new religions: The varieties of later experiences. *Diskus: The Journal of the British Association for the Study of Religions* 12. www.basr.ac.uk/diskus/diskus12/Barker.pdf.

Beckford, James 1985. *Cult Controversies: The Societal Response to the New Religious Movements*. London: Tavistock.

Bromley, David and Larry Shinn 1989. *Krishna Consciousness in the West*. Lewisburg, PA: Bucknell University Press.

Cohen, Stanley 1972. *Folk Devils and Moral Panics: The Creation of the Mods and Rockers*. Oxford: Blackwell.

Coleman, Lee 1985. Using psychiatry to fight 'cults': Three case histories, in: Brock Kilbourne (ed.) *Scientific Research and New Religions: Divergent Perspectives*. San Francisco, CA: AAAS, Pacific Division, pp. 40–56.

Das, Subhananda 1978. *A Request to the Media: Please Don't Lump Us In*. Los Angeles, CA: International Society for Krishna Consciousness, Office of Public Affairs.

Fautré, Willy (ed.) 2011. *Japan: Abduction and Deprivation of Freedom for the Purpose of Religious De-conversion*. Brussels: Human Rights without Frontiers International.

Galanter, Marc 1989. *Cults: Faith, Healing, and Coercion*. New York, Oxford: Oxford University Press.

Giambalvo, Carol, Michael Kropveld and Michael Langone 2013. Changes in North American cult awareness organizations, in: Eileen Barker (ed.) *Revisionism and Diversification in New Religious Movements*. Farnham: Ashgate, pp. 227–45.

Glock, Charles and Robert Bellah (eds.) 1976. *The New Religious Consciousness*. Berkeley: University of California Press.

Harvey, Sarah and Suzanne Newcombe (eds.) 2013. *Prophecy in the New Millennium: When Prophecies Persist*. Aldershot: Ashgate.

Horowitz, Irving (ed.) 1978. *Science, Sin, and Scholarship: The Politics of Reverend Moon and the Unification Church*. London: MIT Press.

Judah, Stillson 1974. *Hare Krishna and the Counterculture*. New York: Wiley.

Kilduff, Marshall and Ron Javers 1978. *The Suicide Cult: The Inside Story of the Peoples Temple and the Massacre in Guyana*. New York: Bantam.

Kirkham, David (ed.) 2013. *State Responses to Minority Religions*. Aldershot: Ashgate.

Lheureux, N. L. et al. 2000. *Report on Discrimination against Spiritual and Therapeutical Minorities in France*. Paris: Coordination des Associations des Particuliers Pour la Liberté de Conscience.

Lifton, Robert J. 1961. *Thought Reform: A Psychiatric Study of 'Brainwashing' in China*. London: Gollancz.

Lindholm, Tore, Cole Durham and Bahia Tahzib-Lie (eds.) 2004. *Facilitating Freedom of Religion or Belief: A Deskbook*. Leiden: Brill.

Lofland, John 1966. *Doomsday Cult: A Study of Conversion, Proselytization, and Maintenance of Faith*. New York, London: Irvington.

McGuire, Meredith 2002. *Religion: The Social Context* (5th edition). Belmont, CA: Wadsworth.

Moore, Rebecca 2006. Peoples Temple: A typical cult?, in: Eugene V. Gallagher and W. Michael Ashcraft (eds.) *Introduction to New and Alternative Religions in America*. Westport, CT: Greenwood Press, pp. 113–34.

Needleman, Jacob 1970. *The New Religions*. Garden City, NY: Doubleday.

Niebuhr, Richard 1929. *The Social Sources of Denominationalism*. New York: Holt.

Noesner, Gary 2010. *Stalling for Time: My Life as an FBI Hostage Negotiator*. New York: Random House.

Patrick, Ted 1976. *Let Our Children Go*. New York: Ballantine.

Richardson, James T. 1996. 'Brainwashing' claims and minority religions outside the United States: Cultural diffusion of a questionable concept in the legal arena. *Brigham Young University Law Review* 4, 873–904.

——— 1998. The accidental expert. *Nova Religio* 1(2), 31–43.

——— 2006. Governmental reports on minority religions: An assessment and guidelines, in: Pauline Côté and T. Jeremy Gunn (eds.) *The New Religious Question: State Regulation or State Interference?* Brussels: Peter Lang, pp. 273–84.

——— (ed.) 2004. *Regulating Religion: Case Studies from around the Globe*. New York: Kluwer Academic/Plenum.

Robbins, Thomas and Dick Anthony 1982. Deprogramming, brainwashing and the medicalization of new religious movements. *Social Problems* 29(3), 283–97.

Roszak, Theodore 1970. *The Making of a Counter Culture: Reflections on the Technocratic Society and Its Youthful Opposition*. London: Faber and Faber.

Rothstein, Mikael 2004. Regulating new religion in Denmark, in: James T. Richardson (ed.) *Regulating Religion: Case Studies from around the Globe*. New York: Kluwer Academic/Plenum, pp. 229–31.

Schein, Edgar 1956. The Chinese indoctrination program for prisoners of war: A study of attempted 'brainwashing'. *Psychiatry* 19, 149–72.

Shupe, Anson and David Bromley 1980. *The New Vigilantes: Deprogrammers, Anti-cultists, and the New Religions*. Beverly Hills, CA: Sage Publications.

—— 2006. *Agents of Discord: Deprogramming, Pseudo-science, and the American Anti-cult Movement*. New Brunswick, NJ: Transaction.

—— (eds.) 1994. *Anti-cult Movements in Cross-cultural Perspective*. New York: Garland.

Stewart, David (ed.) 2003. *Waco: Ten Years After*. Georgetown, TX: Southwestern University.

van Eck Duymaer van Twist, Amanda 2015. *Perfect Children: Growing Up on the Religious Fringe*. New York: Oxford University Press.

Wallis, Roy 1976. *The Road to Total Freedom: A Sociological Analysis of Scientology*. London: Heinemann.

—— 1984. *The Elementary Forms of the New Religious Life*. London: Routledge and Kegan Paul.

Wilson, Bryan 1961. *Sects and Society: A Sociological Study of Three Religious Groups in Britain*. London: Heinemann.

—— 1970. *Religious Sects: A Sociological Study*. London: Weidenfeld and Nicholson.

—— (ed.) 1967. *Patterns of Sectarianism: Organisation and Ideology in Social and Religious Movements*. London: Heinemann.

Wright, Stuart 1987. *Leaving Cults: The Dynamics of Defection*. Washington, DC: Society for the Scientific Study of Religion.

—— 2007. *Patriots, Politics, and the Oklahoma City Bombing*. Cambridge: Cambridge University Press.

Wuthnow, Robert 1976. *The Consciousness Reformation*. Berkeley: University of California Press.

3 CESNUR

A short history

Massimo Introvigne

I am often asked when I first became interested in religious minorities, which in Italy means, for all practical purposes, any religion other than Catholicism. As far as I remember, I can date the prehistory of this interest to 1964, when a leading Italian publisher, Rizzoli, published an encyclopedia known as *The Great Religions of the World* (*Le grandi religioni del mondo* 1964). You could go to the nearest kiosk and buy weekly installments for a sum roughly similar to €0.50, then bind the installments in six richly decorated volumes. I decided I wanted to collect these installments – and still keep the volumes in my library today, with their bright red covers. Although I now realize that they included several mistakes, the photographs are still great to look at. I was, at that time, nine years old.

Why exactly should an otherwise normal boy of nine spare money to buy, in addition to his usual comics, the installments of *The Great Religions of the World*? I think I acquired an interest in "strange" religions from the travel accounts of my mother, an almost compulsive traveler who came back from exotic places, from Bali to Polynesia, with artifacts whose meaning often seemed to have something to do with religion. I also read novels by authors such as Emilio Salgari (1862–1911), a novelist who largely defined Italy's popular culture for several generations, and Rudyard Kipling (1865–1936). I had read all their novels dealing with India before I was ten. The age was perhaps an excuse for not realizing that they were not the best guides to Hinduism and other Eastern religions.

A later book I remember as very influential on me was a novel for teenagers by Luigi Ugolini (1891–1980), *The Island Nobody Found* (Ugolini 1950), which featured Haiti and the mysterious world of voodoo. I borrowed this book from my junior high school's library at age eleven, and only recently managed to find a copy for the CESNUR library. With surprise, in rereading it after more than forty years, I realized that the author's picture of voodoo as barbaric and dangerous was not intended at all to make it look fascinating. But the novel was well written, and I found voodoo quite interesting without seeing all the implications.

The second crucial event for seriously considering the study of religion was my attendance between 1970 and 1973 at an intellectually stimulating high school, the Social Institute (Istituto Sociale), the Jesuit high school of Turin. This was the post–Vatican II Roman Catholic Church, and Jesuits came in all shapes and doctrinal variations. In 1972, while in that high school, I joined Alleanza Cattolica, a conservative Catholic group I am still a member of. The presence in the same milieu of liberal Catholic organizations and Jesuits, including the future Cardinal Carlo Maria Martini (1927–2012), created a lively debate. It benefited both me and other pupils. Some of them eventually went on to become well-known Italian politicians.

Equally stimulating were, a few years later, another Jesuit institution, Rome's Gregorian University, where I earned my BA in philosophy in 1975, and the well-known Capranica College, often referred to as "the breeding ground of Catholic bishops." In fact, many of my friends there *did* become bishops, but the college was starting to open its doors to laymen wishing to stay there while studying at the Gregorian. The latter institution was not only about Catholicism: a Chinese Jesuit offered, and I attended, some of the finest courses on Chinese religions I ever came across.

My interests were not confined to religion. While at the Gregorian, taking advantage of the intricate interrelations between the Italian and Vatican academic systems, I had already enrolled in the law school of the University of Turin, where I became a Dr. Juris in 1979. My dissertation on American philosopher John Rawls (1922–2002) eventually became my first published book and the first book on Rawls published in a language other than English (Introvigne 1983). My mentor was Professor Enrico di Robilant (1924–2012), a colorful, larger-than-life character: a refined gentleman, a scion of an old Turin family, and a daredevil mountaineer. He was also a fine scholar of philosophy and sociology, who introduced me to the notion of the social construction of reality, including legal reality. At that time the University of Turin, as did most Italian universities, did not include a school of sociology. The basic principles of social science – including political science and law – were taught in a variety of other schools.

Rawls got me interested in the United States, and in the interaction between religion, politics, and society there. Following a family tradition, I spent my summers during high school and college traveling around the world and visiting, in addition to many states of the United States, Eastern Europe, the Middle East, India, and North Africa, getting again in touch – although of course not very deeply – with a number of different religions, as well as with Soviet state atheism.

Toward the end of my college years I came to an important conclusion, which was to prove crucial for my future life – and for CESNUR. I decided that the Italian academic system in the 1970s simply had no room for a career devoted to studying contemporary religions different from Roman Catholicism. I didn't want to give up the study of religions, but I also needed to make a living. I decided to become an attorney, devoting a substantial amount of time (roughly half) to religious studies, funding this interest from the income of what I hoped would be a decent legal career. This worked quite well, and in the next decade and beyond allowed me to donate to CESNUR whatever was necessary to make its ends meet. My final choice of intellectual property law as my preferred legal field offered the renewed opportunity of traveling around the world, and I often combined visits to clients of my legal practice and others with visits to religious groups and scholars in the same countries.

The only other folks interested in minority religions in Italy were Roman Catholic counter-cultists who dealt principally with the Jehovah's Witnesses, who had been phenomenally successful in Italy in the 1960s and 1970s. They were of course not called counter-cultists at that time. I myself introduced the distinction between a Christian counter-cult and a secular anti-cult movement in 1990. In 1993, I proposed this distinction to an international audience in an article I was asked to write by Danish Lutheran counter-cultist Johannes Aagaard (1928–2007) (Introvigne 1993).

I was an active Roman Catholic, and didn't have any initial trouble in cooperating with the counter-cultists. In fact, I was one of the founders in 1985 of what is still the largest Italian Catholic counter-cult organization, GRIS (acronym of Group for Research and Information on Sects, although the name was later changed to Group for Socio-religious Research and Information), and was among those who legally incorporated it in 1987. It soon came out, however, that the approach I intended to adopt in studying minority religions was different from what the counter-cultists wanted to do. I was taught in college that one has to let any group at first speak for itself. When I asked an old leader of the Catholic controversy against Jehovah's Witnesses, an otherwise kind and good man, how many active Witnesses he had interviewed, he responded none, neither did he intend to do this in the future. This was, to put it mildly, a serious methodological problem. When I noticed that something called the brainwashing theory, which I immediately disliked, was penetrating from the secular anti-cult into the Catholic counter-cult movement, I decided that I should look elsewhere for more congenial company.

A significant event was my discovery of the Mormon History Association (MHA), an international association devoted to the study of Mormonism, led by somewhat liberal Mormons and including several non-Mormons. I discovered that such an organization existed in 1986, by perusing journals in several Salt Lake City bookstores during a visit I made there in connection with my legal business. Happily, in 1987, the MHA was meeting, for the first time in its history, in Europe, in Oxford, and I decided to attend the conference. There, I met Jean-François Mayer, a Swiss historian of religions, and Michael W. Homer from Salt Lake City, who just as I did was dividing his time between working as an attorney and studying issues related both to Mormonism and other minority religions, particularly Spiritualism.

The Oxford conference was the start of long-lasting friendships and scholarly cooperations with both Mayer and Homer. I also met important figures of the Mormon history community such as Leonard J. Arrington (1917–1999), perhaps the most important Mormon historian of the twentieth century, whom I interviewed several times in the following years and who was very generous with his suggestions and encouragement. Just as I was interested in new religious movements, at least one new religious movement did take an interest in my first endeavors. The Unification Church invited me to some of its events (I always paid my travel and accommodation expenses, as I would keep doing in the future), and the information I gathered in the process resulted in my first small monographic book about an NRM, *Reverend Moon and the Unification Church* (Introvigne 1987).

Mayer had experienced similar problems in Switzerland in trying to cooperate with the Christian counter-cult community, and shared a dislike of brainwashing theories and anti-cultism. We decided we needed a new organization of our own, and CESNUR, the Center for Studies on New Religions, was born in 1988. I approached a friendly Italian bishop, Monsignor Giuseppe Casale – soon to become famous as the most liberal Italian bishop in matters of politics – who agreed to contribute money and to host the new organization in his dioceses: first Vallo della Lucania and then Foggia, where he was transferred in late 1988. Casale believed that the Catholic Church needed, before passing any judgment, reliable information on "new" or little-known religions. He also had an academic background as an historian, and little patience with what he regarded as the amateur approach of many counter-cultists. For these reasons, he welcomed the idea of an academic organization collecting information on new religious movements, even if one of the founders (Mayer, an Eastern Orthodox) and many of the first scholars involved were not Catholic. With Casale's help, we organized the first CESNUR conference in Vallo della Lucania in 1988. The attendance did not exceed a dozen, and only three persons (myself, Mayer, and an Italian Roman Catholic priest, Father Ernesto Zucchini) presented papers.

Undaunted, we went on and proceeded both to legally incorporate CESNUR and to call a second conference in Foggia for the same year, 1988. In the meantime, Mayer had attended several international conferences and, enlisting the help of Michael Homer, we were able to bring to Foggia – and to CESNUR – the two most famous international scholars in the field of new religious movements, Eileen Barker and J. Gordon Melton. We started learning about their respective organizations, Barker's INFORM, the Information Network Focusing on Religious Movements, and Melton's ISAR, the Institute for the Study of American Religion. Both collected information on new religious movements active in their respective countries, the United Kingdom and the United States, and INFORM also offered advice to concerned parents and law enforcement personnel, organizing frequent and well-attended educational events. We became their disciples and friends, and tried to do something similar in Italy. Although not comparable to Melton's at that time, I had assembled a decent collection of books and ephemera on religious minorities, and started organizing it with the aim of transferring it out of my home as the nucleus of a future public library. Although we did not have the resources or the prestige of INFORM, we were also interested in providing to Italian media, law enforcement personnel, and families reliable information about controversial minorities.

These aims started appearing more realistic when, in 1989 and 1990, I published two volumes, for a total of some 900 pages, which were the first Italian encyclopedias about, respectively, new religious movements and what I proposed to call new magical movements, *The New Religions* (Introvigne 1989) and *The Magician's Hat* (Introvigne 1990). The books sold quite well, and I used the royalties to hire a secretary, who welcomed visitors to my library in Turin and supplied information. She was based in a room of my home, and that situation created family problems when a second child, a daughter, joined my first son in 1993 (two additional children would be born in later years). I then moved the library to an external office, and that move allowed the hiring, in addition to the secretary, of a scholar in residence. The first such scholar was Veronica Roldán, a sociologist from Argentina whom I had met at the CESNUR conference we organized in 1994 in Recife, Brazil. She then moved to an academic career in Rome, and we hired PierLuigi Zoccatelli, a fellow member of Alleanza Cattolica who came from Verona in 1996 and was a crucially important addition to CESNUR.

CESNUR became more well-known with the creation of a Web site in 1997 and the launch in the same year of a collection of short books on religious movements and denominations with a Turin Catholic publisher, Elledici. This collection went on to include forty-two titles, which sold in excess of 140,000 copies and were written by well-known international scholars including – besides Mayer and Homer – J. Gordon Melton, Karel Dobbelaere, Antoine Faivre, James Santucci, Mikael Rothstein, Susan Palmer, Margit Warburg, Jane Williams-Hogan, and Constance Jones, among several others. By the end of the 1990s CESNUR published the large majority of scholarly books available in Italian on new religious movements. A near monopoly had been established in the field, more for a lack of competition than in pursuance of a deliberate project.

This prominence didn't go unnoticed in the anti-cult community. Although our publication of a book in 1996 criticizing the French report on cults of the same year triggered a strong reaction, with French academics associated with CESNUR interviewed by policemen who rang their bells at six in the morning, sooner or later this would probably have happened at any rate. Anti-CESNUR criticism became a specific variety of anti-cultism, although it happened mostly on the Internet and was picked up by offline media only outside Italy: very rarely, if ever, did Italian mainline journalists take any interest in these campaigns.

Ironically, while the anti-CESNUR Web sites insisted in depicting us as "cult apologists," by the end of the 1990s we were largely moving to other areas, although we still crossed swords occasionally with the remaining champions of the brainwashing theory. What we had learned from years of fruitful interaction with the Italian media was that Italy lacked a reliable map of religious minorities in general, not only new religious movements. Italy, in particular, was home to the richest variety of Pentecostal bodies (and had the largest Pentecostal community) in Europe, but nobody had mapped this phenomenon, which concentrated particularly around Naples and in Sicily. Immigrant ethnic Christian churches and Islamic movements also remained largely unmapped. We started collecting data on all religious bodies existing in Italy, and eventually published in 2001 the first edition of the 1,000-page *Encyclopedia of Religions in Italy* (the second edition would follow in 2006, and the third in 2013). It became the single most reviewed nonfiction book in Italy in that year (CESNUR 2001).

In 2001, of course, something else also happened: 9/11, which in Italy as elsewhere diverted public resources and funding from the study of NRMs to the study of radical Islam. Unlike in France or the United Kingdom, most scholars of Islam in Italy were very reluctant to study contemporary phenomena, preferring the safer waters of the first Muslim centuries. We had mapped Italian Islam, including its most radical brand, for the encyclopedia, and regarded several Islamic groups as new religious movements within Islam. We decided, to some extent, to play by the new rules, and produced several books and educational events about groups such as the Muslim Brotherhood or Al Qa'ida, in addition to general studies of the relationship between religion and violence.

In 2003, the publication of Dan Brown's *The Da Vinci Code* (Brown 2003) – which for CESNUR was, in a way, not less important than 9/11 – generated enormous interest in secret societies and esoteric groups. We were fortunate in having at CESNUR PierLuigi Zoccatelli, a world-renowned expert on obscure esoteric organizations. On the other hand, I had a long-lasting interest in popular culture and supernatural fiction (including comics), and was able to document, including by organizing exhibitions in several Italian cities, how folk conspiracy theories went from dime novels and comics to Dan Brown and beyond. Research on groups such as the Illuminati and the Priory of Sion mentioned in Dan Brown's novels attracted unprecedented crowds to CESNUR events, and landed my book on the matter (Introvigne 2005), courtesy of Dan Brown, on the Italian best seller list.

The Da Vinci Code represented a unique opportunity that will probably never repeat itself, but the cooperation of CESNUR with the leading international scholars of esoterica (including Antoine Faivre, Wouter Hanegraaff, Jean-Pierre Laurant, and Marco Pasi) remains an established feature of the Center, and started well before Dan Brown. In addition, and thanks to our cooperation with Rodney Stark, Laurence Iannaccone, and other scholars of the so called religious economy persuasion, we started collecting data on secularization and on the meaning and future of religious pluralism in general. Some of our research was no longer directly correlated to NRMs, as evidenced by the project we completed in 2008, funded by an Italian bank, on Chinese immigrants to Turin, their daily life, and their religion (Berzano et al. 2010).

Thanks to funding available for social research by the Region of Sicily, we produced several books about religion on the island, including two well-reviewed surveys about the reliability of statistics of those attending regularly Catholic Mass (Introvigne and Zoccatelli 2010) and about different brands of atheism in Sicily (Introvigne and Zoccatelli 2012). The work in Sicily led CESNUR to engage in quantitative and qualitative research about Catholicism, including on the tragic phenomenon of pedophile priests and the reactions they generated. In 2013, we became quite well-known, not only in Italy, for two surveys on what we called the "Francis effect," that is, the positive impact of the new pope in generating a new interest in the Catholic Church among the lapsed Catholics and the unchurched (see Introvigne 2013). Apart from specialized publications, these surveys were mentioned by several hundred daily newspapers and other media throughout the world.

Unfortunately, with the economic crisis the Sicilian funds dried out. But new opportunities for research opened. We were always interested in the relationships between new religious movements and the visual arts. Our cooperation with Marco Pasi and other scholars of esotericism led to the realization that some comparatively small movements, such as the Theosophical Society, had a disproportionate influence on the genesis and evolution of modern art. In the 2010s, we devoted considerable energies to projects in this field. They are important, and part of a mainstreaming of the study of new religious movements. Just as the "old" religions, they have their own art and contribute to a larger patrimony of visual culture.

In 2011, quite surprisingly since previously this position had been held by diplomats or politicians rather than by scholars, I was called to serve as the representative of the Organization for Security and Co-operation in Europe (OSCE) for combating racism, xenophobia, and intolerance and discrimination against Christians and members of other religions. Besides making for a long business card, the year at the OSCE offered the opportunity for considering religious liberty from a larger political and international perspective, going beyond the new religious movements and extending in particular to persecutions and assassinations of Christians in African and Asian countries. I served at the OSCE in the year of the Lithuanian presidency, and this offered a welcome opportunity to explore Baltic new religious and esoteric movements, a subject CESNUR had already started studying in the previous years, with two conferences held respectively in Vilnius and Riga (Tallinn would follow suit in 2015).

Taking advantage of my OSCE experience, the Italian Ministry of Foreign Affairs appointed me in 2012 as chairperson of the newly instituted Observatory of Religious Liberty. CESNUR has been involved in some of its initiatives, and I believe that, considering the problems anti-cultism created within the framework of a general hostility to religious minorities, old and new, in several world regions, religious liberty is a promising field for our future studies. Also in 2012, I joined the faculty of the Pontifical Salesian University in Turin as a professor of sociology of religious movements and sociology of religion, and the interaction with students coming from different countries and continents offered new opportunities, particularly for looking at new religious movements in Africa and Asia.

All these changes are reflected in CESNUR's yearly conferences, which continue to be an important opportunity for scholars of different countries to meet and interact. The practice of changing venue every year, seeking the cooperation of local universities all over the world, including outside of Europe and North America (Brazil, Taiwan, Morocco, South Korea), created new friendships with scholars we previously did not know. But it is also worth noting that a core group of NRM scholars attended almost all CESNUR conferences since their beginning in 1988.

Things change. Visiting the Chicago History Museum some years ago, I learned about the fact that the first cellular phone, Motorola's Cellular One (a big thing, larger and heavier than the average home cordless of today), was shipped from a Chicago factory in 1983. True, the Japanese claim they sold cellular phones in Tokyo even before, but that was not the same technology we know, and after all some Japanese claim they also invented spaghetti before the Italians. Be it as it may, I bought my first cellular phone only in 1991. CESNUR was founded by scholars with no cellular phones, no laptop computers, no e-mail. My children would hardly believe that a world without cell phones and e-mail ever existed, but this was the world, or at least our world, when CESNUR was born. This gives us pause to consider the enormous changes in the past decades, which have obviously affected also how religious movements develop and how we see and study religion.

On the other hand, we do believe that research on NRMs, anti-cult and counter-cult movements, esotericism, minority religions, and religious pluralism is still a needed task. While some "old" NRMs lose members or disappear, "new" NRMs arise every day and need to be studied. Those who deny that there is a future for the study of NRMs tend to ignore hundreds of new movements, which have never been the subject of reliable scholarly studies. They may also ignore that studying NRMs has been for all these years, and happily remains, a lot of fun.

References

Berzano, Luigi, Carlo Genova, Massimo Introvigne, Roberta Ricucci, and PierLuigi Zoccatelli 2010. *Cinesi a Torino. La crescita di un arcipelago.* Bologna: Il Mulino.

Brown, Dan 2003. *The Da Vinci Code.* New York: Doubleday.

CESNUR 2001. *Enciclopedia delle religioni in Italia.* Leumann (Torino): Elledici. Third edition, Torino: Elledici, 2013.

Introvigne, Massimo 1983. *I due principi di giustizia nella teoria di Rawls.* Milan: Giuffré.

——— 1987. *Il reverendo Moon e la Chiesa dell'Unificazione.* Leumann (Turin): Elledici. Translated as *The Unification Church*, Salt Lake City: Signature Books, 2000.

——— 1989. *Le nuove Religioni.* Carnago (Varese): Sugarco.

——— 1990. *Il cappello del mago. I nuovi movimenti magici dallo spiritismo al satanismo.* Carnago (Varese): Sugarco.

——— 1993. Strange Bedfellows or Future Enemies. *Update & Dialog*, 3, 13–22.

——— 2005. *Gli Illuminati e il Priorato di Sion. La verità sulle due società segrete del 'Codice da Vinci' e di 'Angeli e demoni'.* Casale Monferrato: Piemme.

——— 2013. *Il segreto di Papa Francesco*. Milan: Sugarco.
——— and PierLuigi Zoccatelli 2010. *La Messa è finita? Pratica cattolica e minoranze religiose nella Sicilia Centrale*. Caltanissetta and Rome: Salvatore Sciascia Editore.
——— 2012. *Gentili senza cortile. 'Atei forti' e 'atei deboli' nella Sicilia Centrale*. Caltanisssetta: Lussografica.
Solmi, Antonio, ed., 1964 *Le grandi religioni del mondo 1964*. 6 vols. Milan: Rizzoli.
Ugolini, Luigi 1950. *L'isola non trovata*. Turin: SEI.

Appendix

List of CESNUR conferences and host organizations

1988 (1) Vallo della Lucania, Italy – Theological Seminary of Vallo della Lucania
1988 (2) Foggia, Italy – University of Theology of Southern Italy
1989 Foggia, Italy – University of Theology of Southern Italy
1990 Lugano, Switzerland – School of Theology of Lugano
1991 Buellton, California – ISAR
1992 Lyon, France – Université de Lyon II
1993 London School of Economics, London – INFORM
1994 Recife, Brazil – Federal University of Pernambuco
1995 Rome – University of Rome "La Sapienza," School of Sociology
1996 Montreal, Québec – University of Montreal
1997 Amsterdam – Free University of Amsterdam
1998 Turin, Italy – Industrial Union of Turin
1999 Bryn Athyn, Pennsylvania – Bryn Athyn College
2000 Riga, Latvia – University of Riga
2001 London School of Economics, London – INFORM
2002 Salt Lake City and Provo, Utah – University of Utah and Brigham Young University
2003 Vilnius, Lithuania – University of Vilnius
2004 Waco, Texas – Baylor University
2005 Isola delle Femmine (Palermo), Italy – Secretariat for Culture, Region of Sicily
2006 San Diego, California – San Diego State University
2007 Bordeaux, France – Université Michel de Montaigne Bordeaux 3
2008 London School of Economics, London – INFORM
2009 Salt Lake City, Utah – Utah State Historical Society
2010 Turin, Italy – University of Turin
2011 Taipei, Taiwan – Aletheia University
2012 El Jadida, Morocco – University of El Jadida
2013 Falun, Sweden – Dalarna University
2014 Waco, Texas – Baylor University
2015 Tallinn, Estonia – University of Tallinn

4   Are the cult wars over? And if so, who won?

Timothy Miller

Anyone over a certain age should remember what many of us have called the cult wars, which raged from the 1970s through the 1980s and well into the 1990s before they died down, although not out. In this chapter, I want to look back at that decades-long series of confrontations and try to figure out where they came from, where they stand today, and what we may or may not have learned from them.

Incidentally, I don't like military language. Hereafter I'll say "cult conflicts," hoping that that term is a little less aggressive than "cult wars." We don't need any more wars.

Cult conflicts are undoubtedly as old as history. Religion goes back farther than any scholar can trace it, and when a new religion comes along it inherently poses a challenge to the established religion, its priesthood and other officials, its institutions, its social position, and its financial resources. Christianity, of course, was initially rejected by both Jews and Romans, whose existing religions it inescapably challenged (Wilken 1984). The people of Mecca were so outraged by the new religion of Muhammad that they ostracized his clan, his base of support, forcing him to flee. When he returned, it was with an army, and his triumph in his hometown came only after he overcame armed resistance. Thereafter Islam spread rapidly, much of that spread coming after armed conflicts with peoples who already had their own established religions. And so forth countless times over the course of history (Esposito 1998).

Religious conflicts of this sort have not been restricted to struggles between established religions and wholly new ones arriving on the scene. Many similar conflicts have involved new *versions* of religions, in which new ways of thinking have challenged the guardians of the sacred established truth. Once Christianity became the official religion of the Roman Empire its Roman leaders used their considerable power to try to eradicate competing versions, of which there were many during the early years of the faith. As years and centuries passed, more innovators appeared, and typically were suppressed. Thus the Cathars of the twelfth through fourteenth centuries were finally eliminated after many violent conflicts (Pegg 2008). Jan Hus, the Bohemian Catholic who questioned some church practices and ideas a century before Martin Luther, was eventually burned at the stake when he refused to recant and submit to church authority (Schattschneider 1974). Such cases are legion in the history of religions.

Given that alternative religions seem to be a cultural constant, it is a safe conjecture that cult conflicts of a sort are endemic to human culture, and we could continue describing many episodes of such struggles. Here, however, we are looking at a particular set of conflicts that arose in the Western world only over the past several decades.

Defenders of the true faith have always been among us, and a major part of defense of "truth" involves eradication of falsehood. The nineteenth century was a time of flowering of religious alternatives in North America and Europe that gave the defenders many new ideas to refute. By the beginning of the century such groups as the Shakers were presenting distinctly unorthodox versions of Christianity, and after its founding in 1830 the Mormon church experienced explosive growth. By the 1840s various Eastern texts began to appear in the West, and at about that time the Oneida Perfectionists began to proclaim a version of Christianity that included a group marriage with hundreds of members. In mid-century spiritualism, which embraced communication with the dead and other psychic phenomena, began a major flourishing, with adherents and dabblers as prominent as Arthur Conan Doyle, Mary Todd Lincoln, and Alfred Russel Wallace. In the 1870s the fertile mind of Helena Blavatsky created Theosophy, and at about the same time Christian Science entered the American spiritual marketplace (Miller 2006).

In this environment the defenders of orthodoxy, meaning mainstream Protestantism, began to single out unorthodox movements for special criticism as they wrote their apologetic works. George Hamilton Combs, in his *Some Latter-Day Religions* (1899), attacked such heresies as Theosophy, otherism (meaning altruism, more or less), pessimism, spiritualism, Mormonism, and socialism. In 1914 Edmond McClure, in his *Modern Substitutes for Traditional Christianity*, similarly attacked not only Theosophy and Christian Science, but also non-miraculous Christianity, rationalism, and Modernism. Objective examinations of such "deviations" were rare, if existent at all, in the first decades of the new century.

But in the 1920s that solid wall of orthodoxy began to exhibit cracks. The year 1923 saw the publication of *Modern Religious Cults and Movements* by Gaius Glenn Atkins. Although its publisher, the Fleming H. Revell Company, was a staunch bastion of evangelical Protestantism, Atkins, although a solid defender of the inherited faith (he was a Protestant minister in Detroit), actually admitted that some of the groups he examined had some value, some insights, even if they fell short of full legitimacy. At the end of his 100-page evaluation of Christian Science, Atkins concedes that it and related groups "have made contributions of real value to our common problem," even though they are "not big enough for the whole either of truth or experience." In a similar vein, in his 1929 book *The Confusion of Tongues*, Charles W. Ferguson, although he too made his disapproval of the "modern Babel" of the new "cults" clear, gave them fair presentations and made reasonable conjectures about their appeal to a segment of the population – conjectures that avoided depictions of maniacal leaders exploiting their gullible followers.

In the following decade more substantial objective surveys began to surface, and with that the literature on new and alternative religions was no longer all in attack mode. Charles S. Braden published the edited volume *Varieties of American Religion* in 1936, and in it included, in addition to such predictable chapters as "Fundamentalism" and "Liberal Protestantism," surveys of seven "modern religious movements in America": Mormonism, Unity, Christian Science, ethical culture, Humanism, spiritualism, and Theosophy. Braden also made the breakthrough of letting actual spokespersons for the various movements and points of view speak for themselves (Braden 1936). The following year Elmer T. Clark's *The Small Sects in America* was published; dividing this subject matter into six categories ("Pessimistic or Adventist Sects," "Perfectionist or Subjectivist Sects," and so forth), Clark brought to light dozens of religious movements that, it is safe to say, were little known to the public, and he did so quite dispassionately (Clark 1937). A bit later Marcus Bach stepped into Clark's territory with several books, including *They Have Found a Faith (1946)* and *Strange Sects and Curious Cults* (1961). Charles Braden published his most important work, *These Also Believe: A Study of Modern American Cults and Minority Religious Movements*, in 1949, building on his earlier survey by covering thirteen religious movements, from Psychiana to the Oxford Group, with eighteen more receiving brief notice in an appendix. Clark, Bach, and Braden all sought to understand, not condemn, the movements they spotlighted.

Such works as these helped inspire a new generation of anti-cultists, who in the process created a good deal of literature intent on exposing the errors and dangers of "cults" that played a major role in transforming the word "cult" from its historic meaning of having to do with rituals and other kinds of religious practice into a heavily pejorative term, one that branded any group so labeled as intrinsically evil. A leading example of their new perspective was J. K. Van Baalen's book *The Chaos of Cults: A Study in Present-Day Isms*, first published in 1938. In a later edition of his book Van Baalen noted the presence of surveys of NRMs by such observers as Braden and Bach, lamenting their "conciliatory spirit." As far as Van Baalen was concerned, the only true religion is ultraconservative Reformed Protestantism; all others stand "in opposition to the Christian, that is, the true religion." The majority of the groups he covered were Christian in some form, but he found them "devious and multiform devices of Satan to tear down the Church of Christ in the Saviour's own Name." The "cults" to which Van Baalen devoted his attention included Theosophy, Christian Science, Swedenborgianism, Mormonism, Jehovah's Witnesses, Unitarianism, and astrology, along with several others. He also included chapters defining "true" Christianity (which appeared to be, essentially, that of Van Baalen's own denomination, the Christian Reformed Church) and outlining ways to present the true faith to the adherents of the "cults." His line of analysis would soon be taken up by many others (Van Baalen 1962: 14–16, 6).

A new shock to the established orthodoxy of the Western world came with the explosion of new religious movements in the 1960s, and it is at this point that the cult conflicts most scholars and other contemporary observers have experienced began. As in earlier decades, new movements with roots in Christianity were in the mix, but now Asian religions were present as well. Their numbers never were and still are not massive, but popular media portrayals often characterized them as growing rapidly, and gave us sensationalized stories of power-hungry leaders, mindlessly obedient followers, and so forth. One theme that rose to the top was that of brainwashing, that these sinister new movements controlled the very minds of their members. Given that kind of media attention, it is not surprising that a fair number of good, upstanding citizens became concerned about this powerful threat to their way of life and their children, and began agitation focused on specific groups, or sometimes on "cults" more generally (Sparks 1977; Hassan 1988).

In the United States one of the most controversial of the new religious movements was the Children of God, which had coalesced around holiness minister David Berg in California. The Children had begun as a coffeehouse ministry in the late 1960s, but soon developed quarters for communal living from which the members conducted street evangelism. They soon became known for their doom-and-gloom predictions of the demise of modern society and for their sackcloth-robed vigils. The movement grew rapidly (Bainbridge 2002).

In 1972 a group of parents, distraught that their adult children had joined the movement, formed what was originally called the "Parents' Committee to Free Our Sons and Daughters from the Children of God Organization," soon truncated to FREECOG. It soon became a lighthouse to which parents of children in a wide range of new religious movements flocked, hoping to "rescue" their children from such relatively new and controversial groups as the International Society for Krishna Consciousness, the Unification Church, and the Love Israel Family. Slowly a narrative took shape – of exploitation of young converts, of isolation of movement members from their birth families, of what came to be called "mind control."

FREECOG soon broadened its focus to cover a variety of religious movements that were being called "cults," although that term was never clearly defined. FREECOG was renamed Volunteer Parents of America (VPA), but soon a new organization appeared and effectively supplanted the VPA: the Citizens Freedom Foundation (CFF), which soon became more than just a sounding board for unhappy parents. The CFF had a paid staff and disseminated its anti-cult message through publications and other outreach activities. And with that the anti-cult movement, as it has since been termed, was hitting high gear. Several other organizations with similar goals soon formed. By 1976 the anti-cult movement had enough clout to enlist U.S. Senator Bob Dole to hold a hearing in Washington that gave the movement its most visible forum to date (Shupe and Bromley 1980).

The new anti-cult movements were joined by an outpouring of anti-cult literature, much of it, as had been the case nearly a century earlier, defending

Protestant orthodoxy against any and all deviations. Evangelical authors such as Walter Martin, whose best-known volume was *The Kingdom of the Cults*, and Bob Larson, author of *Larson's Book of Cults*, wrote dozens (if not hundreds) of books that achieved massive circulation and fueled the work of the anticult organizations. Videos, and later Web sites, also promoted the anti-cult agenda (Martin 1965; Larson 1982).

In the meantime, academics had already checked in. The new religious movements as well as the growing conflict over them provided an excellent setting for research, and studies of several of the new groups soon appeared. By the end of the 1970s some had also taken to studying the new religions' opponents, the multifaceted anti-cult movement. As the academic knowledge base about new religions grew, the majority of the scholars concluded that the prolific popular stereotypes were exaggerated, or simply wrong. Most scholars found that most of the controversial new religious movements really were much like the majoritarian religions in that they were made up mostly of members who had joined voluntarily, freely gave their time and money for the cause, and could (and often did) exit at will. The movements also were not, typically, growing by leaps and bounds. Although academicians think of themselves as impartial investigators, they were soon drawn into the fray as exponents of a point of view – that the "cults" were not terribly unlike other religions, that they were entitled to free exercise of their religions, and that they did not as a whole constitute a menace to their members or to society, even if in specific cases real problems could occur. Radical stuff (Shupe and Bromley 1980).

A few dramatic events exacerbated the conflict. No event was greater than the mass suicide/murder at Jonestown in 1978, in which more than 900 American members of the Peoples Temple lost their lives at the Temple's outpost in Guyana. Although the circumstances surrounding that traumatic event were unique to that organization, anti-cultists seized on the tragedy as conclusive proof that the "cults" did pose a massive threat to society (Hall 1987). Later new religions–related calamities, moreover, were followed by renewal of indiscriminate public outrage about the "cults." The Branch Davidian disaster, in which around eighty persons died in a fire that ended a government siege of their communal headquarters in 1993, resulted mainly in public decrying of the Davidians as the very epitome of dangerous cultists, despite the fact that by any reasonable standard they were much more victims of malicious, or at least misguided, government action than evildoers (Tabor and Gallagher 1995). Two years later, in 1995, when the Japanese new religious movement Aum Shinrikyo carried out a sarin gas attack on the Tokyo subway, similar anti-cult uproars blossomed (Reader 1996). And two more years later the group suicide of the members of Heaven's Gate brought life to the anti-cult cause once again (Chryssides 2011).

Efforts to understand what happened in each case, and to explain that each group is different and not guilty of the sins of another, were drowned out. Over time, the academics who refused to undertake the rush to judgment came to be called "cult apologists" by the anti-cultists, a label that still sees some use.

But for all of that, the noise of the cult conflict does seem somewhat muted these days. I can suggest several reasons for this. First, the globalization of cultures has made an impact here. In the 1960s the new religions were often Asian religions. Although some non-Asian Americans were attracted to Asian religions at least as early as 1893, when Swami Vivekananda of India's Ramakrishna Mission made his dramatic appearance at the World's Parliament of Religions at the Chicago World's Fair, for many years thereafter the number of Asian groups operating in the United States was small, and adherents were relatively few. With huge immigration over recent decades, however, Asians, and with them their religions, have become fixtures of public life throughout the Western world. What is familiar is not very threatening, at least most of the time.

Second, humans do tend to get familiar with their neighbors, and with that process barriers fall away. In my own studies of intentional communities I have found that it is almost universally true that when a communal group moves in, neighbors panic (Miller 1999: 218–24). If anything, the image the word "commune" conjures up is even worse than the image the word "cult" generates, and people expect an overflowing house full of layabouts who do not bathe, take a smorgasbord of drugs, and engage in uninhibited promiscuous sex. Or perhaps they are working on some diabolical plot to take over the world under the direction of a powerful leader. Or perhaps they will simply, by their ominous and undesirable presence, drive down property values in the neighborhood. But in fact "cults," communal and non-communal alike, are inhabited by people with strengths and weaknesses like any other people, and once a religious movement or an intentional community has been in place for a time it is almost always accepted, even welcomed, by its neighbors. The passage of time tends to bring familiarity, and familiarity usually brings acceptance. Mormons, to take a familiar example, were reviled mightily by their neighbors in their movement's early days, to the point that a hostile mob killed their leader. Today, however, Mormons, although still regarded as religious heretics by more than a few adherents of mainstream Christianity in Western countries, are well accepted in home and workplace. Few would object to having Mormon neighbors.

Third, the excesses of the anti-cult movement have to some degree devoured that movement. Deprogramming, in particular, was wretchedly excessive behavior, and its extremity eventually caught up with it. Deprogramming, as it was practiced in the 1970s and 1980s and to some degree thereafter, typically involved abducting a young adult adherent of a religious movement, keeping him or her captive in a secret location, and using strong psychological processes (and sometimes physical abuse) to make the member disaffiliate from the group. However, holding someone prisoner without legal cause is unacceptable in any civilized society, and some of the specific cases were ludicrous, as when parents had a child deprogrammed for political views that differed from their own (Kelley 1983: 311–12). Eventually felony convictions and substantial civil monetary judgments resulted from the acts of deprogrammers, and finally its connections to deprogrammers forced the Cult Awareness Network, the successor to the Citizens Freedom Foundation and America's leading anti-cult organization at the time, into bankruptcy.

Fourth, we no longer argue about brainwashing or mind control. We have learned that brains are hard to wash. Can people be influenced? Certainly. Our society is full of dubious influence, as when slick advertising entices consumers to purchase frivolous goods and services they can't afford. But that doesn't deserve to be called brainwashing. Even the anti-cult movement has abandoned the brainwashing model, as Carol Giambalvo, Michael Kropveld, and Michael Langone note in their article in Eileen Barker's new edited volume in this Ashgate series (Giambalvo et al. 2013).

Fifth, some of the stories of abusive activities shifted from the world of new religions to the mainstream. Anti-cult activists often made allegations of sexual abuse of movement members when compiling their lists of atrocities, but in the 1990s sexual abuse and cover-ups of such sordid activities were more abundant in the Catholic Church than anywhere else. Those cases have tended to crowd the NRMs out of the sensational headlines over the past decade or two.

Sixth, although humans will always be capable of prejudice, it does seem that some overall progress toward tolerance of differences has been made in recent years in the Western world. Not too many years ago it was acceptable in polite society to maintain that persons of African ancestry should not mingle with Caucasians, and even that African Americans were intellectually and morally inferior to Caucasians. Not too many years ago prejudice against Catholics and Jews was open and widespread; in the mid-nineteenth century a substantial political movement sought to eradicate, or at least to minimize the influence of, any who were not Protestant. Not too many years ago women lacked certain basic rights in many Western countries and were widely thought of as the "weaker sex," without the right to vote or hold property. Very recently the rights of gay and lesbian people were tenuous to the point that homosexuality could be mentioned only in whispers. But look at what has happened in all of those cases. I would not argue that we have buried intolerance – far from it. But it does seem that we're progressing on many fronts, and increased religious tolerance may well be part of that progress.

Seventh, the anti-cult movement itself has changed. As I noted earlier, it has backed away from the "brainwashing" model. It has also distanced itself from deprogramming, and when a woman at an International Cultic Studies Association (ICSA) conference in 2008 told of being sexually abused by a prominent deprogrammer, her story was heard without hysterics by an audience that might have reacted explosively a few years earlier. Occasionally members of new religions attend ICSA meetings, and these days they are tolerated, if not wildly welcomed. Giambalvo and colleagues note in their recent article that most ICSA members now recognize "that groups are different [and] that different people react differently to the same group" (Giambalvo et al. 2013: 239). That's a real shift in attitude.

Eighth, the attention span of the public is rarely very long. New crises come along and take people's attention. A huge controversy is often nearly forgotten just a few months later. We had cult conflicts, and now we need something else. One measure of that general decline in interest, for me personally, is that enrollments in my new religious movements classes have been declining for a decade (although of course it could be that my teaching is just getting worse).

Ninth, finally, some of us who were involved in one way or another in the cult conflicts took positive steps toward seeking understanding, if not agreement, with those who saw things differently than we did. Here I would like to hold Eileen Barker and Gordon Melton out as exemplars. Barker began talking with people whose point of view differed from her own, and her efforts at dialogue have now been in place for many years. Similarly Melton has reached out. I was quite surprised when he showed up at a meeting of the American Academy of Religion with Ron Enroth, the anti-cult academic with whom he had authored a book. I'm not sure that collaboration continues, but the point is that bridges were built. Talk to someone, and stereotypes and preconceptions tend to break down.

All of that said, I'm not sure that the conflict is entirely over in the public mind. Billy Graham, whose widely circulated column reaches millions in the United States, recently wrote that despite the seeming disappearance of some "cults," "other cults are just as active as ever, and new ones are being formed all the time" (Graham 2013).

Such progress as we may have made is not equally distributed across the Western world. France and Belgium, especially, have continued their anti-cult policies and actions. And September 2015 saw a major police raid on the Twelve Tribes community in Klosterzimmern, Germany. The raid was reminiscent of an earlier raid at Island Pond, Vermont, in the United States, in 1984, in which more than 100 children were removed from the community but quickly returned when a court found no cause for their removal (Swantko and Wiseman 1995). Both of the raids were based on allegations of physical abuse of children and, in the German case, the admitted fact that the Twelve Tribes communities were homeschooling their children, something not allowed under German law. Twelve Tribes members freely admit that they impose physical discipline on their children, mainly in the form of spanking. An undercover opponent recently released a video of corporal punishment he had taken surreptitiously in the German community, and it showed a small stick being used to spank the children (Paterson 2013). Unless we maintain that all physical punishment is abusive, we will argue about the point at which punishment moves into the territory of actual abuse. But the point here is that we have not progressed much in the thirty years since the Island Pond raid.

Even in the academy we who see ourselves as standing for freedom of religion and innocence until proven guilty haven't fully prevailed. Among ourselves we have an outlook that is widely shared, but our message hasn't penetrated very far. I am sometimes amazed at how often academics uncritically adopt the popular media view of "cults." Most scholars of new religious movements avoid the word "cult" because it represents a judgment rendered before evidence is heard, but the word is quite alive and well among most of our colleagues with other specialties than our own. Despite the best efforts of many of us, "cult" is still the word denoting new religions even for most academics. And I dare say the great majority of academics share the standard public opinion that the Branch Davidians were zombies who followed a deranged charismatic leader and caused their own deaths rather than that they were victims of a botched and misguided government raid, as most of those who have studied the case closely have concluded (Wessinger 2000: 56–119).

So are the cult conflicts really over, and if so, what was the outcome? I can only conclude that the conflict seems to have died down somewhat, but it is still with us, and certainly no one can so far claim victory. We still have work to do.

References

Atkins, Gaius Glenn 1923. *Modern Religious Cults and Movements*. New York: Fleming H. Revell.
Bach, Marcus 1946. *They Have Found a Faith*. Indianapolis, IN: Bobbs-Merrill.
——— 1961. *Strange Sects and Curious Cults*. New York: Dodd, Mead.
Bainbridge, William Sims 2002. *The Endtime Family: Children of God*. Albany: State University of New York Press.
Braden, Charles 1936. *Varieties of American Religion: The Goal of Religion as Interpreted by Representative Exponents of Seventeen Distinctive Types of Religious Thought*. Chicago: Willett, Clark.
——— 1949. *These Also Believe: A Study of Modern American Cults and Minority Religious Movements*. New York: Macmillan.
Chryssides, George 2011. *Heaven's Gate: Postmodernity and Popular Culture in a Suicide Group*. Farnham, Surrey, England: Ashgate.
Clark, Elmer T. 1937. *The Small Sects in America*. New York: Abingdon.
Combs, George Hamilton 1899. *Some Latter-Day Religions*. Chicago: Fleming H. Revell.
Esposito, John L. 1998. *Islam: The Straight Path*. Oxford: Oxford University Press.
Ferguson, Charles W. 1929. *The Confusion of Tongues*. London: William Heinemann.
Giambalvo, Carol, Michael Kropveld, and Michael Langone 2013. Changes in North American Cult Awareness Organizations, in: Eileen Barker (ed.) *Revisionism and Diversification in New Religious Movements*. Farnham, Surrey, England: Ashgate, 227–45.
Graham, Billy 2013. Cults Are Still as Destructive as Ever, *Kansas City Star*, October 10, 2013.
Hall, John R. 1987. *Gone from the Promised Land: Jonestown in American Cultural History*. New Brunswick, NJ: Transaction Books.
Hassan, Steven 1988. *Combatting Cult Mind Control*. Rochester, VT: Park Street Press.
Kelley, Dean M. 1983. Deprogramming and Religious Liberty, in: David G. Bromley and James T. Richardson (eds.) *The Brainwashing/Deprogramming Controversy: Sociological, Psychological, Legal and Historical Perspectives*. New York: Edwin Mellen.
Larson, Bob 1982. *Larson's Book of Cults*. Wheaton, IL: Tyndale House.
Martin, Walter 1965. *The Kingdom of the Cults*. Minneapolis, MN: Bethany Fellowship.
McClure, Edmund 1914. *Modern Substitutes for Traditional Christianity*. London: Society for Promoting Christian Knowledge.

Miller, Timothy 1999. *The 60s Communes: Hippies and Beyond.* Syracuse, NY: Syracuse University Press.

——— 2006. New Religious Movements in American History, in: Eugene V. Gallagher and W. Michael Ashcraft (eds.) *Introduction to New and Alternative Religions in America*, volume 1, History and Controversies. Westport, CT: Greenwood, 1–22.

Paterson, Tony 2013. Germany's Twelve Tribes Sect, Cameras Catch "Cold and Systematic" Child-Beating, *The Independent*, September 10, 2013; available at www.independent.co.uk/news/world/europe/in-germanys-twelve-tribes-sect-cameras-catch-cold-and-systematic-childbeating-8807438.html (accessed 1/17/2014).

Pegg, Mark Gregory 2008. *A Most Holy War: The Albigensian Crusade and the Battle for Christendom.* New York: Oxford University Press.

Reader, Ian 1996. *A Poisonous Cocktail? Aum Shinrikyo's Path to Violence.* Copenhagen: Nordic Institute of Asian Studies.

Schattschneider, Allen W. 1974. *Through Five Hundred Years: A Popular History of the Moravian Church.* Bethlehem, PA: Comenius Press.

Shupe, Jr., Anson D., and David G. Bromley 1980. *The New Vigilantes: Deprogrammers, Anticultists, and the New Religions.* Beverly Hills, CA: Sage Publications.

Sparks, Jack 1977. *The Mind Benders.* Nashville, TN: Thomas Nelson.

Swantko, Jean, and Ed Wiseman 1995. Messianic Communities, Sociologists, and the Law. *Communities: Journal of Cooperative Living*, 88, 34–35.

Tabor, James D., and Eugene V. Gallagher 1995. *Why Waco? Cults and the Battle for Religious Freedom in America.* Berkeley: University of California Press.

Van Baalen, J. K. 1962. *The Chaos of Cults: A Study in Present-Day Isms.* Grand Rapids, MI: Eerdmans. Originally published in 1938 and updated periodically.

Wessinger, Catherine 2000. *How the Millennium Comes Violently: From Jonestown to Heaven's Gate.* New York: Seven Bridges.

Wilken, Robert Louis 1984. *The Christians as the Romans Saw Them.* New Haven, CT: Yale University Press.

5 From deviance to devotion
The evolution of NRM studies

George D. Chryssides

The study of new religious movements (NRMs) has made great strides in the past century. Half a century ago colleges and seminaries in the United Kingdom were only beginning to include the study of 'comparative religion', as it was then called, in addition to the staple diet of Christianity. The study of new religions was not on the horizon, and would not have been considered a worthy topic for study, despite the fact that Mormons and Jehovah's Witnesses had embarked on their major evangelising work in the United Kingdom, and were gaining public attention. Even though topics like ancient Egyptian religion did not directly impinge on the average student's life, it was nonetheless studied, but NRMs were firmly excluded, despite the fact that it might have seemed reasonable for clergy to be able to advise their congregations about what they believed and how to respond. This chapter seeks to trace the beginnings and developments of the modern study of NRMs, starting with very early pioneering attempts, and to examine possible future trends. Because of the proliferation of literature that now exists on the subject, comprehensiveness is impossible, but I shall comment on the main strands, incorporating academic writing, anti-cult and counter-cult critiques and more sympathetic popular attempts to understand the phenomenon.

Despite new religious movements' exclusion from college syllabi until recent times, a small body of literature has existed on the topic for slightly more than two centuries. One very early study was that of John Evans, a Baptist minister and founder of a small school in Islington, London. Evans' *A Sketch of the Several Denominations into which the Christian World Is Divided* first appeared in 1795, and was expanded into *A Sketch of the Denominations of the Christian World* in 1807, going through numerous editions. As well as Catholics, Protestants, Scotch and English Presbyterians and Greek Orthodox Christians, Evans includes Swedenborgians, Quakers, Universalists, Muggletonians and Methodists, among numerous others. These were, of course, new religions in Evans' time: Swedenborg had his first vision in 1757, and John Wesley's first Methodist Conference had taken place only fifty years earlier. Evans tells us little about how he collected his data, apart from acknowledging the use of the library of a Samuel Brent of Rotherhithe: one presumes that his research was predominantly literature-based. Evans believed that there was a common essence in religions, while acknowledging that they were not all alike (Evans 1808: v, 236), and his aim was to encourage tolerance and respect for all who sought religious truth in their own ways.

Several decades later, a book bearing the title *Unorthodox London: Faces of Religious Life in the Metropolis* (1874) by C. Maurice Davies appeared. Davies was variously an Anglican clergyman, a headmaster and a journalist who turned to spiritualism in later life. This book was the result of extensive fieldwork, possibly the first field study of minority religious organisations, and was a description of various communities which the author found in the city, including Tabernacle Ranters, Particular Baptists, Swedenborgians, Christadelphians, spiritualists, the West London Synagogue and the Greek Church in London Wall – quite a varied mixture! Like Evans, Davies was not unsympathetic in his treatment of these new religious movements: he simply regarded them as somewhat eccentric curiosities on London's religious landscape. Subsequent literature was more hostile. The late nineteenth century and early twentieth century saw a proliferation of material accusing the emergent new religions or 'cults' of heresy, typically comparing them with the beliefs of mainstream Christianity or finding ancient heresies to attribute to them. The Watch Tower Bible and Tract Society was one principal target. Hostility was due to a number of factors: theologically, they distanced themselves from mainstream Christianity, initially on account of their eschatological views, particularly the denial of eternal torment in hell, and their belief that death for the wicked was no more than oblivion. Additionally they were perceived as an organisation that did little to benefit the community, but merely promoted their own beliefs about scripture. This unpopularity was fuelled by the press, who gave high publicity to several controversial incidents involving founder-leader Charles Taze Russell. Russell took part in two theological disputations with prominent members of the clergy, and transcripts of these debates were published in the press and subsequently released in book form (Russell and Eaton 1903; Russell and White 1908). One of the debaters, Dr E. L. Eaton (a Methodist Episcopal clergyman), contended that the stenographer had failed to do justice to his side of the discussion, and accordingly followed up the debate with his own published critique of Watch Tower biblical exegesis (Eaton 1911).

Christianity's status as the world's largest religion, coupled with its preoccupation with sound doctrine and the elimination of heretical thinking, tended to ensure that its places of learning generally focused on systematic theology and biblical interpretation, with little room for the teaching of other faiths, let alone NRMs. In England in the mid-1950s there were only sixteen university lecturers who taught the study of world religions (Cunningham 1990: 22). In the United States religious studies was still just emerging as its own field distinct from biblical studies or anthropology. Theology could in no way encompass NRMs: if that Queen of the Sciences aimed at discovering the truth about God, organisations like the Church of Jesus Christ of Latter-Day Saints (Mormons) and Jehovah's Witnesses appeared to offer error rather than truth.[1] Comparatively speaking, they were numerically small, and these new Christian movements used the Bible, offering an interpretation of scripture that seemed patently erroneous, in contrast with the true interpretation already taught in theological seminaries. It is understandable that mainstream Christian literature should take the form of critiques of these 'modern heresies'. In R. A. Torrey's edited collection of tracts, written between 1901 and 1915, titled *The Fundamentals – A Testimony to the Truth* (and giving the name 'fundamentalism' to the movement that followed), a few contributors offered critiques of Mormonism, the Millennial Dawn movement,[2] spiritualism and Christian Science. In 1913 the Rev. Lewis B. Radford delivered the Moorhouse Lectures in St Paul's Cathedral, Melbourne, which set out to criticise Seventh-Day Adventism, theosophy, Christian Science and the Eastern doctrines of karma and reincarnation, subsequently published as *Ancient Heresies in Modern Dress*.[3] Other early studies included William C. Irvine's *Timely Warnings* (1917 – later re-titled *Heresies Exposed*), and Gaius Glenn Atkins' *Modern Cults and Religious Movements* (1923). The oft-cited *The Chaos of the Cults*, by J. K. van Baalen, a minister of the Christian Reformed Church in North America, first appeared in 1938, undergoing various editions until 1962. In 1954 the Society for the Propagation of Christian Knowledge (SPCK) published a series of short booklets, authored by the Anglican clergyman Kenneth N. Ross, targeting Jehovah's Witnesses, Christian Science, spiritualism and astrology. Ross offered more detailed critiques of these and other NRMs of this period in subsequent pamphlets and in a short book titled *Dangerous Delusions* (1961), based on a series of lectures given at the University of Durham in 1960. The earlier twentieth-century writers tended to use terms like 'heresy' and 'sect', since they were endeavouring to compare the tenets of their targeted NRMs with mainstream Christian doctrine. However, the term 'cult' gradually gained currency, particularly in the wake of the new wave of NRMs, many of which made no claims to relate to the Christian faith. The earliest known use of the term 'cult' in the context of NRM studies goes back to the late nineteenth century, and is found in A. H. Barrington's *Anti-Christian Cults* (1898).

Such attacks on these new religions continued into the 1960s, the best known of these later examples being Anthony A. Hoekema's *The Four Major Cults* (1963). Hoekema was a professor of systematic theology and his book is a detailed exposition and critique of Christian Science, Jehovah's Witnesses, Mormonism and Seventh-Day Adventism. Other writers treated the NRMs as curiosities or exoticisms, for example Elmer T. Clark's *The Small Sects in America* (1937) and Marcus Bach's *Strange Sects and Curious Cults* (1961). Yet most of the material published on NRMs before the late 1960s was produced from specific Christian denominational perspectives, and like the anti-heretical writings of the early Church fathers, was polemical in nature.

These writings were characterised by a number of features. First, their assessment of NRMs was almost invariably negative. One exception was Charles Samuel Braden's *These Also Believe* (1949), which covers a range of NRMs, seeking to treat them objectively, while at the same time discussing the extent to which they agree with Christian doctrine. Second, most works tended to give more emphasis to critique rather than exposition, and in some of these studies, such as Horton Davies' *Christian Deviations*, one learns little about the beliefs and practices of the NRMs themselves. Third, the key question for the majority of these writers seemed to be the NRMs' lack of doctrinal soundness. To some degree this was encouraged by the NRMs themselves, some of which had produced their own doctrinal writings, such as The Book of Mormon, Mary Baker Eddy's *Science and Health* and numerous volumes by Adventist and Watch Tower authors offering new biblical interpretation, particularly on the theme of eschatology. The public disputations involving Charles Taze Russell and his successor, Joseph Franklin Rutherford, highlighted the point that the key issues were doctrinal ones. This challenging of NRM doctrines continues among Christian evangelicals. In the post-war period the best known evangelical Christian critiques included Horton Davies' *Christian Deviations* (1954) in Britain, and – perhaps even better known, and certainly much more extensive – Walter Martin's *The Kingdom of the Cults*, first published in 1965 and revised several times until Martin's death in 1989.

Although these paper heresy trials continued, the years after World War Two saw a number of changes in NRM studies. The topic began to attract interest among academics, initially sociologists, and particularly in the field of sociology of deviance. Probably the best-known study is Leon Festinger, Henry Riecken and Stanley Schachter's *When Prophecy Fails* (1956), followed by John Lofland's *Doomsday Cult* (1966), and research by Robert Balch and David W. Taylor in the 1970s on the group which was at that time called Human Individual Metamorphosis (HIM). All three studies were undertaken covertly, and all were studies of groups that were little known at the time. Festinger and Lofland used pseudonyms for the groups and their leaders, although it is now well known that Festinger's study was of Dorothy Martin's group, Sananda, and that Lofland describes the early days of the Unification Church in California's Bay Area. Balch and Taylor only used the nicknames of Heaven's Gate leaders Marshall Herff Applewhite and Bonnie Lu Nettles, and the group's better-known name Heaven's Gate was not employed until later in the group's history. Other landmark studies include James A. Beckford's *The Trumpet of Prophecy* (1975), and Eileen Barker's important *The Making of a Moonie* (1984). Beckford's study is a sociological analysis of the Jehovah's Witnesses, while Barker aims to establish the process by which seekers joined and left the Unification Church – examining whether the recruiting process might be described as 'brainwashing', or whether joining was undertaken by rational choice.

In the meantime, anti-cult literature was also changing, for three principal reasons. First, the new wave of NRMs from the 1960s onwards raised new issues about conversion and belonging. Several of these NRMs targeted youths rather than families, and offered communal living, requiring a break from one's conventional family life, education and lifestyle. Second, the mass deaths at Jonestown, Guyana in 1978 caused widespread scaremongering about the possible dangers of NRM membership. The power of a single leader to persuade more than 900 of his followers to commit mass suicide was almost impossible to grasp, and it was understandable that the news coverage of the Peoples Temple disaster should cause the public to resort to 'brainwashing' explanations. Encouraged by the studies of Robert Jay Lifton, who was a psychiatrist in the U.S. Air Force during the 1951–3 Korean War, the anti-cult movement (ACM) adopted Lifton's eight components of 'thought reform' as the 'marks of the cult' – and continues to champion these, despite their lack of support by NRM scholars (Lifton 1961; cf. Cult Information Centre 2014). Third, as familiarity with Christian doctrine declined, many were less interested in theological critique of such movements, but were more concerned about their lifestyle and the demands they made on followers. Hence a new genre of anti-cult literature addressed issues like brainwashing, coercion, lifestyle, separation from families and so on.

Back in academia, NRM studies developed beyond sociological study. The application of the methodologies used in the study of religion lagged behind sociological approaches, but an increasing interest arose in the worldviews NRMs espoused. Although socially they might appear deviant, it did not follow that they had a bizarre or incoherent worldview. On the contrary, my own fieldwork demonstrated that asking probing questions to NRM followers almost invariably resulted in very lucid answers. Indeed, one of the fascinating aspects of NRM studies is that the initial impression that NRM adherents hold naïve and unpromising ideas has been overturned by the subsequent discovery that they hold coherent systems of thought.

Some of the major NRMs have taken the initiative in engaging with academia. The Latter-Day Saints had already established their own tradition of scholarship, not least in the establishment of Brigham Young University in Utah. In 1993 the International Society for Krishna Consciousness (ISKCON) established the *ISKCON Communications Journal*, to which academics were invited to contribute, and which served to give academic credibility to the organisation.[4] The Oxford Centre for Hindu Studies, established in 1997, has as its director Shaunaka Rishi Das, an ISKCON devotee. Possibly the most ambitious attempts to gain an academic foothold were those of the Unification Church (UC). When the church began to hold conferences in the 1970s and 1980s to which academics were invited, part of the agenda was to enable some of its up-and-coming scholars to expound *Divine Principle* to a critical academic audience, taking aboard questions and criticisms to which they could devise responses. Such incursions into academia served a number of functions. The Unification Church gained a higher profile, giving itself a place in the academic community, and associating itself with well-known scholars in sociology, theology, religious studies and politics, among other disciplines. Putting themselves in dialogue with these scholars meant members were not merely the subjects of sociological enquiry, but partners in dialogue, enabling their own students to present Unificationism on an equal footing. A number of their own young converts had at that time embarked on postgraduate studies, and were working towards PhD degrees, which most of them successfully completed. Their role in assisting with these seminars was thus conducive to their own training; subjecting the doctrines to external criticism not only strengthened their own ability to defend their faith, but provided fuel for further academic writing on behalf of the UC. The Unification movement[5] had set up its own publishing houses – New Era Publications, Paragon Press, the Rose of Sharon Press and the Unification Theological Seminary's own press. Many of these publications addressed general issues relating to theology and the study of religion, but they also enabled Unificationists to present material on their own theology and lifestyle, and thus put themselves on the same footing as accounts of mainstream religions. Some attendees at UC conferences published their material about the organisation with more established and less controversial publishers.

One important but often neglected influence on NRM studies lies in the field of missiology. Even before NRM studies acquired its own distinctive identity, scholars working on indigenous and primal religions had noted the influence of Christian mission in producing syntheses of the Christian message with the ideas of indigenous cultures. NRMs were not to be regarded as a distinctively Western phenomenon, but rather as a global one. Accordingly, work done by scholars such as Harold W. Turner highlighted the emergent religious movements in Africa and Australasia, and Turner's collection of scholarly writings on new religions in primal societies remains an important resource at the University of Birmingham, UK. Turner's collection spanned a large variety of NRMs that had arisen globally, many of which are less well-known, since they did not have an uptake by Westerners. Examples include the Ghost Dance movement, cargo cults, the Cao Dai of Vietnam, the Rastafari and the Unification Church, which was itself the product of interaction between Christian mission and indigenous Korean religion. Native American religion, initially the province of missiologists, gained momentum amongst Western NRM scholars as its ideas and practices became popular amongst certain Western seekers.[6] The present author's *The Advent of Sun Myung Moon* (1991) was an attempt to apply the methodology of the study of religion to a new religious movement: the subtitle 'The origins, beliefs and practices of the Unification Church' signalled that it was an attempt to account for its origins by combining part of the history of Korean Christian mission with the UC's beliefs and practices, many of which drew substantially on folk shamanism in its country of origin. Additionally, the book was the result of fieldwork and dialogue with the organisation's members.

When NRM studies gained a foothold in university and college syllabuses – a trend that gained momentum from the early 1990s – finding a good basic student textbook that attempted to combine broad coverage with objectivity was a serious problem. One or two publications existed that were not 'cult critiques', such as the Anglican priest Kenneth Leech's *Youthquake* (1973), which took as its starting point the psychedelic revolution of the youth counterculture of the time, and discussed its interest in Zen, the Hare Krishna movement and various Indian gurus, occultism and emergent ideologies such as gay liberation and nuclear disarmament. Leech's survey ended with the Jesus Revolution and how the church should respond. Also popular was journalist Stephen Annett's *The Many Ways of Being* (1976) – a useful compendium, but rather more like an extended directory than a discursive treatment of NRMs, and it fairly soon became outdated and went out of print. Eileen Barker's (1989) *New Religious Movements: A Practical Introduction* was a useful resource, published in the wake of the founding of the Information Network Focusing on Religious Movements (INFORM) in 1988, and aimed principally at the new organisation's stakeholders rather than an undergraduate readership – although this book continues to be recommended in several higher education courses countrywide. In 1996, David V. Barrett published his *Sects, 'Cults' and Alternative Religions*, which gave extensive coverage to a very wide variety of NRMs; it was expanded into an even larger volume, *The New Believers*, in 2001. Barrett's books are slightly journalistic in style, reflecting his background as a popular writer, but they were certainly the most comprehensive surveys at that time – and of course in the present academic climate where 'impact' is of key importance, informing a wider public is as desirable as writing for students and academic colleagues. The present author's *Exploring New Religions* (1999) was an attempt to provide an academic portrayal of a range of NRMs, although like most works in this field, it became slightly dated in not too long. A number of other introductions have followed, and some of these – such as Douglas E. Cowan and David G. Bromley's *Cults and New Religions* (2008) and Paul Oliver's short *New Religious Movements: A Guide for the Perplexed* (2012) – have the merit of combining exposition with a number of issues in NRMs requiring discussion.

One important development in NRM studies has been the increasing specialisation within the field. It has swiftly been recognised that there is no such thing as a 'cult expert', any more than one can be a literature expert or a science expert, and ACM spokespersons who continue to use this label only underline their own charlatanry. Since it is estimated that there are at least 2,000 new religious groups in the United States, around 600 in Britain, at least 10,000 in Africa, and at least 8,000 in Japan, it would be ludicrous to suppose that any single person could be an NRM expert. Additionally, over and above the specific NRMs, societal issues require individuals' specialist expertise, for example legal issues, gender issues, psychological issues, media treatment of religions and many more. This range of expertise is something that Ben Zeller and the present author tried to bring out when *The Bloomsbury Companion to New Religious Movements* (2014) was commissioned. In this volume some thirty authors, reflecting various specialisms, have contributed articles on topics as diverse as race and ethnicity, children and generational issues and healing, as well as specific categories of NRMs, such as African NRMs, Japanese NRMs, UFO religions and what Carol Cusack has called 'invented religions' (Cusack 2010).

A further development gaining momentum in NRM studies is the increasing presence of NRM insiders as scholars, as well as ex-member researchers, and some of the contributors to the *Bloomsbury Companion* are themselves insiders. This is certainly a far cry from the perception of the NRM member as belonging to a bizarre cult, as numerous NRMs have now demonstrated their ability to provide their own scholarship. One could also cite individual academics who support new forms of spirituality, including Graham Harvey, Damien Keown, Kennet Granholm and Steven J. Rosen (Harvey 1997; Keown 2001; Granholm 2005; Rosen 2007). Whether NRM members are drawn to academia because of faith seeking understanding, or whether their studies of NRMs – which can often involve participant observation – draw them in to the organisation they are studying, is an interesting question to which there is probably no single answer. The insider-scholar, of course is no new phenomenon, since until recently it could be generally assumed that scholars of Christianity were uniformly Christian.

It is tempting to end this discussion of trends in NRM scholarship with speculations about possible future trends in the field. However, rather than making uncertain predictions, I believe it is possible to identify present trends and gaps in the field that need to be filled. It is clear that NRM studies has the complexity that will continue to draw on the specialisms that have contributed to it – sociology, anthropology, theology and religious studies and, more recently, cultural and media studies. Relatively little has been written on how NRMs express their ideas in music and literature – an area which, I believe, merits further study.[7] Just as in the study of mainstream religion, there are contributions by both insiders and outsiders, it seems likely that – at least with some NRMs – we will see continuing scholarship and dialogue from both. NRMs themselves are likely to generate their distinctive brands of scholarship, reflecting their fundamental convictions. We have already seen the rise of Mormon and of Vedic archaeology, for example, reflecting different views of history that come from these forms of spirituality.

As in many fields of study, gaps become evident. One area that has been neglected is the 'old new religions'. Little work has been done on the Christadelphians, and scholars have undertaken remarkably little serious scholarship on the Jehovah's Witnesses. Adventism has been little explored, except by Adventist scholars who have their own presuppositions and agendas. The old new religions may seem less exciting to some than the Moonies, Hare Krishnas, Scientologists and the Jesus People, but they remain gaps that academic study needs to fill, and which it is hoped will be on the future agenda in NRM studies. The development of the Internet, with easier availability of electronic versions of texts, has undoubtedly heralded a transformation in the way scholars can conduct research. With the increased ease of availability of archival material online, it is possible to access and to search an entire body of literature, and in many cases old copies of publications by groups such as the Watch Tower organisation. It is no longer always necessary, or efficient, for scholars to visit a large library archive and pore through mountains of old documents; electronic searching can very quickly establish how an organisation's teachings and practices develop over time, and when and where key topics are discussed. The Internet has also facilitated wider communication amongst researchers, and made the study of NRMs a truly global venture. Those who read our work are therefore entitled to have much higher expectations about its compass and its accuracy.[8]

Finally, if the ACM still appears committed to the theory of brainwashing and 'marks of the cults', is Christian evangelical counter-cult literature equally intransigent? There may be signs of change. John Morehead has recently written an article titled 'Walter Martin Was Wrong: A Critique and Alternative to the Counter-cult Approach to Cults' (2013). In this article he argues against the heresy-rationalist model that has typically characterised counter-cult literature. This model, he contends, has been influenced by biblical injunctions to beware of false Christs and false teachings (e.g. Matthew 7:15–23; Acts 20:26–31), but Morehead believes that a confrontational approach is both inappropriate and ineffectual. When Jesus adopts a confrontational stance, it is with the Pharisees and Sadducees, who were fellow Jews, and when Elijah confronts the Baal prophets, he is opposing the religious officials that are supported by the king and queen of his country (1 Kings 18:16–40). When we look at Jesus' own relationships with those of other faiths, Morehead argues, we find that he does not accuse the Samaritan woman of false belief and practice (John 4:1–28), and he is willing to heal the Roman centurion's servant and the Canaanite woman's daughter (Matthew 8:5–13; 15:21–28). Paul, despite being a Jew, adopts an inclusive stance to the Gentiles, interpreting the Jewish law in an inclusive way. Morehead therefore argues for 'right affection' and dialogical method, seriously questioning whether NRM members have ever been persuaded to abandon their faiths by the methods adopted by Martin and others.

A further impetus for change in NRM studies has been the increased attention to forms of spirituality lacking clear congregational or membership boundaries. The New Age movement, the revival of paganism and druidism, the rise of cyber-religions, the growth of irreligion and the increasing numbers of people who describe themselves as 'spiritual but not religious' have called into question the notion of NRMs as membership organisations with insiders and outsiders. Richard Dawkins' claims that 'religion' does more harm than good seem to presuppose that religion is some kind of 'thing' that is clearly distinguishable from other activities that do not belong to that category – an extremely dubious assumption. These developments do not merely widen the scope of NRM studies, but call into question categories that have traditionally been used in the field. Future debate in the field of NRM studies is therefore likely to entail serious discussion about what is spiritual or religious, what terms should be used to describe devotion (if these indeed are appropriate terms), and whether we can continue to draw boundaries such as 'insider' and 'outsider'. These are some of the methodological issues which students of NRMs, and indeed of religion more widely, can expect to find on our future agenda.

Notes

1 In addition to the new Christian NRMs, theosophy was a popular target for counter-cult writers. The Theosophical Society was established in 1975 in New York.
2 This was the name frequently given to followers of Charles Taze Russell, being the title of his series of books, subsequently renamed *Studies in the Scriptures*. The organisation became known as Jehovah's Witnesses in 1931.

3 Although Seventh-Day Adventism is now more favourably regarded by mainstream Christians, it was initially unpopular on account of its eschatology. In particular, the notion that Christ cleansed the heavenly sanctuary in 1844 suggested that Christ's crucifixion did not complete his atoning work.
4 The journal ceased publication in 2005.
5 The term 'Unification movement' describes the partnership between the Unification Church and wider bodies, including academics. A substantial number of volumes produced by these publishing houses was authored or edited by scholars who were not members of the Unification Church.
6 A relatively early study of how religious syncretism gave rise to Japanese NRMs is McFarland (1967).
7 For example, there has been no attempt to ascertain whether or how L. Ron Hubbard's techno-religious ideas might be expressed in his fiction, and works of fiction had an important role in the dissemination of Zen in the United States and Europe, and also in the New Age. The British Association for the Study of Religions published a special edition on religion and music in 2014, accessible at www.religiousstudiesproject.com/DISKUS/index.php/DISKUS/issue/view/1, but as yet there are few other examples of such incursions.
8 A more negative aspect, however, is the increased ease of self-publishing and the facilities to make one's efforts available to all through distributors such as Amazon. This has given rise to a proliferation of extremely poor critiques of organisations like the Jehovah's Witnesses, which add nothing to one's understanding or to debate about the teachings and practices.

References

Annett, Stephen 1976. *The Many Ways of Being*. London: Abacus.
Atkins, Gaius Glenn 1923. *Modern Cults and Religious Movements*. Old Tappan, NJ: Fleming H. Revell.
Bach, Marcus 1961. *Strange Sects and Curious Cults*. New York: Dodd Mead.
Balch, Robert W. 1998. The Evolution of a New Age Cult: From Total Overcomers Anonymous to Death at Heaven's Gate, in: William W. Zellner and Marc Petrowsky (eds.) *Sects, Cults, and Spiritual Communities: A Sociological Analysis*, Westport: Praeger, pp. 1–24.
―――― 2002. Making Sense of the Heaven's Gate Suicides, in: David G. Bromley and J. Gordon Melton (eds.) *Cults, Religion, and Violence*. Cambridge: Cambridge University Press, pp. 209–28.
Barker, Eileen 1984. *The Making of a Moonie*. Oxford: Blackwell.
―――― 1989. *New Religious Movements: A Practical Introduction*. London: HMSO
Barrett, David V. 1996. *Sects, 'Cults' and Alternative Religions*. London: Blandford.
―――― 2001. *The New Believers: Sects, 'Cults' and Alternative Religions*. London: Cassell.
Barrington, A. H. 1898. *Anti-Christian Cults*. Milwaukee, WI: Young Churchman.
Beckford, J. A. 1975. *The Trumpet of Prophecy*. Oxford: Blackwell.
Braden, Charles S. 1960. *These Also Believe: A Study of Modern American Cults and Minority Religious Movements*. New York: Macmillan.
Chryssides, George D. 1991. *The Advent of Sun Myung Moon*. London: Macmillan.
―――― 1999. *Exploring New Religions*. London: Cassell.
―――― and Zeller, Benjamin E. (eds.) 2014. *The Bloomsbury Companion to New Religious Movements*. London: Bloomsbury.
Clark, Elmer T. 1937. *The Small Sects in America*. New York: Abingdon.

Cowan, Douglas E. and Bromley, David G. 2008. *Cults and New Religions*. Oxford: Blackwell.
Cult Information Centre 2014. *What Is Mind Control?* Available at www.cultinformation.org.uk/question_what-is-mind-control.html. Accessed 30 September 2014.
Cunningham, Adrian 1990. Religious Studies in the Universities – England, in: King (ed.), *Turning Points in Religious Studies*, pp. 21–31.
Cusack, Carole M. 2010. *Invented Religions: Imagination, Fiction and Faith*. Farnham: Ashgate.
Davies, C. Maurice 1874. *Unorthodox London: Or Phases of Religious Life in the Metropolis*. London: Tinsley Brothers.
Davies, Horton 1954. *Christian Deviations: Essays in Defense of the Christian Faith*. London: SCM.
Eaton, E. L. 1911. *The Millennial Dawn Heresy*. New York & Cincinnati: The Methodist Book Concern.
Evans, John 1795. *A Brief Sketch of the Several Denominations into Which the Christian World Is Divided, Accompanied with A Persuasive to Religious Moderation*. London: B. Crosby. Available at https://play.google.com/books/reader2?id=0CJdAAAAcAAJ&printsec=frontcover&output=reader&hl=en&pg=GBS.PP2. Accessed 25 August 2015.
––––––– [1807] 1808. *A Sketch of the Denominations of the Christian World*. Boston: Beals. Available at https://archive.org/details/sketchofdenomin00evan. Accessed 29 September 2014.
Festinger, Leon, Riecken, Henry W. and Schachter, Stanley [1956] 2008. *When Prophecy Fails*. London: Pinter and Martin.
Granholm, Kennet 2005. *Embracing the Dark: The Magic Order of Dragon Rouge*. Åbo Åbo Akademi University Press.
Harvey, Graham 1997. *Listening People, Speaking Earth: Contemporary Paganism*. London: Hurst & Co.
Hoekema, Anthony A. 1963. *The Four Major Cults: Christian Science, Jehovah's Witnesses, Mormonism, Seventh-Day Adventism*. Exeter, England: Paternoster.
Irvine, William C. 1955. *Heresies Exposed*. Neptune, NJ: Loizeaux. (Originally published as *Timely Warnings*, 1917).
Keown, Damien 2001. *The Nature of Buddhist Ethics*. 2nd edn. Basingstoke: Palgrave.
King, Ursula (ed.) 1990. *Turning Points in Religious Studies*. London: T & T Clark.
Leech, Kenneth 1973. *Youthquake: The Growth of a Counter-culture through Two Decades*. London: Sheldon Press.
Lifton, R. J. [1961] 1989. *Thought Reform and the Psychology of Totalism: A Study of Brainwashing in China*. Chapel Hill: University of North Carolina Press.
Lofland, John 1966. *Doomsday Cult: A Study of Conversion, Proselytization, and Maintenance of Faith*. Englewood Cliffs, NJ: Prentice-Hall.
Martin, Walter 1965. *The Kingdom of the Cults*. Minneapolis, MN: Bethany House.
McFarland, H. Neill 1967. *The Rush Hour of the Gods: A Study of New Religious Movements in Japan*. New York: Macmillan.
Morehead, John W. 2013. Walter Martin Was Wrong: A Critique and Alternative to the Counter-cult Approach to Cults. *Journal of Asian Mission* 14(1): 3–28.
Oliver, Paul 2012. *New Religious Movements: A Guide for the Perplexed*. London: Continuum.
Radford, Lewis B. 1913. *Ancient Heresies in Modern Dress*. Melbourne: George Robertson.
Rosen, Steven J. 2007. *Krishna's Song: A New Look at the Bhagavad Gita*. Westport, CT: Greenwood.
Ross, K. N. 1954. 'Astrology'; 'Christian Science'; 'Jehovah's Witnesses'; 'Spiritualism' [pamphlets]. London: SPCK.

—— 1961. *Dangerous Delusions*. Oxford: Mowbray.
Russell, C. T. and Eaton, E. L. 1903. *Complete Report of the Great Religious Debate between Rev. E. L. Eaton, D. D., and Pastor C. T. Russell, V. D. M., on the Subject of 'Eschatology'*. Reprinted from *The Gazette*, Allegheny, PA, 19 October. Available at https://ia700406.us.archive.org/21/items/RussellVsEatonDebate/1903_Russell_Eaton_Debate.pdf. Accessed 27 September 2014.
Russell, C. T. and White, L. S. 1908. *Russell-White Debate: A Public Discussion between Pastor Charles T. Russell (Millennial Dawn) of Allegheny, Pa., and L. S. White (Christian) of Dallas, Tex.* Cincinnati, OH: F. L. Rowe.
Torrey, R. A. and Dixon, A. C. et al. (eds.) [1901–15] 2003. *The Fundamentals: A Testimony to the Truth*. Grand Rapids, MI: Baker Books.
Turner, Harold W. 1992. *Bibliography of New Religious Movements in Primal Societies*. Boston: G. K. Hall.
Van Baalen, Jan Karel 1962. *The Chaos of Cults: A Study in Present-Day Isms*. Grand Rapids, MI: Eerdmans.

6 Writing on and researching new religious movements

A view from the American academy

Benjamin E. Zeller

When I first decided to research new religious movements (NRMs) I was a graduate student pursuing a terminal master's degree at Harvard Divinity School. I crafted a list of the major scholars working in the field with whom I might consider studying for my PhD. I wanted to stay in the United States, as my interests lay in NRMs in that region, as well as within the discipline of religious studies. Imagine my chagrin when I discovered that almost none of the American religious studies scholars with whom I shared common research interests in the study of NRMs worked in departments with viable doctoral programs. I contrasted this experience with that of friends and colleagues studying Buddhism, Christian Patristics, or the Hebrew Bible, all of whom had an embarrassment of riches in their choices of doctoral programs. I will briefly return to my own experience at the end of this chapter, as it serves – at least for me – as a frame, showing how the study of NRMs in the American academy is both peripheral and in some ways unique.

The academic study of new religious movements in the U.S. context has undergone a remarkable transition over the past three decades. Despite its origins in the sociological study of religion, the main researchers are now institutionally located within religious studies departments. Yet at the same time, several forces have resulted in the study of NRMs becoming diffuse throughout religious studies, rather than solidifying as a mature subfield. This results in both a concentration of scholars within religious studies departments and a dispersal of such NRM scholars across different subfields of religious studies. Such subfields include religions in North America, religion and culture, and the study of individual religious traditions or regions, such as Chinese religions.

Here I consider the reasons for this transition, the underlying economic and social factors, and the ramifications for how scholars research NRMs. Effects have been both positive and negative, with a plurality of approaches and methodologies now characterizing the study of NRMs, but simultaneously the lack of subfield cohesion has resulted in a centrifugal effect. This profoundly impacts how scholars engage NRMs as a subject, since researchers' locations shape their methodologies, approaches, topics, and perspectives. I conclude that the lack of cohesion therefore has had effects that are beneficial as well as detrimental to the maturation and stabilization of the academic study of new religious movements.

The origins of the field

The study of NRMs in the Anglophone world emerged primarily from the sociological models of Weber and Troeltsch, and ethnographic work in the 1970s (Chryssides and Zeller 2014). A rising number of American sociologists of religion in the 1970s came to focus on the study of NRMs, including David G. Bromley, Anson D. Shupe, Jeffrey K. Hadden, Thomas Robbins, Robert W. Balch, and James T. Richardson, among others. They tended to consider issues of direct relevance to broader sociology of religion, such as conversion/defection, socialization, and intergroup social ties. They also situated the study of new religions within the major sociological theories concerning the contemporary religious context, such as secularization, deviance and alienation, sectarianism, and social movements (Glock and Bellah 1976; Robbins and Anthony 1981). The very name "new religious movements" in fact indicates how social movement theory underlay the origin of the field. Certainly non-sociologists, such as historians J. Gordon Melton and Robert Ellwood, psychologist Dick Anthony, and archivist J. Stillson Judah were involved in the early days of the study of NRMs in the United States, and each contributed methodological diversity and perspectives, but overall the field originated and remained housed within departments of sociology among faculty and graduate students.

This sociological emphasis had obvious effects on the study of NRMs. By the late 1970s, American sociologists of religion with interests in NRMs produced a flurry of groundbreaking articles published in the most important social scientific journals, including *American Sociological Review, Journal for the Scientific Study of Religion, Sociological Analysis*, and *American Behavioral Scientist*. The majority of these first publications focused on sociological typologies, theories of social or religious deviance, models of sectarianism, and the study of social processes such as conversion, socialization, and apostasy. Often the research produced was deeply influential. John Lofland and Rodney Stark's "Becoming a World-Saver: A Theory of Conversion to a Deviant Perspective," an article based on their research on the Unification Church, fundamentally shaped how American sociologists of religion model conversion even today, as David Bromley has noted (Lofland and Stark 1965; Bromley 2001). Beyond this, the early research by Rodney Stark and William Sims Bainbridge on new religious movements served as the foundation for their highly influential comprehensive sociological theory of religion, which they dubbed rational choice theory, and which Stark and Roger Finke later extended (Stark and Bainbridge 1979; Stark and Finke 2000). To be clear, American sociologists did not work in isolation, and American sociology of religion was deeply influenced by British and to a lesser extent Continental research as well. British sociologists of religion focusing on new religious movements such as Colin Campbell and Eileen Barker affected American developments through their empirical studies and theoretical models. Campbell's concept of "cultic milieu" became a standard analytic tool among American sociologists (Campbell 1972); Barker's work on the Unification Church served as one of the primary quantitative studies influencing the development of transatlantic sociology of new religious movements (Barker 1981, 1984). Based on these scholars' research and publications, by the early 1980s one could safely speak of the study of NRMs as no longer an emergent field, but one quickly establishing itself as a subfield within the heart of American and even transatlantic sociology.

The authors of the majority of these studies based their work on either ethnography or surveys, and used theoretical models rooted in the classic literature of sociology of religion, especially the work of Max Weber and his successors. Obviously such choices emerged from their training in departments of sociology, and they followed academic norms appropriate to the sociology of religion. This resulted in tightly focused studies delving into one or several social dynamics of new religions. Early publications such as Thomas Robbins and Dick Anthony's studies on Asian mysticism, drug use, and the counterculture provide good examples of this form of scholarship (Robbins 1969; Robbins and Anthony 1972). Similarly, sociologist E. Burke Rochford Jr.'s extended ethnographic and qualitative studies of the Hare Krishna movement yielded extensive publications on theoretical and thematic studies of this new religion (Rochford 1983, 1989, 1995).

Such research broke new ground particularly in the study of concepts valuable to the social scientific study of religion, such as conversion/apostasy, socialization, secularization, and sectarianism. Yet scholars' tight focus on matters sociological had other results too. As Robert W. Balch wrote of his research into the new religious movement that would come to be called Heaven's Gate:

> When I lived with the group in 1975, I was so absorbed by the minutia of everyday life that I didn't think much about its beliefs. They were simply a given. Although I recognized that the belief system shaped and constrained members' actions, I, like other sociologists, was more concerned with the actions themselves than with the beliefs on which they were based.
>
> (Balch 2014: xii)

That is to say, the focus of sociologists of religion on social forces resulted in studies with obvious lacunae, such as the study of groups' theologies, rituals, mythological structures, and historical contexts. While exceptions existed – most notably the aforementioned Ellwood, Anthony, Melton, and Judah, generally the pattern Balch described held for the broader study of new religious movements.

One cannot ignore the social milieu of the researchers themselves, namely the infamous "cult wars" of 1970s America, featuring deprogrammers, concerned parents, anti-cult organizations, and evangelical Christian missionaries on one side; and the proponents of specific new religious movements, civil liberties, and youth culture on the other. Sociologists of religion found themselves in the middle. Researchers soon found themselves co-opted and relabeled as "anti-cultists," on one hand, or as "cult apologists," on the other. Because sociologists of religion came to dismiss the various models of brainwashing as invalid on empirical grounds, many found themselves accused of supporting the NRMs they were studying (Bromley 2001; Palmer 2001; Robbins 2001; Richardson 2014). As a result, scholars of NRMs became not only pulled into academic, legal, and popular debates about "cults," but also drawn toward research agendas considering issues related to the sociology of conversion, membership, and defection and the study of ex-members who had been forcibly deprogrammed. With new religions accused of abusive recruitment and socialization techniques, scholars naturally focused on such issues. Such topics therefore became the mainstays of research on NRMs.

The shift to religious studies

The decade that followed – the mid-1980s into the 1990s – witnessed an academic shift as increasing numbers of researchers trained in the interdisciplinary field called *religious studies* took an interest in the study of new religions, while simultaneously interests among American sociologists shifted in new directions. This transformation led to new topics, methodologies, and approaches represented in the academic writing about new religious movements.

Religious studies draws from multiple disciplines, including sociology, anthropology, history, theology, ritual studies, area studies, gender studies, and media studies (Elliott 2013). The field itself came of age in the United States during the 1960s from a confluence of factors: increasing student interest; the growth of the secular academic interest in religion rather than theology; legal recognition by the Supreme Court in 1963 that the First Amendment's prohibition against religious establishment permitted the academic study of religion in state-sponsored universities; and increased funding from both private and public educational institutions for the study of and teaching in this new field (Long 1985; Murphey 1989; Bivins 2012).

The 1960s religious counterculture, but even more so the 1978 Jonestown deaths, drew increased attention from scholars toward the topic of new religions within the inchoate religious studies field (Moore 2014). In the immediate years that followed the Jonestown deaths, scholars of religion with training in history, theology, comparative methods, and what had been called "history of religions" – generally meaning specialists in the study of the world's largest or most influential religious traditions – took an interest in new religious movements. With considerable effort and some contention, participants in this new NRM studies subfield were able to found a program unit of the American Academy of Religion (AAR) in 1984 that focused on the topic. As a program unit, the new group had semi-permanent status within the Academy, and was able to host paper sessions at the annual meeting of the AAR. With a presence at the United States' national professional association and guild for religious studies, the NRM program unit represented the gradual acceptance of the study of new religions as a legitimate subfield. Subsequently an increasing number of American religious studies scholars began to look to the phenomenon as an area of research. The subfield coalesced within this program unit, and the success of the program unit led directly to the creation of the field's new journal, *Nova Religio: Journal of Alternative and Emergent Religions*, in 1997.

The effects of these developments on the scholarship of NRMs cannot be overstated. The AAR group created an academic community in the United States wherein scholars of NRMs in the religious studies field – including historians, theologians, comparativists, and anthropologists as well as sociologists and social psychologists – could cohere. *Nova Religio* subsequently created a written forum wherein such scholars could write for each other as well as a general audience, and develop more cohesion as a subfield within religious studies. The journal's first issues featured debates over the relationship of NRMs to violence, politics, gender, nationalism, and the Internet, among other new topics. *Nova Religio*'s first volumes also highlighted issues of continuing concern among sociologists, such as brainwashing, charisma, and exit costs. The journal also provided an avenue for the publication of case studies on specific groups using methodologies ranging from ethnographic to historiographic to literary.

Simultaneous to the rise of religious studies, sociologists of religion began to turn to other topics during the late 1980s and 1990s. The rise of evangelicalism and the religious right, increasing religious tensions within the political sphere, and immigration captured increasing interest among American sociologists of religion. Between 1970 and 1975, the leading American journal for the sociology of religion, the *Journal for the Scientific Study of Religion* (*JSSR*) published twelve articles on NRMs. From 1975 to 1980, it published nineteen articles, and from 1980 to 1985, twenty-two articles. Yet from 1985 to 1990, it published only thirteen, from 1990 to 1995 only nine, and from 1995 to 2000, only eight articles. The pattern clearly shows an increase in interest in topics related to NRMs during the late 1970s until 1975, followed by a decrease as interests shifted elsewhere.

The handoff of NRMs as a topic from sociologists to religious studies scholars resulted in an increase of focus on cultural, theological, and historical issues. One can look to the articles published in the first five years of *Nova Religio* for evidence of this transformation. The journal published a mix of articles using historical, textual, and gender studies approaches as well as sociological ones. The vast majority of articles focused on case studies of specific new religions, drawing broader issues from these studies as related to themes such as the relation of NRMs to the state, gender and sexuality, and the Internet and technology. Several clusters of articles focused on methodological issues in the study of NRMs, ranging from research ethics, to engagement with legal or law enforcement authorities, to theoretical models. Important, *Nova Religio* shifted away from quantitative studies, and the social scientific research it publishes is generally qualitative. While the *Journal for the Scientific Study of Religion* and similar social scientific journals continued to publish quantitative studies on NRMs, albeit in lesser numbers, *Nova Religio*'s focus on qualitative social scientific and humanistic research resulted in two developments: a proliferation of diversity of approaches to the study of NRMs, but also a decline in the number of quantitative studies of the topic.

Economic and institutional factors

One direct effect of the increasing shift to a religious studies perspective among scholars working on NRMs has been the bifurcated existence of many of these scholars. While NRM studies has become a generally accepted subfield within religious studies, it is nevertheless not one of the major subfields within the field, at least if one looks to which AAR program units are largest and hold the most permanent status and what fields have the most tenure-track lines. Such major subfields are generally limited to biblical studies, ancient Mediterranean religion, Islamic studies, South or East Asian religions, North American religions, medieval religions, and increasingly religion and culture (i.e., critical theory). The lack of inclusion of NRM studies within the list of the major subfields has a very real effect: graduate departments organize faculty and students within these subfields, and institutions hiring scholars and researchers look to fill positions in accordance with these subfields. Of the major graduate institutions producing scholars in religious studies, none has "NRM studies" as an organized subfield. As a result, graduate students seeking to study NRMs or faculty wishing to train graduate students fit themselves within one of the existing subfields. The current generation of scholars focusing on NRMs therefore defines itself always in two ways: scholars of NRMs as well as scholars within another subfield. (The same is true of researchers in other emergent subfields, such as ritual studies or religion and media studies.)

This has repercussions. On the positive side, NRM studies is not ghettoized and becomes integrated within broader academic conversations. Researchers writing on NRMs consider broader audiences, and engage in conversations with scholars well outside the subfield of NRM studies. This increases academic diversity and breadth of research topics and approaches. One finds articles on NRMs published in journals focusing on Asian religions, North American religions, and cultural studies, for example. Yet at the same time, this acts as a centrifugal force on the study of NRMs themselves, with colleagues spending half or more of their time engaged in the professional obligations, networking, and research of their "other" subfield.

Further, though some graduate programs have in recent years transitioned to interdisciplinary approaches, eschewing official subfields altogether, this is not the case in terms of how most colleges and universities hire their faculty. Scholars of NRMs need to eat, and they need jobs. There are no jobs in the study of NRMs in religious studies departments in the American academy, or at least there are none defined as such. American scholars studying NRMs hold chairs in Christian studies, Asian religious studies, comparative religion, theology, history of religions, and numerous other subfields. Because tenure-track lines are few and academic administrations are seldom willing to create new ones, there is little possibility of this changing. As a result, junior scholars of new religions must market themselves as working in other subfields in order to secure funding and jobs.

An examination of the archived job advertisements from recent years illuminates precisely this problem. The vast majority of hiring departments and job candidates in religious studies engage in their search through the employment services of the American Academy of Religion. Through the aid of that organization I was able to access the past decade of data in the form of the advertisements for job searches that employers posted for the annual meeting of the AAR. These advertisements included not only the text of the advertisement, but also lists of subfields that the hiring institution identified as relevant to the position. This includes the "NR" code, which the AAR uses for "New Religions." I was able to search for not only the NR code, but any reference to new religious movements or particular new religions within the text of the job advertisements themselves. Important, institutions advertising through the AAR may select multiple desired subfields, and the inclusion of "NR" among the coded subfields for a job advertisement does not mean that the position necessarily focused on or even required expertise in NRMs. New religions were always merely one among several desiderata. Analyzing these data revealed several important patterns in how departments and institutions categorize and describe job opportunities relevant for scholars of NRMs.

Overall during the period of 2004–2014, institutions advertised approximately 100 job opportunities each year across the entire field of religious studies at the AAR's annual meeting, with the height coming in the year immediately preceding the Great Recession of 2008. The 2009–2010 and 2010–2011 academic years featured the lowest number of job opportunities posted through the AAR for religious studies scholars of the past decade owing to not only the economic collapse but also a short-term separation of the AAR annual meeting from that of its sister organization, the Society for Biblical Literature (SBL).[1] During this ten-year period, institutions advertised through the AAR an average of two positions each year that explicitly called for expertise in NRMs as either a required or a possible qualification.

Table 6.1 Number of positions relevant to NRM scholars advertised at AAR annual meeting, compared to total number of positions advertised at annual meeting.

Year	Number of NRM positions advertised at AAR annual meeting	Total number of positions advertised at AAR annual meeting
2004–2005	5	108
2005–2006	1	136
2006–2007	2	155
2007–2008	7	136
2008–2009*	4	93
2009–2010*	2	36
2010–2011*	0	59
2011–2012	0	83
2012–2013	2	92
2013–2014	2	92

*During these years the American Academy of Religion did not meet with the Society for Biblical Literature, meaning that the total number of positions does not include most jobs in biblical studies or theology.

The 2004–2005 job year seems on the face of it like an excellent one, with five advertised positions at the AAR tagged by the "NR" label. Yet looks can be deceiving, for only one of those, an assistant professor position at California State University, Bakersfield, explicitly mentioned NRMs as a preferred area of competence. The advertisement noted that the university sought to hire in religion and society, and that the new hire would "regularly teach Introduction to Religion and survey courses in Western or Eastern religions. S/he will also teach upper-level courses that may include Sociology of Religion, Psychology of Religion, Women and Religion, New Religious Movements, African American, Hispanic, or Native American Religions, Myth and Symbolism, and our heavily enrolled course on death" (AAR 2004). While it is hard to celebrate the inclusion of NRM studies in such a long list, at least the advertisement included the topic. The other four positions that included the NR tag did not mention NRMs as desired or required areas of competence. Two institutions sought new faculty with training in North American religious diversity and pluralism, one was a short-term post-doc in "any area of religion" excluding those already represented at the institution, and the final position sought an expert in "biblical or New Testament studies," although it called for secondary competence in "feminist religious thought, African-American religion, Native American religion, or Latin American religion" (AAR 2004). In fact, none of these institutions hired a specialist in new religious movements.[2]

The 2005–2006 and 2006–2007 academic years were bleak for job seekers in the NRM field, with only one institution mentioning NRMs in job advertisements each year. The job advertised in 2005, like several from the previous year, called for expertise in North American religious diversity, explicitly mentioning "American religious history, new religious movements, popular culture, Black Church, gender issues, fundamentalism" (AAR 2005). The following year a position in religious practice listed NRMs alongside several other areas of competence such as diasporic religions and race/ethnicity as possible areas of hire. A third advertised position, an entry-level one for the teaching of world religions, included the AAR's NR tag but did not explicitly mention NRMs (AAR 2006). Of these positions, none of the eventually hired candidates were self-described NRM scholars, although one of the individuals hired did have a secondary interest in NRMs. The 2007–2008 job season improved somewhat, with three positions in North American religions either tagged with the NR field or listing new religious movements among possible areas of specialization within the North American religions specialization. Additionally, two quite broad advertised positions in Islam and one in Judaic studies included the NR tag without noting NRMs in the descriptions, and another advertised position described as "open" listed new religions along with twenty-seven other possible subfields. The inclusion of new religions in these broad searches indicates a positive development that institutions recognized the study of new religions as embedded within multiple other subfields, although of course it also speaks to the centrifugal nature of the professionalization of the study of new religions (AAR 2007).

The 2008–2009 job year represented the last academic year wherein searches for tenure-track faculty hires were approved before the economic collapse. Although university administrations canceled some of these searches, it was at first an excellent year for candidates in the NRM field, with six advertised positions either listed in the AAR's NR category or mentioning NRMs as possible areas of hire. However, the overall area of specialization for five of these six jobs was American religion. A sixth was a position in religion and society (AAR 2008). Combined with the three previous years of available positions, a clear pattern emerges that the majority of job opportunities for scholars of NRMs required specialization in North American religions. Of the scholars of North American religions hired for these positions, none identify themselves as specialists in new religions, although one had a secondary interest in the subfield.

The years since the 2008 collapse have been bleak for academic job hunters of all types, including religious studies generally, and new religions specialists particularly. The 2009–2010 year featured two opportunities explicitly mentioning NRMs. One was a repeat of a canceled search from the previous year. Both this and the second job fell within the rubric of American religions (AAR 2009, 2010). The next academic year featured one job mentioning NRMs as an area of interest, specifically a position in the religions of China seeking an expert in Chinese religions broadly but able to teach on new religions of China and Taiwan in addition to her or his specialty. The 2011–2012 academic year yielded one opportunity for scholars of NRMs, again in Chinese religions, that included "popular folk sects and new religious movements" among the desirable areas of research expertise (AAR 2011). In the final year of my analysis, the 2012–2013 academic year, only three full-time positions in religious studies enumerated NRMs as among the desired possible fields of study. These three jobs – one in church history, one in North American religions, and one in Chinese religions – all listed NRMs among secondary areas of focus, alongside numerous other possibilities. Of the candidates receiving these positions few had any direct connection to new religions, which is hardly surprising given that the advertised positions themselves were in other subfields.

Assessing the past decade as a whole, therefore, one finds a clear pattern: young scholars researching new religious movements stood the best chance of securing a tenure-track position in religious studies if they worked within the broader subfield of American religions, and to a lesser extent religion and society, or Chinese religions. North American religious diversity provided the most traction for potential job seekers, since specialists in NRMs with that area of expertise could leverage their experience studying minority religions in the United States. However, specialists in the study of new religions in other geographic regions with the exception of China had less luck. While certainly they could – and anecdotally, some did – position themselves as scholars of broader geographic regions, no hiring departments explicitly called for NRM specialists in such searches. The onus fell on junior scholars of new religious movements to show that they were primarily experts in, for example, African religions or Japanese religions, Finally NRM scholars with more sociological interests fared somewhat better, with several opportunities available to young scholars with such interests. Yet here the NRM field reverted to its origin, and rather than highlighting how the study of new religions has transformed and developed over the past three decades, the prevalence of such positions indicates that broader American religious studies scholars still think of new religions primarily from the perspective of sociology, or perhaps North American religious diversity.

A caveat on this research: the methodology I have used results in missing some job announcements. Hiring institutions do not advertise every academic job related to the study of religion through the AAR, nor do they always advertise at the annual meeting. Yet departments of religious studies, wherein one finds the vast majority of open positions in the study of religion, generally advertise their open positions through the AAR and interview candidates at its annual meeting. Therefore, the majority of religious studies jobs during the years I considered were advertised through the AAR and included in the data set that I considered.

Despite this, I have compared and cross-referenced between the AAR's listings and the self-reported number of job opportunities reported on the social networking "Job Wiki" site, a Web site wherein job searchers and employers anonymously post updates on specific opportunities and the progress made in the interview and selection process. For the 2011–2012 and 2012–2013 academic years the Wiki listed 160 and 163 available full-time positions in religious studies, respectively, whereas the AAR listed 92 for each year (Academic Jobs Wiki 2012, 2013). While the difference in listed opportunities may seem high, in fact many of the opportunities self-reported in the Wiki were either administrative positions or jobs requiring confessional identities. The actual numbers of tenure-track positions in religious studies at American colleges and universities listed in the Wiki for both the 2011–2012 and 2012–2013 academic years were approximately 110, depending on how one determines the criteria. Important, none of the additional jobs listed on the Wiki was of relevance to the study of NRMs. I was also able to compare the data set I received from the AAR with a more comprehensive data file of jobs advertised throughout the year and not only at the annual meeting. Overall, the numbers are quite similar, and I am confident that I missed very few – if any – advertised positions in religious studies.

None of this is to say that specialists in NRMs did not receive new jobs during these years. Many – including myself – did. Yet these American scholars of NRMs must by the nature of their positions define themselves as something other than specialists in new religious movements. They must teach classes outside the subfield of NRM studies, and must advise and work with students in far different subfields. In my own case, I fall within the quite popular American religious diversity subfield, which given the data was quite fortuitous. Not everyone is as lucky, or shares the same interests.

Table 6.2 Number of positions relevant to NRM scholars advertised at AAR annual meeting, compared to positions listing NRMs as desired subfields advertised throughout year.

Year	Number of positions including NRMs as possible area of interest advertised at AAR Annual Meeting	Advertisements selecting "new religious movements" as primary or secondary/additional field of specialization over entire academic year
2004–2005	5	8
2005–2006	1	6
2006–2007	2	15
2007–2008	7	7
2008–2009*	4	0
2009–2010*	2	0
2010–2011*	0	0
2011–2012	0	1
2012–2013	2	4
2013–2014	2	0

*During these years the American Academy of Religion did not meet with the Society for Biblical Literature, meaning that the total number of positions does not include most jobs in biblical studies or theology.

Conclusions

All this being said, what predictions might one offer for the future of the study of NRMs in the American academy? Before answering, one must recognize industry-wide transformations. The overall trajectory in American higher education has been toward contingent faculty, a euphemism for part-time adjuncts. The plight of adjuncts was recently highlighted in a *New York Times* article that focused on the economic situation of highly trained individuals working without benefits, health insurance, or a promise of future employment for the equivalent of $3,000 a course (Swarns 2013). Unfortunately, market forces and institutional realities mean that the use of adjuncts is likely to increase rather than decrease. This problem affects every academic field, although humanities and social science departments face special burdens. The increasing number of NRM scholars who must work as contingent faculty results in such scholars having less time to engage in traditional academic research. They are ineligible to apply for many grants and fellowships, and they are disadvantaged in those for which they are able to apply. The paucity of funding means such scholars are less likely to engage in immersive ethnography, quantitative studies, and longitudinal work. While the AAR and related scholarly organizations have made efforts to develop models of nontraditional scholarship, the basic fact is that the professional study of religion in the United States assumes a tenure-track model, and those positions are becoming fewer and fewer. NRM scholars will continue to face that hurdle.

There seems little chance that universities will create new tenure-track lines in the study of new religious movements. Therefore, young scholars of new religions will need to continue to define themselves as studying some other subfield in order to secure employment, or else look at "alt-ac" (alternative academic) positions such as those in research institutions, digital humanities, and so forth. Specialists in other emergent subfields in the study of religion, such as religion and popular culture, ritual studies, or transnational religions, surely face the same task, so scholars of new religions are hardly alone. Within our subfield of new religion studies, the field of North American religions has historically offered the most opportunities, but there is no reason that trends must continue. Specialists in Islamic new religions may find themselves in demand in the future. The increasing global relevance of power of the BRICs – Brazil, Russia, India, and China – could mean that the study of new religions in those regions is well positioned for the future. Yet the decline of the cult wars themselves, and the seeming disappearance of new religions from the cultural radar – replaced with concerns over religious terrorism – may indicate that the study of new religious movements could remain relatively marginalized into the foreseeable future.

The author thanks Ryan Woods at the American Academy of Religion for providing the relevant employment data used in this study, and for feedback on the analysis itself. He also thanks the participants at the 2014 INFORM Anniversary Conference, "Minority Religions: Contemplating the Past and Anticipating the Future," for feedback on an earlier version of this chapter.

Notes

1 While I was not able to access SBL data, approximately twenty to thirty job opportunities each year fall exclusively within biblical studies, and therefore the AAR numbers from these years reflect the loss of these advertised positions.
2 I was able to track down details using a mix of institutional Web sites, self-reporting on the Academic Jobs Wiki, the social network Academia.edu, and in a few cases by asking colleagues directly. I have omitted names from my analysis.

References

Academic Jobs Wiki 2012. Available at: http://academicjobs.wikia.com/wiki/Religious_Studies_2012–2013.
——— 2013. Available at: http://academicjobs.wikia.com/wiki/Religious_Studies_2013–2014.
American Academy of Religion [AAR] 2004–2006. Openings: Employment opportunities for scholars of religion.
——— 2007. Raw job data set provided by organization.
——— 2008–2010. Job postings: Special annual meeting edition.
——— 2011–2012. Employment center: Special annual meeting edition.
Balch, Robert W. 2014. Foreword, in: Benjamin E. Zeller (ed.) *Heaven's Gate: America's UFO Religion*. New York: New York University Press, pp. xi–xiv.

Barker, Eileen 1981. Who'd be a Moonie? A comparative study of those who join the Unification Church in Britain, in: Bryan Wilson (ed.) *The Social Impact of New Religious Movements*. New York: Rose of Sharon Press, 67–109.

——— 1984. *The Making of a Moonie: Choice or Brainwashing?* Oxford: Basil Blackwell Publishing.

Bivins, Jason 2012. Only one repertory: American religious studies. *Religion* 42(3), 395–407.

Bromley, David G. 2001. A tale of two theories: Brainwashing and conversion as competing political narratives, in: Benjamin Zablocki and Thomas Robbins (eds.) *Misunderstanding Cults: Searching for Objectivity in a Controversial Field*. Toronto: University of Toronto Press, pp. 318–48.

Campbell, Colin 1972. The cult, cultic milieu and secularization, in: Michael Hill (ed.), *A Sociological Yearbook of Religion in Britain*, vol. 5. London: SCM Press, pp. 119–36.

Chryssides, George D., and Benjamin E. Zeller (eds.) 2014. *The Bloomsbury Companion to New Religious Movements*. London: Bloomsbury.

Elliott, Scott S. 2013. *Reinventing Religious Studies: Key Writings in the History of a Discipline*. London: Equinox.

Glock, Charles Y., and Robert N. Bellah (eds.) 1976. *The New Religious Consciousness*. Berkeley: University of California Press.

Lofland, John, and Rodney Stark 1965. Becoming a world-saver: A theory of conversion to a deviant perspective. *American Sociological Review* 30(6), 862–75.

Long, Charles H. 1985. Study of religion in the United States of America: Its past and its future. *Religious Studies and Theology* 5(3), 30–44.

Moore, Rebecca 2014. Jonestown and the study of NRMs, in: George D. Chryssides and Benjamin E. Zeller (eds.) *The Bloomsbury Companion to New Religious Movements*. London: Bloomsbury, pp. 73–88.

Murphey, Murray G. 1989. On the scientific study of religion in the United States, 1870–1980, in: Michel J. Lacey (ed.) *Religion and Twentieth-Century American Intellectual Life*. Cambridge: Cambridge University Press, pp. 136–71.

Palmer, Susan J. 2001. Caught up in the cult wars: Confessions of a Canadian researcher, in: Benjamin Zablocki and Thomas Robbins (eds.) *Misunderstanding Cults: Searching for Objectivity in a Controversial Field*. Toronto: University of Toronto Press, pp. 99–122.

Richardson, James T. 2014. Conversion and brainwashing: Controversies and contrasts, in: George D. Chryssides and Benjamin E. Zeller (eds.) *The Bloomsbury Companion to New Religious Movements*. London: Bloomsbury, pp. 89–102.

Robbins, Thomas A. 1969. "Eastern Mysticism and the Resocialization of Drug Users: The Meher Baba Cult" Journal for the Scientific Study of Religion 8 no 2: 308–17.

——— 2001. Balance and fairness in the study of alternative religions, in: Benjamin Zablocki and Thomas Robbins (eds.) *Misunderstanding Cults: Searching for Objectivity in a Controversial Field*. Toronto: University of Toronto Press, pp. 71–98.

Robbins, Thomas A. and Dick Anthony. 1972. "Getting Straight With Meher Baba: A Study of Mysticism, Drug Rehabilitation and Postadolescent Role Conflict" Journal for the Scientific Study of Religion 11 no 2: 122–40.

——— (eds.) 1981. *In Gods We Trust: New Patterns of Religious Pluralism in America*. New Brunswick, NJ: Transaction Publishers.

Rochford, Jr., E. Burke 1983. Recruitment strategies, ideology, and organization in the Hare Krishna movement, in: Eileen Barker (ed.) *Of Gods and Men: New Religious Movements in the West*. Macon, GA: Mercer University Press, pp. 283–302.

——— 1989. Factionalism, group defection, and schism in the Hare Krishna movement. *Journal for the Scientific Study of Religion* 28(2), 162–79.

——— 1995. Hare Krishna in America: Growth, decline, and accommodation, in: Timothy Miller (ed.) *America's Alternative Religions*. Albany: State University of New York Press, pp. 215–22.

Stark, Rodney, and William Sims Bainbridge 1979. Of churches, sects, and cults: Preliminary concepts for a theory of religious movements. *Journal for the Scientific Study of Religion* 18(2), 117–33.

Stark, Rodney, and Roger Finke 2000. *Acts of Faith: Explaining the Human Side of Religion*. Berkeley: University of California Press.

Swarns, Rachel L. 2013. Crowded out of ivory tower, adjuncts see a life less lofty. *New York Times*, January 20, p. A11. Available at: www.nytimes.com/2014/01/20/nyregion/crowded-out-of-ivory-tower-adjuncts-see-a-life-less-lofty.html?_r=0.

7 The law, the courts, religious freedom, and the evolving pattern of jurisprudence in Western societies

James T. Richardson

Since new religious movements (NRMs) burst on the scene in the 1960 and 1970s various patterns of jurisprudence have emerged involving such groups as well as other minority faiths. Those patterns vary greatly, but overall I discern movement toward more tolerance of NRMs and other minority faiths in many Western nations.[1] This jurisprudential pattern seems to involve a recognition and protection of more religious freedom for minority faiths in these regions. Some key rulings of various courts in Europe, especially the European Court of Human Rights (ECtHR), reveal this pattern. Also, in the United States the federal courts and the U.S. Supreme Court have issued significant recent rulings that offer more freedom for small and nontraditional religious groups to function. And in an effort to influence the U.S. Supreme Court in its rulings concerning religious freedom, the U.S. Congress has entered the fray on behalf of religious groups through passage of major laws such as the Religious Freedom Restoration Act (RFRA) in 1997 and the Religious Land Use and Institutionalized Persons Act (RLUIPA) in 2000. All of these court-related actions seem to demonstrate that the much-discussed "judicialization of politics" (Tate and Vallinder 1995; Hirschi 2006) also applies in the area of religion, where courts have been able to exert considerable influence over the definition and role of religion in contemporary Western societies.[2]

First, I will briefly describe recent developments within Europe, and then I will discuss recent developments within the United States.

The situation in European regions

Western Europe offers sharp contrasts concerning tolerance for minority faiths, varying from the more tolerant Netherlands and Italy, to paternalistic Germany, and officially secular France (see chapters in Richardson 2004 and in Lucas and Robbins 2004). Add to that mix Greece, where proselytizing remains a criminal offense (Richardson and Garay 2004), and the pattern concerning religious freedom is indeed complex. Place the newly freed nations from the Central and Eastern European parts of the Soviet Bloc in the mix and the situation is even more complicated (Lykes and Richardson 2014; Richardson and Lee 2014). For example, Russia, while initially quite open to different religions post-1990, quickly reverted to a society where the Russian Orthodox Church (ROC) demanded its traditional dominant position, and Russian politicians were quick to assist (Shterin and Richardson 1998, 2000; Richardson, Krylova, and Shterin 2004). Poland's loyal Catholic opposition to Soviet domination quickly evolved after the Soviet Union dissolved to a situation where the Church tried to enforce Catholic values in every sphere of Polish life (Daniel 1995; Richardson 1997). Hungary was at first open to minority faiths and took an officially positive view of religious freedom and the role of religion in society. But of late the situation has changed dramatically. Severe restrictions have been placed on minority faiths, with many losing official recognition as a result (Baer 2012, 2013; Uitz 2012). Yet other nations that the Soviet Union once dominated have reacted differently. The Baltic countries, particularly Latvia and Estonia, have demonstrated that religious freedom for minority religions is a highly valued concept (Krumina-Konkova 2004; Ringvee 2009; Barnett 2010; Alisauskiene 2011; Richardson and Lee 2014). Thus the variegated pattern concerning religious freedom in Europe became much more challenging to understand with the decision of many formerly Soviet-dominated countries to seek membership in the Council of Europe (COE). However, even in this very complicated situation signs appear that religious freedom may be gaining traction, through efforts of some national courts, but especially the European Court of Human Rights, which is the judicial arm of the Council of Europe established to enforce the European Convention of Human Rights and Fundamental Freedoms. The ECtHR finally, after forty years of ignoring Article 9 of the Convention, began to find violations of that article in 1993 (Richardson 1995; Evans 2001). Since then the ECtHR has been able to work in concert with some constitutional courts in the region to promote religious freedom, as will be described (Richardson and Lykes 2012; Lykes and Richardson 2014; Richardson and Lee 2014).[3] Whether the efforts of various national courts and of the ECtHR will continue is uncertain, of course, as is the question of whether governments will respond positively to court decisions that further religious freedom. But at present a pattern of decisions shows promise for those valuing religious freedom.

First, a few sample court cases from national courts in Western European countries bear mentioning. Germany's powerful constitutional court ruled in 2005 in favor of Jehovah's Witnesses gaining significant formal recognition as a "corporation under public law" within the German legal system, thus ending a fifteen-year legal battle (Besier 2009). The decision came in spite of the German penchant for paternalism regarding religious participation. In France, a recent October 2013 decision by the French Supreme Court upheld the request of Jehovah's Witnesses for access to prisons through a system of volunteer chaplains.[4] And recently (December 2013) in the United Kingdom, in a case over whether a Scientologist could legally officiate in a marriage ceremony, the Supreme Court rendered a decision that Scientology was a religion.[5] The decision represents a major shift from the official position of Scientology in the

United Kingdom, as it was just a few decades ago that the United Kingdom would not allow Scientologists to immigrate.[6]

Next, a few widely separated key decisions of the ECtHR concerning Western European nations that were a part of the original Member States of the Council of Europe will be discussed. Obviously the first to mention because of its timing is the famous 1993 *Kokkinakis* case from Greece. That case was perhaps a deliberate effort for the court to send a message to the nations newly emerging from the burdens of Soviet domination that Article 9 guaranteeing freedom of thought, conscience, and religion would no longer be ignored. Greece's criminalizing of proselytizing made it a handy example to use, and that example was followed over the years with many other decisions finding Article 9 violations, with nearly all of them coming from newer members of the COE from Central and Eastern Europe (or Greece) (Richardson and Garay 2004; Richardson and Shoemaker 2008).

Only recently did the ECtHR finally find an original member state, France, guilty of violating Article 9. In June 2011, the court ruled that France had, by actions its tax authorities took to force huge tax payments on contributions, violated Article 9 with the Jehovah's Witnesses. The Aumist religion and another religious group, the Evangelical Missionary Church, also won similar cases in the ECtHR, and all three were awarded large amounts of damages (Lykes and Richardson 2014). This series of decisions marked the first time a major original member state of the COE had suffered defeat in the Strasbourg Court in an Article 9 case.

The recent spate of Article 9 decisions seems to be based not so much on the concept of individual religious freedom, but on preserving the right of religious organizations to exist, as Australian legal scholar Carolyn Evans (2010) and former ECtHR justice Lech Garlicki (2007) have claimed. This could help explain why there are few Article 9 decisions from original member states (except Greece), but many from Central and Eastern Europe, where serious efforts have been mounted to force minority religious groups to leave, curtail their activities, or even suffer legal dissolution. This focus on preserving the right of religious organizations to exist is well illustrated by a series of cases brought and won by the Jehovah's Witnesses, who have amassed an impressive record before the ECtHR, with more than thirty victories to date (Richardson 2014). A series of cases also demonstrates the role of the ECtHR in preserving the right of religious organizations to exist, as well as the interactions that can occur between constitutional courts and the ECtHR, if conditions are ripe for such cooperation (Sadurski 2009; Richardson and Lee 2014).

Russia, as the Soviet Union was imploding, passed laws and approved constitutional provisions modeled after Western documents guaranteeing religious freedom, and indeed, many minority faiths came to Russia in the early 1990s and flourished. But the period of openness did not last long, and a much more restrictive law was approved in 1997 that included among other requirements one that made reregistration mandatory (Durham and Homer 1998; Shterin and Richardson 1998, 2000). This provision was clearly designed to allow the

Russian bureaucracy to deny reregistration, and that is what happened for a number of groups that had come into Russia in the early 1990s and been legally registered. Repeated efforts to reregister were denied, and authorities in some regions of Russia also undertook other ways of harassing newer and smaller religious groups. This led to several legal actions by some of those religious groups, including the Society of Jesus, the Salvation Army, the Jehovah's Witnesses, and Scientology, as well as other groups. These suits nearly always failed at the local trial court level, but some were then taken to the Russian Constitutional Court, where a few were successful, with the court ruling that the reregistration requirement could not be enforced on groups that had been properly registered when the 1997 law was passed (Richardson and Shoemaker 2008).

However, even with these victories in the Constitutional Court, the Russian bureaucracy still refused to allow reregistration, leading to several cases being taken to the ECtHR. The ECtHR sided with the Constitutional Court, ruling against Russia in a series of cases with unanimous and strongly worded judgments. And it even ruled in favor of Scientology although the Russian Constitutional Court had rejected a Scientology case. Russia has reluctantly paid the small amounts of damages ordered and has allowed reregistration in some cases, which are positive signs. However, as is well known, Russia is chaffing under these rulings, in part because of opposition by the ROC to the secular tenor of many of the ECtHR's rulings (Kahn 2004).

As several scholars have noted, Russia is being influenced more and more by the rulings of the ECtHR in the area of religion and in other areas as well (Burkov 2012). So the long-term effects of Russia joining the COE remain to be seen. However, if Russia succumbs to the influence of the ECtHR as the court attempts to enforce the European Convention, it would be reasonable to assume that other nations in the region will also move in the direction of allowing more minority religious groups to function. And, as noted with the three recent ECtHR cases from France, even original member states are also caught up in the efforts of the court to enforce Article 9, especially if the very existence of a religious organization is at stake.

U.S. legislation and jurisprudence

Two issues bear discussing regarding major jurisprudential patterns in the United States. One is the way so-called brainwashing legal cases were eventually forced out of courts by two major federal court rulings (with considerable assistance by scholars). A second issue concerns the legislative and judicial response to a major Supreme Court decision in 1990 that seemed to dramatically limit protections for religious freedom in America.

As most may be aware, for a time in the United States, courts accepted brainwashing-based claims against NRMs as valid and granted large damage awards to plaintiffs in civil suits against NRMs such as Hare Krishna, the Unification Church, and Scientology (Anthony 1990; Richardson 1991, 1993; Anthony and Robbins 1992). Such outcomes caused consternation for scholars (and professional organizations). Some scholars who thought such claims were bogus and built on a pseudoscientific theory became involved in legal actions based on so-called brainwashing.[7] Eventually such cases were unsuccessful, failing on evidentiary grounds (Anthony and Robbins 1992; Ginsburg and Richardson 1998). These battles over so-called cult brainwashing were a major battleground between the scholarly community of researchers doing research on NRMs and anti-cult movement organizations and individuals who opposed the spread of NRMs. (See Richardson 1996 for one account of these legal battles.)

The "cult war" legal battles ceased in the early 1990s after a major ruling by a federal judge in 1990 in California finally stopped these kinds of cases. In *U.S. v. Fishman* (1990), a former Scientologist accused of fraud attempted to use a brainwashing-based defense. Margaret Singer and Richard Ofshe, the two major proponents of brainwashing theories as applied to NRM participants, were precluded from testifying that the defendant in the case had been brainwashed into committing criminal acts. NRM scholar Dick Anthony contributed most to this effort, but other scholars were involved in this and similar cases.

The *Fishman* ruling contributed directly to an important ruling in 1991 by the District of Columbia (Washington, DC) Federal Appeal Court in *Green and Ryan v. Maharishi Mahesh Yogi et al.* (1991), which involved the Transcendental Meditation organization. In that civil case a district court had allowed brainwashing-based testimony from Margaret Singer, resulting in a ruling in favor of the plaintiffs. But that ruling was overturned on appeal, which meant that there were two major federal cases, one criminal and one civil, where brainwashing-based testimony was precluded. And one of the rulings was by the most important federal appeals court in the United States, in Washington, DC. These rulings effectively meant an end to brainwashing-based legal claims involving religious groups in both federal and state courts in the United States.

The second issue to discuss concerns legislative efforts to overcome a ruling by the U.S. Supreme Court in 1990 that seemed to limit severely religious freedom–based claims in the United States. The *Employment Division v. Smith* decision in 1990 involved peyote use in a religious ritual by two members of the Native American Church in Oregon, which resulted in their dismissal from jobs as substance abuse counselors. They filed for unemployment compensation and were denied, so they sued in Oregon courts and won. But the Oregon attorney general appealed the case all the way to the U.S. Supreme Court, which ruled against the plaintiffs and issued a ruling stating that a law that was otherwise neutral on its face was constitutional even if its application resulted in harm to a religious group or practice. The ruling dismissed the traditional approach normally used in freedom of religion cases, including the "strict scrutiny" review and the "compelling interest" and "least restrictive means" tests.[8]

The *Smith* decision led in turn to the nearly unanimous passage by Congress of the Religious Freedom Restoration Act (RFRA) in 1993, which restored the traditional tests used in jurisprudence concerning religious freedom cases involving governmental entities. But in 1997 the Supreme Court ruled this new RFRA law unconstitutional in the *Boerne* case as applied to local and state governments (Richardson 1999). The case involved an effort by a Catholic church to expand and renovate its building, which was located in a designated historical district in a suburb of San Antonio, Texas. The church lost at the local level, won at the appeals court level, but then lost at the U.S. Supreme Court, striking a blow against traditional views of religious freedom in America, as least as applied to local and state governments.[9]

However, a somewhat differently constituted Supreme Court (several new members) in a later case did unanimously support RFRA as it applied to federal agencies in a case involving a small Brazilian religious group in New Mexico that used *hoasca*, a substance that included an illegal drug. This case is apparently the first instance when a religious freedom claim defeated a claim related to the infamous "War on Drugs," so it represents an important milestone (Richardson and Shoemaker 2014), and demonstrates that the courts in America are supportive of religious freedom if the laws are written in such a way as to sanction such freedoms.

Congress, upset by the Supreme Court's overruling of RFRA, eventually tried to "correct" the impact of the *Boerne* case on local and state governments by passing the Religious Land Use and Institutionalized Persons Act (RLUIPA) unanimously on the same day (July 27, 2000) in both houses of Congress. Since its passage RLUIPA has been criticized by legal scholars and others who think it much too broad and granting too much power to religious groups in our society (Hamilton 2014). Note that heretofore both land use decisions and the treatment of prisoners had been left to the individual states to manage, with little interference from the federal government. However, RLUIPA explicitly stated that religious land use claims should prevail over most efforts of local and state governments to control the building of religious facilities in certain areas. This part of RLUIPA has facilitated the building of meeting houses for a number of minority religious groups, including Muslim groups, throughout the United States (a development itself somewhat controversial in some circles) (see Note 2007).

RLUIPA also guaranteed that persons who are institutionalized have religious freedom rights as well. This latter idea, which was quite controversial as the new law was being considered, garnered unanimous support from the Supreme Court in a prison case out of Ohio, *Cutter v. Wilkinson* (2005), which resulted in a ruling in favor of a set of prisoners in Ohio who sued, claiming that their religious rights under RLUIPA were being violated because prison officials were not allowing them to practice their religions. The plaintiffs included a Satanist, a Wiccan, a member of Asatru, and a member of the Church of Jesus Christ-Christian, a white supremacy group. This ruling in favor of unpopular and controversial religious minorities clearly shows that religious freedom is important to the Supreme Court, even when the groups bringing the legal action are somewhat exotic and their views counter those of mainstream America.

Thus it appears that the U.S. Supreme Court has moved considerably in the direction of protecting religious freedom rights for minority faiths since the *Smith* decision in 1990. Whether this is a result of the changing membership of the court (with the death of Antonin Scalia, a Catholic, in February 2016, it now has five Catholics and three Jews, and, for the first time, no Protestants at all!), an example of the members of the court "getting the message" from Congress that religious freedom is important to Americans, or some other reason can be debated. Whatever the reason(s), the trajectory toward more religious freedom in the United States seems reasonably clear. Minority religions do not win every case, but current federal (and state-level – recall the mini-RRA laws passed by many states) legislation and jurisprudence about those statutes suggest that religious freedom concerns have gained momentum in America, much to the consternation of some (Hamilton 2014).

Conclusion

This descriptive presentation of developing patterns of jurisprudence in Europe and America offers modest grounds for thinking religious freedom is gaining momentum in at least some parts of the world, and that the courts are playing a major role is defining the meaning of religious freedom in the West.[10] This is a controversial claim, of course, especially in the light of such arguments as that of Winnifred Sullivan (2005) about the impossibility of religious freedom, given the many controversies and conflicts about the meaning of the term in contemporary societies. Her point is well taken, and is demonstrated by decisions from the same courts to which I referred earlier, where confusion about the meaning of religious freedom is revealed.[11] However, I would argue that there is an overall coherence to recent major court decisions in both Europe and the United States, and that a pattern of increasing tolerance is discernable.

There are several caveats to offer before proponents of religious freedom celebrate too much. One concern is that these major cases discussed from the two regions do not mean that all minority religious groups and participants win their cases. That is definitely not the case (and sometimes perhaps they should not prevail for reasons that have nothing to do with religious freedom). Minority religious groups continue to struggle in many parts of the world, especially where once powerful religions are regaining strength and influence, as in formerly Soviet-dominated nations in Central and Eastern Europe. But even in that part of the world some constitutional courts and the ECtHR seem focused on protecting the right of minority religious groups to exist and function.

Another caveat concerns Islam, and the growing disquiet about Islam in many Western nations. There have been controversies in several Western nations with Muslim minorities about wearing religious clothing and symbols, food preparation, circumcision practices, the building of mosques, and the application of provisions of Shari'a dealing with family matters (see Berger 2013; Possamai, Richardson, and Turner 2015 for discussions). In America, for instance, conservative religious groups who strongly supported RFRA and RLUIPA have had second thoughts now that RLUIPA's implications for the building of mosques have become known. The growing focus on Islam in Western societies could represent a major test of how those societies treat minority religions in the future.

A third caveat concerns the puzzle of why the patterns I discern are occurring. Governments are expected to "manage" the growing religious pluralism in societies in order to control conflict and potential violence (Richardson 2004). Why that management has in some nations and regions seemed to result in more tolerance for minority faiths requires explanation. I and others have written elsewhere about the sociological conditions that seem to foster religious freedom (Richardson 2006a, 2006b). I believe those conditions should include considerable focus on the important role of the courts and the legal system, as well as the history and culture of the society. Roger Finke (2013) also has addressed judicial systems, highlighting the important role of the judicial autonomy for the development of religious freedom. The patterns discerned in this brief paper would seem to fit well with the logic on my earlier theorizing, as well as that of Finke.

Only time will tell what will happen in the future in this important arena, and why, but the patterns described herein seem to promise expansion of religious freedom in at least some parts of the world. Scholars who value religious freedom and organizations such as INFORM and CESNUR must continue to be vigilant and to develop objective, research-based information on religious groups to share in whatever forum it might be relevant, including the courts.

Notes

1 This chapter will focus on the United States and Europe, including Central and Eastern Europe. However, I believe the comments made here also would pertain to other nations oriented toward the West in terms of values and legal considerations. See Moon (2014) for discussions of this issue in Canada, Bouma (2011) for discussion of Australia's positive view of religious freedom, and Ahdar (2006) for an assessment of the situation in New Zealand. For an overall assessment of the state of religious freedom around the world, see the annual International Religious Freedom Reports of the U.S. Department of State available at www.state.gov/j/drl/rls/irf/.
2 It perhaps goes without saying that many scholars of religion and organizations such as INFORM, CESNUR, and others have played a role in the development of the jurisprudential patterns described herein. Some organizations have furnished important information to parliaments and other legislative bodies, and a number of scholars have engaged in public discussions of religious freedom and have served as consultants to courts and as expert witnesses.
3 See Scheppele (2003) and Sadurski (2008) for a discussion of the growing and important role of constitutional courts in formerly Soviet-dominated Central and Eastern Europe, and Richardson and Shterin (2008) and Richardson (2006a) for a discussion of the role of these courts in Hungary and Russia.
4 The case was decided on October 16, 2013, by the Council of State, the highest administrative law court in France. See www.droit-tj.fr/spip.php?article349 accessed on August 29, 2014.

5 *R (on the application of Hodkin and another) v. Registrar General of Births, Deaths and Marriage*, judgment given on December 11, 2013.
6 The European Court of Justice agreed with the UK ban on Scientologist immigration in the *van Duyn* case in 1974, but the official UK ban was ended in 1980.
7 The conflict was chronicled in a special print symposium of *Nova Religio* in 1998 that included articles by Massimo Introvigne, Thomas Robbins, this author, and others.
8 These tests mean that if a governmental entity is to interfere with someone's religious activities, it must demonstrate a compelling governmental interest to justify such actions, and the government must also show that it is using the least restrictive means to accomplish the governmental purpose.
9 The *Boerne* decision led to a number of states passing "mini-RFRAs" as well, but the effect of those state statutes is unclear at this time.
10 I am not naïve about the severe restrictions on religious freedom that exist in other parts of the world, where proselytizing and changing one's religion can even be defined as a capital offense. This chapter is focused on parts of the world that differ considerably from what is found in places such as China, Iran, or other countries with strict regulation of religious activities and groups (see Pew Research Foundation 2014).
11 See Evans (2001) for a critical assessment of the ECtHR jurisprudence that demonstrates considerable confusion on the meaning of religious freedom and how it should best be protected.

References

Ahdar, Rex. 2006. "Reflections on the path of religion-state relations in New Zealand." *Brigham Young University Law Review*, 2006: 619–59.
Alisauskiene, Milda. 2011. "Freedom of religion in the Baltic states." In Andras Mate-Toth and Cosima Rughinis (eds.), *Spaces and Borders: Current Research on Religions in Central and Eastern Europe* (pp. 141–9). Berlin: De Gruyter.
Anthony, Dick. 1990. "Religious movements and brainwashing litigation: Evaluating key testimony." In T. Robbins and D. Anthony (eds.), *In Gods We Trust* (pp. 295–344). New Brunswick, NJ: Transaction Books.
———. and Thomas Robbins. 1992. "Law, social science, and the 'brainwashing' exception to the Frist Amendment." *Behavioral Sciences & the Law*, 10: 5–30.
Baer, David. 2012. "The fate of Hungary's deregistered churches." Accessed May 20, 2013 at: http://hungarianspectrum.wordpress.com/2012/08/13/david-baer-the-fate-of-hungarys-deregistered-churches/
———. 2013. "Testimony concerning the condition of religious freedom in Hungary." Submitted to the U.S. Commission on Security and Cooperation in Europe (the Helsinki Commission), March 18. Accessed May 20, 2013 at: http://hungarianspectrum.wordpress.com/2013/03/20/testimony-of-h-david-baer-texan-lutheran-university-for-the-record/
Barnett, Simon. 2010. "Religious freedom and the European Convention on Human Rights: The case of the Baltic states." *Religion, State and Society*, 29: 91–100.
Berger, Maurits. 2013. *Applying Shari'a in the West*. Leiden: Leiden University Press.
Besier, Gerald. 2009. "How to understand religious freedom in Germany." *Religion-Staat-Geselllschaft*, 10: 325–36.
Bouma, Gary. 2011. *Being Faithful in Diversity*. Adelaide: ATF Press.
Burkov, Anton. 2012. "Russia." In Leonard Hammer and Frank Emmert (eds.), *The European Convention on Human Rights and Fundamental Freedoms in Central and Eastern Europe* (pp. 425–77). The Hague: Eleven International Publishing.

Daniel, Krystyna. 1995. "The church-state situation in Poland after the collapse of communism." *Brigham Young University Law Review*, 1995: 401–19.

Durham, Cole and L. Homer. 1998. "Russia's 1997 law on freedom of conscience and on religious associations: An analytical appraisal." *Emory International Law Review*, 12: 101–246.

Evans, Carolyn. 2001. *Freedom of Religion under the European Convention on Human Rights*. Oxford: Oxford University Press.

———. 2010. "Individual and group religious freedom in the European Court of Human Rights: Cracks in the intellectual architecture." *Journal of Law and Religion*, 26: 321–43.

Finke, Roger. 2013. "Origins and consequences of religious freedom: A global overview." *Sociology of Religion*, 74: 297–313.

Garlicki, Lech. 2007. "Collective aspects of the religious freedoms: Recent developments in the case law of the European Court of Human Rights." In A. Sajo (ed.), *Censored Sensitivities: Free Speech and Religion in a Fundamentalist World* (pp. 217–33). The Hague: Eleven International Publishing.

Ginsburg, Gerald and J. T. Richardson. 1998. "'Brainwashing' evidence in light of *Daubert*." In Helen Reece (ed.), *Law and Science* (pp. 265–88). Oxford: Oxford University Press.

Hamilton, Marci. 2014. *God versus the Gavel: The Perils of Extreme Religious Liberty*. Cambridge: Cambridge University Press.

Hirschi, Ran. 2006. "The new constitutionalism and the judicialization of pure politics." *Fordham Law Review*, 75: 721–34.

Kahn, J. D. 2004. "Russia's 'dictatorship of law' and the European Court of Human Rights." *Review of Central and East European Law*, 29: 1–14.

Krumina-Konkova, Solveiga. 2004. "New religious minorities in the Baltic states." In Phillip Lucas and Thomas Robbins (eds.), *New Religious Movements in the 21st Century* (pp. 117–27). New York: Routledge.

Lucas, Phillip and Thomas Robbins. 2004. *New Religious Movements in the 21st Century*. New York: Routledge.

Lykes, Valerie and J. T. Richardson. 2014. "The European Court of Human Rights, minority religions, and new versus original member states." In J. T. Richardson and Francois Bellanger (eds.), *Legal Cases Involving New Religious Movements and Minority Faiths* (pp. 171–201). Burlington, VT: Ashgate.

Moon, Richard. 2014. "The constitutional protection of religious practices in Canada." In David Kirkham (ed.), *State Responses to Minority Religions* (pp. 231–42). Burlington, VT: Ashgate.

Note. 2007. "Religious land use in the Federal Courts under RLUIPA." *Harvard Law Review*, 120: 2178–99.

Pew Research Foundation. 2014. "Which countries still outlaw apostasy and blasphemy?" May 29. Accessed August 28, 2014 at: http://us1.campaign-archive2.com/?u=434f5d1199912232d416897e4&id=9518ebe5f5&e=2cc60d08b4.

Possamai, Adam, J. T. Richardson, and Bryan Turner. 2015. *The Sociology of Shari'a*. New York: Springer.

Richardson, James T. 1991. "Cult/brainwashing cases and the freedom of religion." *Journal of Church and State*, 33: 55–74.

———. 1993. "A social-psychological critique of 'brainwashing' claims about recruitment to new religions." In J. Hadden and D. Bromley (eds.), *Handbook of Cults and Sects in America* (pp. 75–97). Greenwich, CT: JAI Press.

———. 1995. "Minority religions, religious freedom, and the new pan-European parliamentary and judicial institutions." *Journal of Church and State*, 37: 39–59.

———. 1996. "Sociology and the new religions: 'Brainwashing,' the courts, and freedom of religion." In Pamela Jenkins and Steve Kroll-Smith (eds.), *Witnessing for Sociology* (pp. 115–34). Westport, CT: Praeger.

———. 1997. "Minority religions in former Communist countries: A sociological analysis." In I. Borowik and G. Babinski (eds.), *New Religious Phenomena in Central and Eastern Europe* (pp. 257–82). Krakow: Nomos.

———. 1999. "The Religious Freedom Restoration Act: A short-lived experiment in religious freedom." In D. Guinn, C. Barrigar, and K. Young (eds.), *Religion and Law in the Global Village* (pp. 142–64). Atlanta, GA: Scholars Press.

———. 2004. *Regulating Religion: Case Studies from around the Globe.* New York: Kluwer.

———. 2006a. "Religion, constitutional courts, and democracy in former Communist countries." *The Annals of the American Academy of Political and Social Science*, 603: 129–38.

———. 2006b. "The sociology of religious freedom: A structural and socio-legal analysis." *Sociology of Religion*, 67: 271–94.

———. 2014. "In defense of religious rights: Jehovah's Witness cases from around the world." In Stephen Hunt (ed.), *Handbook of Global Contemporary Christianity* (pp. 285–307). New York: Brill.

Richardson, James T. and Alain Garay. 2004. The European Court of Human Rights and former Communist states." In D. Jerolimov, S. Zrinscak, and I. Borowik (eds.), *Religion and Patterns of Social Transformation* (pp. 223–34). Zagreb: Institute for Social Research.

Richardson, James T., Galina Krylova, and Marat Shterin. 2004. "Legal regulation of religion in Russia: New developments." In J. T. Richardson (ed.), *Regulating Religion: Case Studies from around the Globe* (pp. 247–58). New York: Kluwer.

Richardson, James T. and Brian Lee. 2014. "The role of the courts in the social construction of religious freedom in Central and Eastern Europe." *Review of Central and Eastern Europe Law*, 39: 291–313.

Richardson, James T. and Valerie Lykes. 2012. "Legal considerations concerning new religious movements in the 'new Europe.'" In Peter Cumper and Tom Lewis (eds.), *Religion, Rights and Secular Society* (pp. 293–322). Cheltenham, UK: Edward Elgar.

Richardson, James T. and Jennifer Shoemaker. 2008. "The European Court of Human Rights, minority religions, and the social construction of religious freedom." In E. Barker (ed.), *The Centrality of Religion in Social Life: Essays in Honour of James A. Beckford* (pp. 103–16). Aldershot: Ashgate.

———. 2014. "The resurrection of religion in the U.S.? The 'tea' cases, the Religious Freedom Restoration Act, and the war on drugs." In J. T. Richardson and Francois Bellanger (eds.), *Legal Cases Involving New Religious Movements and Minority Faiths.* Burlington, VT: Ashgate.

Richardson, James T. and Marat Shterin. 2008. "Constitutional courts in post-Communist Russia and Hungary: How do they treat religion?" *Religion, State, & Society*, 36(3): 251–67.

Ringvee, Ringo. 2009. "Legal aspects of state-church relations in the Baltic states, and the Jehovah's Witnesses." *Religion, Staat, Gesellschaft*, 10: 249–65.

Sadurski, Wojciech. 2008. *Rights before the Courts: A Study of Constitutional Courts in Post-Communist States in Central and Eastern Europe.* Dordrecht: Springer.

———. 2009. "Partnering with Strasbourg: Constitutionalisation of the European Court of Human Rights, the accession of Central and East European states into the Council of Europe and the idea of pilot judgments." *Human Rights Law Review*, 9: 397–453.

Scheppele, Kim. 2003. "Constitutional negotiations: Political contexts of political activism in post-Soviet Europe." *International Sociology*, 18: 219–38.

Shterin, Marat and James T. Richardson 1998. "Local laws on religion in Russia: Precursors of Russia's national law." *Journal of Church and State*, 40: 319–41.
———. 2000. "Effects of the Western anti-cult movement on development of laws concerning religion in post-Communist Russia." *Journal of Church and State*, 42: 247–72.
Sullivan, Winnifred Fallers. 2005. *The Impossibility of Religious Freedom*. Princeton, NJ: Princeton University Press.
Tate, Neal and Torbjorn Vallinder. 1995. *The Global Expansion of Judicial Power*. New York: New York University Press.
Uitz, Renata. 2012. "The pendulum of church-state relations in Hungary." In Peter Cumper and Tom Lewis (eds.), *Religion, Rights and Secular Society* (pp. 189–214). Cheltenham, UK: Edward Elgar.

8 Is an anti-cult movement emerging in Croatia?[1]

Dinka Marinović Jerolimov and Ankica Marinović

Two cult-awareness groups (CAGs) registered as non-governmental organisations (NGOs) have appeared in Croatia during the past few years, emphasising the struggle against cults and sects in their programmes: The Centre for Information on Sects and Cults (CISK) and The Guardian Angels. We started a case study focussing on this type of social response to new religious movements (NRMs), with the aim of exploring the potential for development of an anti-cult movement in Croatia.

Introduction

Soon after their appearance in the United States in the 1960s and the beginning of the 1970s, new religions spread across Western Europe as well. Following this pattern, counter-movements, as one type of social response to NRMs, also appeared as 'cultural imports' from the United States. Nevertheless, considerable differences exist among European countries concerning minority religions, particularly in their treatment in laws and official reports, which are historically and culturally embedded.

The post-Communist European countries were not exempted from these phenomena, particularly after democratisation processes started in 1989. The increase in the number of NRMs in post-Communist countries is one of the features of religious changes these countries share (Borowik and Babiński eds. 1997). But there are differences in the legal status of these new groups, in their number and in social and legal responses to their appearance, which reflect different historical, cultural and religious situations in those countries (Richardson ed. 2004). Despite these differences, minority religions are generally publicly perceived as a social problem across Europe.

Theoretical concepts

The anti-cult movement (ACM) comprises secular organisations focussed on the actions NRMs take and is based on the assumption that the majority of these movements are destructive to individuals, families and societies (Chryssides and Wilkins 2006; Richardson and Introvigne 2007). Its focus on the *behaviour* of NRMs differentiates this secular anti-cult movement from the counter-cult movement (CCM), which focusses on group *doctrines* and consists primarily of conservative Christian anti-cultists, ministers and laypeople (Introvigne 1995). Key elements of the ACM include: ideology (the brainwashing or mind control thesis[2]), formation of counter-movement organisations, rituals (deprogramming) and testimony from apostates (Richardson and Introvigne 2007: 95). Removing 'cults' and 'sects' from the category of religion and framing cult-related problems as 'economic', 'political' or 'psychological' is one of the aims of ACM (Beckford 2001).

Reaction and engagement of parents and relatives of participants in NRMs, together with activities of anti-cult groups and individuals, supported by mostly negative media coverage, has resulted in perceiving NRMs as a social problem. The media have played a crucial role in constructing (mostly negative) public opinion about NRMs, especially when they support ACM efforts to promote concern and even moral panic[3] about NRMs. An exaggeration of events, distortion and stereotyping in presenting NRMs are usual tools employed in media accounts. Scholars of religion are usually left out, while in-depth, serious investigative reporting has seldom occurred (Beckford 2001; Beckford and Cole 1988; Richardson and Introvigne 2007).

Finally, particularly important for our case study is Barker's (2002, 2007) ideal-type of cult-awareness groups (CAGs), which focus on the harm destructive cults do. CAGs are one of the ideal-types of cult-watching groups (CWGs) which disseminate information about cults. In our discussion we will compare characteristics of groups analysed in our case study with Barker's ideal-type.

Methodology

Different methods were used in this study: analysis of events and actions of the groups and actors involved, semi-structured interviews with different actors, analysis of documents (conference papers and letters to political authorities), analysis of web pages of organisations and selected media coverage (video materials and interviews). Interviews with leaders of the two groups analysed were conducted during September 2014 by telephone and e-mail.

The case study

Social and religious context

During the Communist period (1945–90), religion and churches in Croatia (a part of the former Yugoslavia) had been viewed negatively, were suppressed in the private sphere and did not have any social impact. Religion, however, did not disappear from people's lives; it was widely spread in traditional forms across all segments of society. In the context of confessional differences (Catholic, Orthodox, Muslim), Croatia was, together with Slovenia, the most religious part of the former Communist Yugoslavia. The post-Communist transitional context in Croatia, as well as in most other post-Communist countries, has been marked by a considerable increase of declared religiosity (Marinović Jerolimov 2001; Zrinščak et al. 2000).

According to the 2011 Croatian census, 86.28 per cent declared themselves Catholic, 4.44 per cent Orthodox, 1.47 per cent Muslim, while slightly more than 1 per cent belongs to other religious communities. A diverse minority religious scene includes forty-six registered and legally recognised religious communities, together with at least a similar number of religious and spiritual groups, more or less visible in the public sphere, which are not registered yet.[4]

Until recently when two CAGs appeared, no anti-cult organisations existed in Croatia. But an example of the initial instance of moral panic occurred in 1988 in Zagreb, the capitol of Croatia.[5] Media spread the story about previously unknown group 'Crna ruža' ('Black Rose') within the youth subculture, whose members were inspired by occult ideas, listened to dark (gothic) music, and wore black clothes, make-up, crosses and pentagrams. The panic escalated after the suicide of a girl member (Goldberger et al. 2010: 46). After the police reports showed the most accurate accounts of events, and the real number of acts and actors involved, the panic cooled down (Goldberger et al. 2010).

Nevertheless, from the 1990s we can list a few cases whose appearance stimulated some of the elements characterising an anti-cult moral panic, especially involving ISKCON and TM. They used stereotypes and prejudices against NRMs, highlighting their threat to Croatian traditional national and religious values. The Catholic Church representatives contributed to anti-cult discourse in those cases as well. But they remained only 'a few-day stories' (Goldberger et al. 2010).

Relevant legal documents

After the establishment of an independent Croatia on 25 June 1991, all religious communities registered during socialism have been re-registered automatically, according to previous 'socialist law', valid until a new law was passed in 2002. This *interregnum* enabled registration of a certain number of new religious communities, including, for example, the Church of Scientology.

The Constitution of the Republic of Croatia proclaims the separation between church and state, and defines and guarantees religious freedom and the protection of religious rights. It emphasises the equality of all religious communities before the law and ensures their right to freely perform religious services in public under the protection and assistance of the state (The Constitution of the Republic of Croatia 2001, articles 14, 17, 39, 40 and 41).

After Croatia established a diplomatic relationship with the Holy See in 1992, regulation concerning the Catholic Church was completed by signing four agreements between the government of Croatia and the Holy See. By signing first the agreements of mutual interest with the dominant Catholic Church, the government recognised its special historical and cultural role and social position.

In 2002 the Religious Communities Act was finally approved. Besides conditions needed for registering (500 members and being registered for five years as an association of citizens), it includes a ban of intolerance and prejudice and requires that religious communities must not act against legal order, public morality, life and health or other rights and freedoms of their followers and other citizens.

Between 2002 and 2010 the government of the Republic of Croatia signed agreements about issues of mutual interest with another sixteen religious communities which assured government support for their finances and created better conditions for their religious activities in general.

In December 2004 the government approved 'the Instruction', an act in which additional new conditions for concluding agreements on issues of mutual interest for religious communities have been determined. But among the consequences of the Instruction were discrimination against some minority religious groups which sued the Republic of Croatia in the European Court of Human Rights (ECHR). After the ECHR ruling in favour of three communities, they finally concluded agreements with the government in 2014 (Marinović and Marinović Jerolimov 2012).

Analysis of two anti-cult groups: CISK

The dynamic of processes in which two CAG groups and associated individuals were involved is of particular interest, because they can help us to answer the question of the potential for further development of an ACM in Croatia.

The first group, the Centre for Information on Sects and Cults (CISK), was registered in 2007, although it was founded in 1997, according to information on its website.[6] This group is affiliated with FECRIS, the European Federation of Centres of Research and Information on Sectarianism. The leader of CISK in Croatia, Branka Dujmi -Delcourt, is also a member of the governing board of FECRIS, lives in Belgium, and occasionally comes to Croatia. She told us that the members are all volunteers, but was not prepared to give information about their number or the finances of the organisation. Also, she gave us only information that could be found at the CISK website.[7] No address of the organisation is posted, only an e-mail address.

On its website CISK is presented as an affiliated member of FECRIS and the latter is described as an international NGO with participative status in the Council of Europe since 2005 and special counselling status in the UN Economic and Social Council. The goals of CISK are declared as: 1) collecting information and research on the position, existence and temptations of individuals and families in modern society; 2) monitoring, researching and informing citizens about the activities, existence, organisation and possible consequences of actions of so-called alternative movements, sects and cults, and individuals who belong to them; 3) research and information on organisations or individuals that use methods of manipulation and fraud, thus abusing generally recognised human rights and freedoms in the areas of culture, art, ethics, health, economic existence and everyday personal and family life while leaving man and a family in a state of physical, emotional, spiritual and economic dependency, exhaustion and crisis.

A comparison between religion and sects is also posted on the website in which religions are valued positively, as opposed to cults, which are valued negatively.

The post 'How to recognise a sect' indicates how CISK perceives them, using extensive anti-cult vocabulary combined with a picture of a sheep as a metaphor for sect followers.

Dujmić-Delcourt's activities as leader of CISK include organising a conference in Rijeka, establishing a network of supporters, writing letters to politicians and officials and giving interviews in the press, for Internet sites, and for (mostly commercial) TV stations. We present here examples of the content of conferences and letters sent to authorities.

The conference 'The Destructive Groups and Youth' was held at the University of Rijeka on 26 November 2010 with the support of FECRIS and Rijeka County. Participants included the president of FECRIS, presidents and representatives of similar organisations from Europe[8] and CISK, an MP from Australia, representatives of the University of Rijeka and Rijeka County, psychiatrists, psychologists, social workers, psychotherapists, a paediatrician, a nutritionist, a neurologist, a physician and a Catholic theologian.

At the beginning eight leaders of anti-cult organisations addressed the conference, stressing that sects, particularly Scientology, are dangerous for society, the family and individuals. In the second session, 'The Impact of Destructive Groups on Vulnerable Persons', various experts from Croatia participated, but experts in religious studies were not invited.

The conference resulted with a formal declaration that states: 1) their goal is prevention of illegal activities of destructive groups; 2) vulnerable groups are children, adults, the elderly, the ill and the poor; 3) bodies that supervise the work of legalised destructive groups should be set up; 4) a mere likelihood that a certain group is destructive is a reason for supervision of destructive groups; 5) regulatory bodies, such as the police and other governmental bodies, should set up an information network with the corresponding European bodies, including records and files containing information on destructive groups and victims; 6) European countries should support and harmonise legislation on destructive groups and organise systematic education of all participants in the education process, including judges, state attorneys, solicitors, police officers and parents; 7) they should also organise education appropriate to age and other features of vulnerable groups; establish one national and four regional centres that would have an advisory role and develop international collaboration; and 8) measures of protection from actions of destructive groups should respect human rights, although repressive measures should be considered too.

On 14 May 2012, the president of FECRIS, Tom Sackville, sent a letter to the president of the Republic of Croatia, Ivo Josipović; the Croatian prime minister, Zoran Milanović; and the speaker of the Croatian parliament, Boris Šprem (Sackville 2012a). The main issue was Scientology, specifically his concern about the Croatian government's decision of 8 March 2012 on preparing the draft of the new Religious Communities Act 'that would change the legal status of 43 religious communities in Croatia'. He expressed his concern about the presence of questionable 'esoteric groups' in the Croatian education system and that publicly financing them could threaten basic human rights and democratic principles.

On 9 July 2012 Sackville sent another letter to Josipović, again concerning the bill.[9] Of particular interest is the following section in the letter:

> We appreciate that much work and effort have been dedicated by the Croatian Government to prepare its adhesion to the European Union. Yet the Council of Europe is concerned that some EU Member States have not, to date, taken measures to face the challenge of cultic abuses; this concern extends to Croatia where the problem of destructive cults has not been recognised.
>
> (Sackville 2012b)

On 18 June 2013 the president of CISK, together with FECRIS, sent an open letter to Josipović, expressing concern that children and youth were in the hands of gurus; that esoteric groups had infiltrated the educational, health and scientific systems; and that violations of constitutional principles were taking place in Croatia.

Dujmić-Delcourt referred to the president's failure to respond to Sackville's previous letter concerning Scientology. She again emphasised that CISK was a member of FECRIS, an international NGO with participating status in the Council of Europe. She provided extensive information about the supposed harmful activities of cult movements and noted that they existed in a 'grey zone' in Croatia. She also demanded an investigation of why 'key Croatian politicians and Ministries publicly and financially support controversial cult organisations and their practices'.[10] Singled out as destructive are the following groups: Scientology, Yoga in Daily Life, Transcendental Meditation, the Art of Living Foundation, the Satya Sai Baba Organisation and Ananda Krya Yoga. CISK and FECRIS insisted on preventing these groups from working with children and youth and abolishing public financing for these groups, as well as terminating the free usage of public space in schools and kindergartens for their activities. The open letter also demanded investigation of several professors, one in primary school and others at the University of Zagreb (including the then rector) 'for abuse of authority, promoting and financing New Age, para-scientific and non-pedagogical methods and techniques in the educational system'.[11] The letter also demanded 'the analysis of work and ethical codex of several scientists for false public interpretation in favour of the Scientology organization which is in Europe charged as a criminal organization, dangerous for the constitutional order'.[12] Answers to the questions included in the demands were sought from the education and teacher training agencies as well (Dujmić-Delcourt and FECRIS 2013).

On 21 May 2014 they sent another open letter to Minister Željko Jovanović. The motive for this letter was an alternative educational approach based on Sai Baba's teaching, included in the programme of one private kindergarten in Split.13 This letter also summarised different allegations from the one previously sent to President Josipović (Dujmić-Delcourt and FECRIS 2014).

Analysis of two anti-cult groups: The Guardian Angels

The second group, The Guardian Angels, was registered in Croatia in 2005 as a non-governmental organisation (NGO). The group was inspired by the personal experience of its leader, Nebojša Buđanovac, with the Satanic group 'Black Rose', which motivated him to organise the group. The group was based on the voluntary work of twenty people, social workers and psychologists. Their goals, accessible at the website of the governmental database of NGOs in Croatia, are as follows: 1) to develop programmes/projects of informal education for children, youths and adults in the area of social pedagogy, rehabilitation, pedagogy, psychology, social work, psychotherapy, arts and culture; 2) to develop socio-pedagogical programmes/projects in order to achieve social strengthening, prevention, social integration and re-socialisation of children, youth and adults at a risk of behavioural disorders and social exclusion.[14]

Concerning sects, they stated their main goal and activity is prevention of suicide through therapy and communication with parents and families of sects' members.

The webpage www.andjeli-cuvari.com, however, has ceased to exist, since the association recently dissolved and the group moved to work on the crisis team of the Croatian Red Cross, in the city of Varaždin. Amongst twenty-eight volunteers, three work with the cases concerning sect membership. They are oriented towards prevention of all kinds of risky behaviour, primarily suicides and family violence, particularly concerning children and adolescents. They are planning to establish similar teams in every county in Croatia. In an interview Buđanovac stated they have been engaged in around thirty cases since their foundation, involving high school pupils and students between fifteen and twenty years old. Cases are 'directly connected to satanic and other sects'. Among the particularly dangerous and aggressive organisations they mention are the Unification Church and the Church of Scientology, 'which systematically brainwash their members'.

When asked for the source of their information about the 'sects', Buđanovac mentioned personal experience, literature, the Internet, ex-members and their families. Specifically asked, he also stated that 'by no means all sects are destructive and most of them are harmless or in worse case oriented to money and profit. But some of them, which can be described as criminal organisations, are their primary target'.

He also pointed to 'the need for stricter control over sects by the establishment of police department for surveillance activities of dangerous and destructive sects, like the one in the Republic of Serbia'. He also labelled Croatia, thanks to its legal regulation, as a 'haven for sects', which can result in unwanted consequences for young people who are particularly easy to manipulate.

Asked about Dujmić-Delcourt's allegations that cult apologists are included among the members of the Croatian government and other politicians, he called these allegations unfounded. On the contrary, 'among politicians there are people directly connected to dangerous sects, so it is a different story.' He also implied that former and present members of the 'intelligence underground' cover up activities of dangerous sects like Black Rose and block investigations of suicide among young people. Some of these members presently occupy high political positions, he added.

The president of The Guardian Angels also participated at a conference in Rijeka, presenting a paper titled 'The Impact of Satanic Sects on the Youth in Croatia'. He also accepted the Rijeka declaration.

In his interviews with newspapers he claims that destructive sects exist in Croatia, and refers particularly to satanic sects, giving examples from cases he dealt with in his practice as a therapist.

We also interviewed actors involved, whether they were directly mentioned in the letters or are working in the domain of human rights, the rights of religious groups or children.[15] All of them reported that their organisations were making no charges against NRMs or groups or individuals promoting alternative healing or nutrition.

Media coverage

In a few cases that occurred in Croatia during the past twenty-five years involving controversial NRMs, the media played an important role in spreading (mostly negative) information about these groups as well as in constructing elements of moral panic (Goldberger et al. 2010). Their presentation was mostly sensationalistic, biased and superficial. Little deep and investigative journalism has been conducted. These cases almost completely refer to media coverage involving the two CAGs discussed here or their representatives. With few exceptions, there was no balanced reporting which included different angles in approach to the case and different experts. Particularly experts in religious studies are missing.

Discussion and concluding remarks

Processes of democratisation and pluralisation in Croatian society resulted not only in further importing of NRMs from the West, but in importing reactions to NRMs as well. Both CISK and The Guardian Angels have provided secular opposition to NRMs they call sects and cults, and have opposed all alternative groups they negatively label as 'esoteric', 'holistic' or 'New Age'. While The Guardian Angels particularly focussed their attention on Satanist groups, CISK is particularly focussed on the Church of Scientology and groups who practice alternative methods of education and healing.

The Guardian Angels was a 'softer' anti-cult group whose activity was only partly engaged in combating NRMs. Nevertheless, when focussing particularly on satanic groups it functioned as a supporter of CISK's activities, either through acceptance of the Rijeka declaration or by accompanying CISK's leader in media interviews and stories.

CISK follows its umbrella organisation, FECRIS, which has managed to impact both popular perception and public policy towards NRMs in France. In order to accomplish that in Croatia, CISK constantly presents sects to the public as a social problem. CISK's goal is to assure social control over all NRMs and to impact regulation of all groups it considers destructive. For CISK, Croatian legislation concerning religious communities (including health care and social legislation, and the educational system as well) is too liberal, enabling registration and unchecked functioning of religious groups which they find destructive sects.

In its materials CISK uses what we call the 'Europe scare'. In order to assure and support the legitimacy of its claims and activities, CISK presents generalised information concerning regulation of 'sects' and 'cults' in France, Belgium, Austria and Germany, without acknowledging that they are actually based on very different experiences and contexts. Also, CISK uses the fact that leaders of such groups are in several cases MPs and high-ranking European politicians and public officials. CISK uses the 'Europe scare' method to warn Croatia that the Council of Europe is concerned because it did not recognise the problem of destructive cults yet.

From the cases presented it is obvious that particularly CISK fits almost completely into Barker's (2002) ideal-type of cult-awareness groups. CISK accuses 'destructive sects' of brainwashing, calls recruits helpless victims, accuses 'sects' of breaking up families, financial malpractice, political intrigue, criminal actions and tendencies, and charges some of them with training members to commit suicide. According to CISK, these characteristics make 'sects' actually or potentially harmful to their own members, to other people and to society in general. Also, CISK implies that such negative actions are not found in traditional religions and tries to denigrate anyone who proposes a different image of the movements, and to define scholars who are not unequivocally against the movement as 'cult apologists'. The only element missing for now in the Croatian anti-cult scene is professional deprogrammers.

The actions CISK advocates clearly and openly aim to assure social control over all religious groups and spiritual movements besides traditional religions, by suggesting different legal regulations. But, keeping in mind that the Croatian anti-cult movement includes not strong groups, but a few active individuals supporting each other, we can say it is still *in statu nascendi*.

As the first work on ACM in Croatia, this chapter is highly 'unfinished' and open for further investigation and discussion. In order to get an insight which is as accurate as possible, more complex and thorough, research is needed.

Notes

1 The authors wish to thank Branko Ančić for his initial research work on this study.
2 After the brainwashing thesis eventually declined, mainly because of the lack of a scientific basis for it (Anthony and Robbins 1995; Melton 2001), ACM experts shifted to different medical terms in order to explain the participation in NRMs, which in that way became "medicalized" (Richardson and Stewart 2004).
3 The term *moral panics* is used to explain situations in which something that has been defined as a social problem becomes the focus of exaggerated attention from media, the public, politicians and legislators, other opinion leaders, law enforcement and action groups (Goode and Ben-Yehuda 1994; Jenkins 1998).
4 During the 1970s, new communities like the Jehovah's Witnesses, Hare Krishnas, Mormons and Seventh-Day Adventists appeared. After 1990, besides evangelical charismatic communities, Buddhist communities, Hindu communities, the a Baha'i community, the Universal Life Church and the Church of Scientology, numerous New Age and spiritual groups also emerged.
5 There is also the counter-cult group within the Croatian Franciscans' province of St Jeronim, 'Croatian Areopag', which supports CISK and follows its activities on its web site (www.areopag.hr).
6 www.cisk.hr
7 She declined to answer the following questions: Are all sects in Croatia destructive? Have you contacted sects you qualified as destructive? How many cases did you have in Croatia? Who informed you about the cases? Have you spoken with members of these sects (how many of them were under age)? What is their education and working status? You stated that you conducted surveys about sects in thirty EU countries. Could you give us information about the samples and where these data could be found? Answers to all these questions she qualified as internal issues of CISK and as private information about the 'victims', but she directed us to EU reports in order to find data we were interested in.
8 La Mission interministérielle de vigilance et de lutte contre les dérives sectaires (MIVILUDES), Union nationale des Associations de Défense des Familles et de l'Individu

victimes de sectes, France (UNADFI), Le Centre d'information et d'avis sur les organisations sectaires nuisibles, Belgium (CIAOSN), and Centre Contre les Manipulations Mentales, France (CCMM).
9 Basically they fear the new law could be even more liberal.
10 Accused are former and actual presidents of the Republic of Croatia, as well as the then vice-president of the Croatian parliament, for giving a reception for Ravi Shankar as well as former President Mesić for giving a reception for *Yoga in Daily Life* guru Swamiji.
11 Accusations of using a practitioner of radiesthesia for checking rooms at the University of Zagreb chancellor's office; using public money for buying biogenerators in one primary school.
12 Here the authors of this article are listed, together with reviewers of their book *Religious Communities in Croatia*. The book presents basic information about (then) forty-one registered religious communities (history, organisation, location, beliefs, practice, education and activities), including the Church of Scientology.
13 The Ministry of Science, Education and Sport supports alternative programmes in private schools (Waldorf, Montessori), but does not finance them. Local authorities are responsible for decisions concerning alternative educational programmes in private kindergartens.
14 www.appluprava.hr/RegistarUdruga/, accessed 8 February 2014
15 These include: the Governmental Office for Religious Communities, Ombudsmen for Children, the Association for Religious Freedom in the Republic of Croatia, The Croatian Helsinki Watch and The House of Human Rights.

References

Anthony, Dick and Robbins, Thomas 1995. Negligence, Coercion and Protection of Religious Beliefs. *Journal of Church and State*, 37, 509–36.
Barker, Eileen 2002. Watching for Violence: A Comparative Analysis of the Roles of Five Types of Cult-Watching Groups, in: David G. Bromley and John Gordon Melton (eds.) *Cults, Religion and Violence*. Cambridge: Cambridge University Press, pp. 123–48.
―――― 2007. Charting the Information Field: Cult-Watching Groups and the Construction of Images of New Religious Movements, in: David G. Bromley (ed.) *Teaching New Religious Movements*. New York: Oxford University Press, pp. 309–29.
Beckford, James 2001. The Mass Media and New Religious Movements, in: Bryan Wilson and Jamie Cresswell (eds.) *New Religious Movements: Challenge and Response*. London: Routledge, pp. 103–19.
―――― and Cole, Melanie A. 1988. British and American Responses to New Religious Movements. *Bulletin of the John Rylands University Library of Manchester*, 70, 209–24.
Borowik, Irena and Babiński, Grzegorz (eds.) 1997. *New Religious Phenomena in Central and Eastern Europe*. Krakow: Nomos.
Chryssides, George D. 2001. Britain's Anti-cult Movement, in: Bryan Wilson and Jamie Cresswell (eds.) *New Religious Movements: Challenge and Response*. London and New York: Routledge, pp. 258–73.
―――― and Margaret Wilkins 2006. *A Reader in New Religious Movements: Readings in the Study of New Religious Movements*. Burlington, VT: Ashgate.
Constitution of the Republic of Croatia, 6 July 2010. Available at www.sabor.hr/Default.aspx?art=2405.
Dujmić-Delcourt, Branka and FECRIS 2013. Letter to Ivo Josipović. (Archive of the Office of the President of the Republic of Croatia).

——— 2014. Letter to Ivo Josipović. (Archive of the Office of the President of the Republic of Croatia).

Goldberger, Goran, Dorota Hall, Lucia Greskova and Rafal Smoczynski. 2010. Societal Responses to New Religious Movements in Poland, Croatia and Slovakia, in: Dorota Hall and Rafał Smoczyński (eds.) *New Religious Movements and Conflict in Selected Countries of Central Europe*. Warsaw: IFiS Publishers, pp. 29–94.

Goode, Eric and Ben-Yehuda, Nachman 1994. *Moral Panics: The Social Construction of Deviance*. Oxford: Blackwell.

Introvigne, Massimo 1995. The Secular Anti-cult and the Religious Counter-cult Movement: Strange Bedfellows or Future Enemies, in: Eric Towler (ed.) *New Religions and the New Europe*. Aarhus, Denmark: Aarhus University Press, pp. 32–54.

Jenkins, Philip 1998. *Moral Panic: Changing Concepts of the Child Molester in Modern America*. New Haven, CT: Yale University Press.

Marinović, Ankica and Marinović Jerolimov, Dinka 2012. What about Our Rights? The State and Minority Religious Communities in Croatia: A Case Study. *Religion and Society in Central and Eastern Europe*, 5(1), 39–53. Available at www.rascee.net.

Marinović Jerolimov, Dinka. 2001. Religious Changes in Croatia: Some Empirical Data from 1972, 1982 and 1999 in the Zagreb Region, in: Irena Borowik and Miklos Tomka (eds.) *Religion and Social Change in Post-Communist Europe*. Krakow: Zaklad Wydawniczy Nomos, pp. 163–80.

Melton, Gordon J. 2001. Anti-cultists in the United States: An Historical Perspective, in: Bryan Wilson and Jamie Cresswell (eds.) *New Religious Movements: Challenge and Response*. London and New York: Routledge, pp. 213–33.

Richardson, James T. 2004. *Regulating Religion: Case Studies from around the Globe*. New York: Kluwer Academic and Plenum Publishers.

Richardson, James T. and Introvigne, Massimo 2007. New Religious Movements, Countermovements, Moral Panics, and the Media, in: David E. Bromley (ed.) *Teaching New Religious Movements*. New York: Oxford University Press, pp. 91–111.

Richardson, James T. and Stuart, Mary 2004. Medicalization and Regulation of Deviant Religions: An Application of Conrad and Schneider's Model, in: James T. Richardson (ed.) *Regulating Religion: Case Studies from around the Globe*. New York: Kluwer Academic and Plenum Publishers, pp. 507–34.

Sackville, Tom 2012a. Letter to Ivo Josipović, Zoran Milanović, and Boris Šprem. (Archive of the Office of the President of the Republic of Croatia).

——— 2012b. Letter to Ivo Josipović. (Archive of the Office of the President of the Republic of Croatia).

Zrinščak, Siniša, G. Črpić and S. Kušar. 2000. Vjerovanje i religioznost. *Bogoslovska smotra*, 2, 233–55.

Part 2
Developments in specific groups

9 From the radical to the routine

The history and future of The Family International (Children of God)

Abi Freeman

The Family International (TFI), formerly known as The Children of God (COG), had its beginnings in the late 1960s as a communal-living movement based on non-traditional Christian teachings. Presenting itself as the Revolution for Jesus (RFJ), the radical teachings and lifestyle of this fledgling movement appealed to the counterculture youth of the time. Its strong emphasis on evangelism saw the group spread globally by the 1970s; its theological trajectory would take it ever further away from mainstream Christianity.

Scholars have typically identified TFI as a world-rejecting new religious movement (NRM) (Fox 2005: 329). Indeed, this has been how TFI sees itself, and its members have taken pride in the dichotomy between themselves and society at large. This outlook was based both on scripture and on the writings of leadership, and had both theological and practical implications.

As it is not possible to do justice to the complex history, structure, controversies and evolving theology of TFI in these few pages, this chapter focusses on the impact of these 'revolutionary' principles, along with the consequences of the abrupt change in the movement's direction in 2010.

The Revolution for Jesus

TFI was founded and led by David Brandt Berg (known in TFI as 'Moses David', 'Mo' or 'Dad'). After his death in 1994, he was succeeded by Karen Zerby ('Maria'), his second wife, and her new partner, Steve Kelly ('Peter Amsterdam'). Berg's writings, and later Zerby's and Kelly's, were known first as *Mo Letters* and then simply as *Letters*. The impact of the Letters cannot be overstated. Considered by TFI members as new scriptures, although not quite on par with the Bible, these writings provided spiritual leadership along with practical and organisational guidance. In the absence of visible leadership – as few members ever met either Berg or Zerby, who largely lived in seclusion – the 'Letters were the leaders' (Berg 1981).

From the beginning, the Letters were filled with revolutionary rhetoric with titles such as *Reformation or Revolution, Jesus People? – Or Revolution* and *Our Declaration of Revolution* (Berg 1970, 1971, 1968, respectively).

These extracts from Berg demonstrate the tone:

> Well, in the Bible they called the followers of Jesus *disciples*, & today I like to call them *revolutionaries*! I think that's a word that really fits, because anybody who really follows the teachings of Jesus Christ is going to be an absolute *misfit* in this present System [TFI's term for society at large], & will be looked on as an utter revolutionary, a radical, a fanatic & an extremist if they really believe & teach & *do* what Jesus & the Apostles did! – And the World will *hear* about them!
>
> (Berg 1986)

> Therefore, we in our worldwide Revolution for Jesus have declared war of the spirit *against* the System's Godless schools, Christless churches and heartless Mammon! Like Jesus, 'Who was manifested that He might *destroy* the *works* of the *Devil*' (1 John 3:8), we are *rebels* against these anti-Christ institutions of man and the Devil and are rebels for the *truth*, rebels for the true naked Word of God!
>
> (Berg 1984)

This uncompromising message struck a chord with the early members, already disenchanted with the mainstream, and the movement grew rapidly in its formative years.

Core membership

In his critical treatment of the early Children of God, John Drakeford claimed that 'A conversation with a member of the Children of God leaves the distinct impression that there is only one real pathway to discipleship – leave the world, sell all your possessions, and, with the proceeds in hand, go to a Children of God colony, turn in your assets, and take up your residence in the community doing full-time Bible study and witnessing' (Drakeford 1972: 88–9).

Joining the movement meant leaving everything behind. For the most part, the first cohort of members dropped out of education, left their jobs and abandoned family ties to travel the world as missionary disciples of Jesus. Members were taught that this was required of disciples of Jesus Christ, who said, 'He that forsakes not all that he has, cannot be my disciple' (Luke 14:33).

Full-time members were known as Disciples, TRFers, Charter Members or Family Disciples at various periods. To avoid confusion I will refer to these highly committed members as 'core members'.

The movement has gone through a cycle of radical structural changes throughout its history, yet these basics remained fairly constant: Core members were expected to be separate from society at large in practical, spiritual and social terms. This was taken quite extremely at some points in TFI history, less so at others.

Generally up until 2010, core members lived in communal homes. Property was shared. Outside employment was not allowed or at least severely discouraged – communities were mostly supported by sales of literature and donations. Children were educated within the communities. Members were discouraged from listening to music or reading books not produced or at least approved by the movement. Television watching was limited. Any friendships with non-members were generally for the purposes of evangelism or winning support. This included the intimate relationships formed as a result of the 'Flirty Fishing' method of personal evangelism in which sexual attraction served as 'bait' for the 'fish' (prospective converts) (Berg 1974b). 'Flirty Fishing' ceased in 1987 when core members were banned from having sexual relations with anyone outside of the TFI communities. Families 'outside' were also kept at arm's length, although this policy in particular varied throughout the years.

A visitor to a TFI community in the 1970s, 1980s, 1990s or even up until around 2010 would have seen variations of the same theme – members were essentially living separately from the society around them, although the degree of separation varied.

Note that although this high commitment of 'revolutionary discipleship' was considered the ideal, the leadership was pragmatic regarding the growth of the movement. Other membership options were less demanding. Berg again:

> **BUT JESUS AND HIS DISCIPLES HAD MANY UNDERCOVER FRIENDS,** members of the **System**—a **great** company of the **priests** and even some of the **Sanhedrin,** the **rulers** and the **rich,** who were their **friends, helpers** and **protectors,** whom God had ordained for this ministry. You **must** remember this and not curse **everyone** who does not **immediately** drop everything and join you. God may know that they would not make very good **full-time** disciples, they would not be wholehearted enough, sacrificial enough, and enthusiastic enough to do a very good job as one of the **inner** circle. But they're still **for** us as **friends!**
>
> (Berg 1974b)

However, most of those associated with TFI aspired to be part of the elite core membership.

Staying separate

Although the fundamental beliefs of TFI were rooted in Christian teaching – indeed the fundamental purpose of the movement was to bring people to faith in Jesus Christ – there was an intentional separation of TFI from mainstream Christianity. Although this was initially predicated upon a rejection of traditional churches that were seen as unfaithful to the original Gospel message (Berg 1969), the evolution of the movement's liberal doctrines regarding sexuality cemented this division.

Berg's teaching of the Law of Love from 1974 onwards freed members from conventional bounds of marriage to engage in heterosexual activity with other consenting adult members. This extended to 'Flirty Fishing,' although in practice this was only until 1987 when sexual relations with non-members were prohibited, partly in response to the emerging AIDS epidemic in wider society (see Kelly 2007).

Berg welcomed the barrier these doctrines and practices established between TFI members and traditional churches:

> WE, LIKE THE EARLY CHRISTIANS, MIGHT HAVE BEEN BROUGHT UNDER BONDAGE TO OLD CHURCH TRADITION by the churches & the Church people if we had not been so radically revolutionary & revolutionarily radical & so shockingly radical that the Church people just totally rejected us & our doctrine & condemned us & ostracised us & refused to believe us! If they would have accepted us we could have gotten sucked back into the churches, but they'll have nothing to do with us, thank God! . . . Sex & nudity & FFing [Flirty Fishing] . . . does the job & keeps us very distinct from the Church people & dead Churchianity & dead Church people & dead Church doctrine!
>
> (Berg 1992)

Much later, Zerby would repeat similar sentiments:

> But let's talk about the church system as a whole. How many pastors, evangelists, missionaries or church members are living communally in love and unity, sharing all things? How many don't lead selfish, private lives, being just as materialistic as the society around them? How many are trusting the Lord completely to supply their needs? How many of them tell their congregations and the world the truth that they *need* to hear, not just what they *want* to hear? How many enjoy the full freedom of the Law of Love? ['Full freedom' refers to consensual adult heterosexual activity outside of marriage.]
>
> It's these things that make the Family different. But compromise gradually roots out all the 'differences' in order to make the Family *just like everyone else*. When that happens, it's death to the Revolution; it's the end of the Family as we know it.
>
> (Zerby 2001)

The revolution within

Revolution was not only a concept regarding TFI's relationship with the world outside; the major structural or theological shifts within the movement were considered revolutions within that revolution. The 'revolution' label was attached to each major structural change, as well as various doctrinal innovations. At least sixty-three Letters up until 2006 had 'revolution' in the title.

The original rulebook for membership was called *The Revolutionary Rules* (1972) and basic beliefs were published in *The Revolution for Jesus Handbook* (1972). The *New Revolution* series of letters in 1975 introduced a wave of internal changes, including a new leadership structure. This was abolished in the major Reorganisation Nationalisation Revolution (RNR) in 1978 at which time the Children of God changed into the Family of Love. There had been a few intervening 'revolutions' including: The Education Revolution, basically setting the movement on course for homeschooling, and The FFing Revolution, encouraging members to practise Flirty Fishing (see Berg 1977).

The Nationalise & Re-organise Security-wise Revolution (NRS) of 1979 was largely a response to the anti-cult publicity following the mass deaths at Jonestown, an event entirely unconnected to TFI (Berg 1979). As a result of the NRS, many members returned to their home countries and took jobs as underground members.

The Fellowship Revolution of 1981 was an attempt to regroup, encouraging members to meet for fellowship, to work together and move again to the mission fields (Berg 1981). As innocuous at this sounds, this developed into one of the most problematic eras in TFI's history, as sexual liberties were taken to an extreme.

We're Still the Jesus Revolution (Berg 1983b) was a reminder of the movement's radical routes, while the Reap Radio Revolution (Berg 1983a) was relatively straightforward guidance about outreach related to the success of the evangelistic *Music with Meaning* radio show. The Honesty Revolution had an impact on members' personal lives, many of whom adopted new names as a result of their spiritual commitments at this time (Berg 1985).

The fervour and zeal of the first generation of converts was rarely replicated by the second generation. Thus the Discipleship Training Revolution was an appeal to the movement's growing cohort of teenagers, born and raised in the movement, who would later become the Second Generation Adults (SGAs) (Berg 1991).

In 1995, The Love Charter codified the movement's beliefs, rules and structure. It was introduced as 'God's call to a Love Revolution' (Berg 1995).

Be True to the Revolution! – Conviction vs Compromise was part of a series of Letters Kelly and Zerby published in Zerby (2001) that attempted to reassert the radical, world-rejecting standards of core membership. These principles are reiterated in this 2004 extract by Kelly, which could as easily have been written at the beginning of the movement. The standards set for discipleship, underpinned by scripture, are maintained. There is no compromise:

> Without living in a Family Home, an individual's discipleship would in most cases weaken; the spiritual strength garnered from living together with other disciples provides an essential element to one's discipleship. The communal Family Home is what sets us apart from the majority of Christians in the world; it is what makes the Family unique; it is where Family discipleship thrives, and it is a vital part of living the discipleship life.

> The Home provides both a supportive environment and fellowship with others to help you live discipleship as defined by the Lord. Full-time 100% discipleship means to go into all the world and preach the Gospel to every creature (Mark 16:15); to be together with those that believe, to have all things common (Acts 2:44–45); to deny yourself and take up your cross daily, and follow the Lord (Luke 9:23–24); to forsake all that you have (Luke 14:33); to come out from among them, and be separate and touch not the unclean thing (2 Corinthians 6:17); to refrain from serving two masters, God and mammon (Matthew 6:24); to lay down your life for the brethren (1 John 3:16); to trust that God will supply all your needs (Philippians 4:19); to continue in the Word (John 8:31–32); to glorify the Father in bearing much fruit (John 15:8); to show that you are a disciple through the love you have one to another (John 13:35).
>
> (Kelly 2007)

This was an idealised picture of Christian discipleship. In practice, the result of these numerous 'revolutions' was that daily life for core members of TFI was governed by a complicated set of regulations.

'Reboot' replaces 'revolution'

The next major restructuring came in 2010. Termed the 'Reboot', it was a surprise for both members and observers. Complex internal regulations were almost entirely abolished; membership was no longer predicated on communal living or a lifestyle regime. Even theology was simplified, with TFI's extensive literature and thousands of Letters withdrawn for internal review.

Following the Reboot, to be a TFI member merely requires assent to a simplified 'Declaration of Faith'. This Declaration largely conforms to traditional Christian teaching, having excluded some of the more unusual theology that had characterised TFI's teachings up until that point. A second requirement is a simple report and monthly contribution or voluntary tithe to the movement or to a member. This is another departure from decades of TFI history: Tithing – giving 10 per cent of one's income – to the central office had been a requirement for core membership up until that point. There are prohibitions against illegal behaviour and activities that could reflect negatively on TFI. Basically this is the sum of all that is required to be a member.

Crucially, there are no more grades of membership; no more core members. There are no longer any requirements to live communally. Furthermore, there are no restrictions on employment or education.

The Reboot and its impact have been accurately described by Gordon Shepherd and Gary Shepherd. They explain:

> The new approach, couched in both social science and self-realization terminology, encouraged individual TFI members to make their own life choices and set their own levels of Christian commitment to missionary

activities. Communitarian living and all its attendant social and moral offshoots would no longer be expected. Individuals could now lead normal lives in secular communities, seek secular education, and hold secular jobs.
(Shepherd and Shepherd 2009)

As a result of the Reboot, TFI essentially became an online community, with websites providing religious reading material, news and a point of contact.

While pockets of TFI members apparently still live in communal homes, no official TFI structure is in place to support them. There remains an informal network of friendship amongst members and former members. Groups of members occasionally gather for fellowships for which they can receive a financial grant from TFI, but again this is not organised from any central office.

There are areas of missionary activity and humanitarian support work, particularly in places such as Africa and Latin America, but these are independent of TFI leadership. People running these successful and worthwhile projects may be TFI members, but these are not TFI projects. If TFI was disbanded completely, these projects would presumably continue.

One structure remains. This is The Family International Services (TFIS). Thirty or forty members of TFIS are spread throughout the globe, working from home, managing the websites and communications. Because their work is paid for on a freelance basis, it is not certain that even all of these TFIS workers are 'true believers', but some are simply doing a job. Others, including editors and designers, do freelance work without necessarily even being members of TFI.

The top leadership also remains: Zerby and Kelly still have overall authority.

Why Reboot?

Exactly how and why the Reboot came about is open to debate. Perhaps the leadership felt that TFI was reaching a breaking point and wished to keep it alive, even a reformed TFI being better than none. There were certainly indications that both first- and second-generation members were dissatisfied with the level of regulation and somewhat exhausted with the never-ending cycle of new programmes and internal restructuring.

The requirements for core membership and the demands on members' personal lives had been introduced over the years as necessary for keeping alive the spirit of the Revolution for Jesus. In the previous decade, the number of internal regulations had escalated, accompanying the adoption of a complex new organisational structure. Most recently, TFI Homes could only retain their coveted 'disciple' status if they passed an internal review or checklist which included scores of detailed questions. These were over and above TFI's governing constitution, the Charter.

Thus the requirements of core membership had grown increasingly onerous. This was a paradox. TFI's message was based on the uncomplicated teaching of Jesus that all behaviour should depend on two simple laws, 'to love God, and to love your neighbour as yourself' (Matthew 23: 37–40), yet the group was governed by a complex system of regulations that not only delineated the movement, but also intruded on members' personal lives.

Difficulties also existed on a practical level. For instance, some Homes were struggling to manage financially. Core members were not permitted to undertake secular employment; limited self-employment was possible but frowned upon. The global economic downturn may well have had an impact, yet the requirement for Homes to support themselves 'living by faith' – seeking out sponsors and selling literature – exacerbated the difficulties.

Whatever the intent, the Reboot fundamentally changed the nature of TFI, changing the outlook for its future as a movement as much as it changed daily life for its members.

Reactions

> Yet, if the Family remains true to its principles, willing to adapt and to experiment but not to compromise, it will survive.
>
> (Bainbridge 2002: 168)

The Reboot changes were presented as an improved means of reaching TFI's ultimate goal of sharing the Gospel. However, taking into account the world-rejecting message throughout the movement's history, it is not difficult to see how this might have been puzzling for members. The same leadership who had insisted on 'conviction, not compromise' a decade earlier now told them:

> The changes being made now should broaden the ways and means available to you to participate in and facilitate the mission. They provide you with more flexibility in how you meet your spiritual needs and advance in your spiritual life. They will give you the opportunity to use different methods and modes of living for and serving the Lord. They will remove the lifestyle barriers and restrictions that, in some cases, may have made it difficult for you to interact with others in mainstream society in a way that makes you relatable, transparent, and better able to meet their needs.
>
> (Zerby and Kelly 2010)

Some members remain confused about the sweeping changes in theology, and why something once considered 'God's Word' is now dismissed, including much of Berg's writings.

Indeed, the Reboot was neither entirely welcome, nor problem-free. Whilst many members were relieved to be liberated from the former strictures, the de-radicalisation of the movement offended a percentage of the older members who still believe in the pure discipleship message in the Gospels, the message that had attracted them to the COG in the first place. Were Peter and Maria staying true to the principles that Berg had promoted, or were they themselves compromising?

But for the greater part, difficulties arising from these changes were practical rather than theological. Those who had been comfortable living in communal homes were faced with the stern realities of supporting and housing themselves. It was not always easy to re-enter mainstream society after twenty to forty years on the edge. Skills learned and honed during their varied life experiences and travels as TFI members are generally good, but may not be transferable. For instance, the member who ran a communal kitchen in a TFI Home may be a great cook and manager, but that alone, without qualifications, may not be enough to secure a job in the catering industry.

These are of course similar challenges as those faced by former members who had left the movement voluntarily over the years. However, it could be said that of those who had remained up until the time of the Reboot, that rather than leaving the movement, the movement had left them. The question remains as to whether the leaders have fulfilled their duty of care to those who spent the best part of their adult lives within the movement and had come to rely on the communal structure.

The following account is a composite of actual members, known personally to me, and illustrates the impact of the Reboot.

The impact of the Reboot: A composite tale

Carol was a typical hippy: long, flowing hair, an easy attitude, dabbling in drugs, living in California, a university drop-out estranged from her family. She initially rebuffed but then embraced the anti-establishment presentation of the Christian message offered by the Children of God (COG), joining the group at the most famous of its early communities – the Texas Soul Clinic (TSC) (see Drakeford 1972). It was 1970 and she was nineteen.

Fast forward to 2010. In the intervening four decades, Carol had left the United States, travelling first to Europe then onwards to Asia. The next sojourn in her journey was South America, and then it was Eastern Europe. By this time she had married twice and had four children. Her second husband, Mark, was British and they spent some time in the United Kingdom, sufficient for her to obtain British citizenship. Another stay in Asia followed.

Their children, born between 1975 and 1982, were adults and had long since left the movement, and so Mark and Carol now found themselves alone back in London.

They had been living communally for forty years as missionaries with the movement, which had long since morphed from the COG to The Family International (TFI). The communal home had housed their church, their friends, their work, their purpose. They had virtually no social life outside.

Except for a few stretches of informal English language teaching, they had not had any conventional employment. Carol spent most of her time taking care of children, helping with the homeschooling of those living in the community, while Mark would be out selling the books, CDs and videos TFI produced. Expenses and income within the community were shared, life was relatively inexpensive, and they seemed to manage. It had been more difficult to make ends meet in recent years, but paying the bills had been a shared responsibility, and something always seemed to turn up.

They had remained members throughout the structural changes that periodically swept through the movement, trusting in the Lord and in the leadership. They did not admit to thinking much about their old age, brushing off questions from their children about saving for a pension, just as they had brushed off similar questions from their parents decades earlier. Why should they worry? They had no plans to leave TFI.

Thus the internal restructuring of 2010 – the Reboot – came as a shock to Mark and Carol. The leadership – Peter and Maria – had explained the reasons at length, but it was difficult to take on board.

For forty years, they had been taught that in order to be disciples of Jesus, they should live communally. Private living as a nuclear family was not only selfish, but also not in conformity with the pattern of the Early Church. Now they were told that communal living was no longer required. What was more, the organisational structure of TFI Homes was being abandoned.

For forty years, they had been taught that in order to be disciples of Jesus, they should avoid secular employment. They should live by faith, not compromise by working for money. Now they were told they could go and get a job to support themselves; in fact, it was more or less essential.

For forty years, they had been taught that in order to be disciples of Jesus, they should be separate from the world, even keep their children separate by homeschooling. Now they were told this wasn't necessary. They could make friends. Children could go to school. Even they could return to university to complete their education.

For forty years, they had been taught that TFI was a unique place to serve the Lord, the best place to be a disciple of Jesus. They had aspired to be one of the elite; now they were told they weren't necessarily the best. Even Peter Amsterdam was taking a course in theology from a mainstream Christian organisation.

Fast forward again, to the present (2014). Mark and Carol are living in a rented flat. Their furniture is second-hand but it's clean. Carol wanted to teach – after all she had been involved in education for many years – but discovered it was not possible without qualifications. She took a course for teaching English as a second language, but the job market is highly competitive, and her age and lack of documented experience have been barriers. Finally she got work as a care assistant in a nursing home. Although she is glad to be helping people, this job is at the low end of the pay scale.

Mark is self-employed, distributing catalogues and taking orders for a mail-order company. He has done quite well – after years of selling TFI products, he's a good salesman. But this is not highly paid work and it is quite physically tiring. He's just turned sixty.

Mark watches a lot of television and isn't interested in religion. He is no longer a member of TFI; he just doesn't seem to care about it. Carol still reports and sends monthly contributions to TFI, and views herself as a member. Every evening she visits the TFI website and reads the postings. Sometimes she chats online with her old friends who are now scattered around the world.

Carol is lonely. Although she is quite happy keeping house, choosing her own meals and schedule, she is depressed by the lack of company that she had always enjoyed in the community. She tried going to an Anglican church, but as much as she appreciates the hymns and services, she finds it as difficult to relate to the church members as they do to her.

It has been decades since Mark and Carol lost touch with their old friends from before joining the COG. It is not easy to forge new friendships, and they are also unaccustomed to making friends purely for social reasons. They keep quiet about their past in TFI. Nobody would understand.

Their children had lived in 'Teen Homes' (TFI communities) from quite a young age. As a result, although they are fond of their parents and visit periodically, close familial ties are lacking. All of them live in the United States; now married and with growing families of their own, they haven't ever considered the possibility that their parents may need help and support as they age. If such help is eventually needed, Mark and Carol will have to rely on the state.

Mark seems content to settle down. Carol would like to be a missionary and return to the developing world, but realises it is unlikely. They are discussing getting involved in some local charities, but they're too busy working to make ends meet to have much time and energy for volunteer work. The unaccustomed stress of making a living has taken a toll on them.

The Jesus Revolutionaries have come home. It isn't what they expected.

Going forward

It is telling that TFI's 2010 restructuring, ushering in the biggest changes in the movement's history, was not even presented as a 'revolution' – quite a contrast to virtually all of the earlier changes. Instead, this restructuring was presented as a reboot, in the same way you reboot your computer: you turn it off, and switch it back on.

Almost six years have passed, and there are not many signs that the organisation has been switched back on. TFI today is still essentially an online network and support group for those who want an active Christian faith, and as such, it is by no means unique. It is not even really an Internet church, as there is no coming together for prayer and worship.

It is difficult to foresee a future for TFI that is much different to what is happening now, and certainly difficult to imagine a return to the earlier communal basis. Out of necessity, most members have long since gone on to other paths, building new lives in society. As of August 2014, only thirty-five members had posted their photos and bios on TFI's member website. Although undoubtedly there are more members who simply did not get around to sharing their pictures, this tiny number is somewhat telling. The circle of those identifying themselves as TFI members is ever-shrinking.

TFI today is a very different organisation from the Revolution for Jesus. Membership is no longer predicated on 'dropping out' of society, living in communes, separated socially and practically from the mainstream. Even theologically, TFI has moved closer to traditional Christianity.

The titles the leadership adopted illustrate the extent of the changes inside TFI. For forty plus years, the COG and then TFI were led by 'prophets' – first David Berg, then Zerby. Lower levels of leadership were 'shepherds'. Now Zerby and Kelly call themselves 'directors'. Not prophets, not even pastors: 'directors'. It is a name devoid of spiritual authority.

'Director' is not the title you would expect of the leadership of a radical new religious movement. It seems that the days when TFI could be identified as a world-rejecting organisation are over.

References

Bainbridge, William Sims 2002. *The Endtime Family, Children of God*. Syracuse, NY: Syracuse University Press.

Berg, David 1969–. *The Mo Letters*. Selection available at www.davidberg.org/moletters; see also www.exfamily.org/pubs/index.html for a fuller selection. Accessed 11 April 2016.

—— 1968. *Our Declaration of Revolution*. Letter 1336.
—— 1969. *Old Church New Church Prophecy*. Letter A.
—— 1970. *Reformation or Revolution*. Letter I.
—— 1971. *Jesus People?–Or Revolution*. Letter 148.
—— 1972a. *The Revolution for Jesus Handbook*. Dallas, TX: Children of God Publications.
—— 1972b. *The Revolutionary Rules*. Letter S.
—— 1974a. *Forsaking All*. Letter 314A.
—— 1974b. *The Little Flirty Fishy*. Letter 293.
—— 1975a. *The Childcare Revolution*. Letter 330B.
—— 1975b. *The Colony Revolution*. Letter 329B.
—— 1975c. *The Disciple Revolution*. Letter 328B.
—— 1975d. *The Economy Revolution*. Letter 330A.
—— 1975e. *The Education Revolution*. Letter 371.
—— 1975f. *The Lit Revolution*. Letter 328A.
—— 1975g. *The New Leadership Revolution*. Letter 329C.
—— 1975h. *New Revolution, the Shake Up!* Letter 328C.
—— 1977. *The FFing Revolution*. Letter 575.
—— 1978. *The Reorganisation Nationalisation Revolution*. Letter 650.
—— 1979. *The Nationalise & Re-organise Security-Wise Revolution*. Letter 747.
—— 1981. *The Fellowship Revolution!* Letter 1001.
—— 1983a. *Reap Radio Revolution*. Letter 1609.
—— 1983b. *We're Still the Jesus Revolution*. Letter 1592.
—— 1984. *Revolution for Jesus*. Letter 1963.
—— 1985. *The Honesty Revolution*. Letter 1926.
—— 1986. *Teens for Christ – Are You One?* Letter 2227.

——— 1991. *The Discipleship Training Revolution*. Letter 2677.
——— 1992. *There's No Way Out But Up!* Letter 2837.
——— 1995. *God's Call to a Love Revolution*. Letter 2963.
Chancellor, James D. 2000. *Life in the Family: An Oral History of The Children of God*. Syracuse, NY: Syracuse University Press.
Drakeford, John W. 1972. *Children of Doom*. Nashville, TN: Broadman Press.
The Family International. Official Website: www.thefamilyinternational.org
The Family International. Governing Documents: http://tficharter.com/
Fox, Judith 2005. 'New Religious Movements', in John R. Hinnells, ed. *The Routledge Companion to the Study of Religion* (pp. 323–36), Abingdon, Oxon: Routledge.
Kelly, Steve 2007. *The Family's History, Policies, and Beliefs Regarding Sex, Part 1*. Letter 3671. Zurich: The Family International.
Kelly, Steve and Zerby, Karen 1994. *The Letters*. Zurich: The Family International.
——— 2004. *Forward, Always Forward! Restructuring the Family of the Future, Part 1*. Letter 3479.
——— 2010. *Lifestyle*.
Melton, J. Gordon 2004. The Children of God: The Family. Salt Lake City, UT: Signature Press.
Shepherd, Gary and Shepherd, Gordon 2009. *The Family International (TFI) 2009 to Present*. Available at www.has.vcu.edu/wrs/profiles/TheFamilyInternational2009-Present.htm. Accessed 9 January 2014.
Van Zandt, David E. 1991. *Living in the Children of God*. Princeton, NJ: Princeton University Press.
Zerby, Karen 2001. *Be True to the Revolution! – Conviction vs Compromise*. Letters 3361–3366. Zurich: The Family International.

10 The Family International
The emergence of a virtual new religious community

Claire Borowik

> If there has been any persistent truth about the Family during its several decades of existence, it has been its almost annual ability to introduce novelty and change. . . . This novelty makes it interesting to scholars, confounds its critics, and prevents even the most careful observers from predicting its future.
>
> (Melton 2004: 62)

At the height of the counterculture era of the 1960s, The Children of God (later known as The Family International) made its dramatic entry onto the religious scene alongside the Jesus People as a Christian fundamentalist, world-rejecting movement of primarily converted hippies. Its anti-establishment stance and rejection of institutional Christianity gave rise to its rupture with the Jesus People and its development as a unique communitarian society, deemed the largest communal experiment engendered by the Jesus Movement (Shepherd and Shepherd 2008: 27). The Family International's uncompromising challenge to potential converts to 'forsake all' and 'drop out' of the 'System', coupled with its heterodox doctrines and antinomian sexual practices led to its designation as the most controversial Christian communal movement to emerge from the 1960s (Miller 1999: 96).

The Family International's history and evolution have been characterized by opposition from its early days of recruitment amongst the hippies of California to its current struggles with adversarial websites and cyber-media. Notwithstanding confrontations with a coalition of irate parents in the early 1970s, alarmist media coverage unleashed by the Jonestown mass murder/suicides in the late 1970s, and government raids and court cases instigated by former members and anti-cultists in the early 1990s, the movement has consistently weathered the storms of adversity and accommodated as needed to survive and propagate its message. By the turn of the twenty-first century, the new cyber-battleground of the 'cult wars' had materialized, which would represent the greatest contemporary challenge to the movement's struggle for legitimacy and its reinvention as a current evangelistic movement.

In 2010, The Family International's directors, Karen Zerby and Steve Kelly (known within the organization as Maria Fontaine and Peter Amsterdam), introduced extensive revisions of long-standing doctrines and practices in a sweeping reorganization known as 'the Reboot'. A salient feature of the Reboot was the virtual dismantling of the movement's previous communal society model and a shift to 'networked individualism' (Wellman 2001: 238), with emphasis placed on themes of autonomy and self-determination. The lack of organizational framework post-Reboot consequentially led to the movement's metamorphosis from a communitarian movement at tension with the surrounding sociocultural environment to a networked community with little formal structure, cohesion or visibility beyond its online presence.

The periodic introduction of radical reorganizations, known as 'revolutions', has been a trademark of The Family International (TFI). The movement has proved highly resourceful and adaptive in responding to contemporary trends and change originating within TFI, as well as those originating from external sources, as evidenced in its evolution from a collection of counterculture youths to a thriving communitarian society that lasted forty years. Revisionism in its foundational interpretations of Christian discipleship and the abandonment of its communal model at the Reboot, however, have produced unprecedented cultural upheaval amongst the membership, resulting in a process of 'identity renegotiation' for members in their reintegration into conventional society (Smith 1998: 100). Nearly six years after the introduction of the Reboot, membership continues to decline and the movement remains largely unstructured. The current-day rebooted TFI community, connected primarily through its online presence, faces new challenges in fostering movement vitality, member retention and cohesion. TFI's ability to effectively recreate itself online and build a vibrant and cohesive community on a virtual platform portends to be a determinative factor in its future evolution and growth.

Brief history

The Children of God was founded in 1968 by David Berg (1919–1994) and his wife, Jane, and four teenaged children. As an ordained minister with the Christian and Missionary Alliance, Berg had become disaffected with organized religion, which he excoriated in his writings as dead 'churchianity' (Berg 1971: 47–8). His independent evangelistic pursuits culminated in a successful ministry to the hippies of Huntington Beach, California, who resonated with Berg's denouncements of the moral decline and decadence of the United States, and his warnings of an imminent apocalypse (Melton 2004: 4). The Children of God witnessed significant growth in its first decade, as several thousand counterculture youths abandoned studies, careers, families and material possessions to 'drop out' of the System. Their street evangelism, musical performances and sackcloth protest vigils led to revival, conversions and international publicity, followed shortly thereafter by controversy, opposition and negative media. From the early to mid-1970s, the Children undertook a diaspora that would lead them to more than 100 countries, where members proved adept at maintaining their unique culture while engaging their host cultures.

Communalism, which Berg understood to exemplify the biblical model of the early Christians in the Book of Acts, was embraced by the movement from its earliest days. Communal households served as faith-based residences relatively insulated from external influences, where the believers congregated, nurtured their faith, conducted their outreach and ministry, and developed a culture aligned to their world view. The practice of 'forsaking all' mandated a renunciation of earthly possessions and secular pursuits, as well as the common-potting of finances, which proved integral to the successful adoption of the communal model and the financing of the communities.

The movement's denunciation of the System and institutional Christianity placed it at the centre of controversy from its earliest days, resulting in a parting of ways with the evangelical Jesus People in the early 1970s (Eskridge 2013: 183). The introduction of heterodox sexual doctrines and practices in the late 1970s would serve both to cement its separation from mainstream Christianity and to place it at a high degree of tension with the surrounding sociocultural environment (Bainbridge 2002: 169). Berg's 'Law of Love' doctrine, premised on the affirmation that Christians have been freed from the strictures of the Mosaic Law, inclusive of biblical prohibitions of sexual relations outside of marriage, served as the theological justification for liberal sexual practices (Berg 1974). Berg's antinomian theology also provided the justification for 'Flirty Fishing,' a form of evangelistic outreach initiated in 1977, which encouraged members to date and interact sexually with outsiders as a means of sharing the salvation message. The practice of Flirty Fishing spawned intense negative media coverage that has lingered beyond its discontinuation in 1987 to the present.

Berg's introduction of liberal sexual theology led to a period of extensive experimentation from 1978–85, as well as polemical speculations in his writings that challenged traditional boundaries and age of consent protections for minors. Although any writings that could be construed to approve of aberrant practices were retracted and systematically expunged from circulation from 1989–94, they would become a source of much of the controversy and stigmatization that has surrounded TFI since the late 1980s. By the early 1990s, the movement was approaching a relatively more conventional view on sexuality (Melton 2004: 11). An early draft of a child protection policy was published in 1986, followed in 1989 by an excommunication policy for those found guilty of child abuse. An official policy statement was published in 1992 with strong denunciations of child abuse, renouncing former literature at variance with this position. Subsequent apologies and acknowledgements to any second-generation members who had experienced sexual misconduct due to Berg's previous writings were published, the most recent of which was published in 2008.[1]

In 1995, a charter of member rights and responsibilities was adopted that codified the movement's beliefs, practices, norms and regulations, and featured an emphasis on the rights of individuals, children and parents. Previous to its publishing, an in-depth examination of the practices, lifestyle, beliefs, education and care of children had been conducted (Bainbridge 2002: 29).

In principle, the Charter granted a higher degree of autonomy to the members and local communities, while identifying essential beliefs from Berg's writings. Its implementation led in turn to a gradual process of democratization, culminating in the introduction of a board structure in 2002 that provided member representation at the regional, national and international levels. The boards embodied a more egalitarian approach to Family governance, enabling grass-roots member participation in decision-making processes, and proved a catalyst for modernization in numerous spheres of Family life (Shepherd and Shepherd 2005: 77).

Throughout the 1990s, the organization became increasingly aware of the critical need to engage the public and recreate itself in the modern, mass-mediated public sphere to overcome the negative imaging of TFI that had prevailed in the absence of promotion efforts on its part. In 1995, TFI launched one of the earlier new religious websites to appear on the Worldwide Web in an effort to leverage this new virtual space to communicate its unique message and to attain legitimacy and representation (Campbell 2013: 17). Shortly thereafter, in 1998, the 'Members Only' website was created, which furnished chat forums, prayer boards and community spaces where members could interact and share artwork, music, mission resources and Christian resources for children and teens. TFI publications, previously only available as paper copies sent by mail, became downloadable on the members-only site subsequent to the adoption of a sophisticated log-in system to ensure that these would not be accessible to outsiders. Numerous websites were gradually created both for and by members, to promote the works of their local communities, cities and countries, as well as to promote TFI's evangelistic message. Notwithstanding numerous concerns expressed throughout the writings of the period regarding the potential risks of spiritual corrosion and moral decline from engaging in the mixed-messaging of the 'Net and the risk of exposure to former members' narratives, overall TFI embraced new communication technologies as strategic tools for evangelization and networking its widely dispersed membership (Campbell and Lovheim 2011: 1089).

The introduction in May 2010 of TFI's most monumental restructuring to date, known as the Reboot, resulted in the virtual dismantling of the communal society model that had been central to TFI's religious identity construction and the perpetuation of its culture and belief system. The Reboot introduced extensive revisions to the movement's doctrines and practices, effectively distancing it from its collectivist approach in favour of personal autonomy and individual empowerment. Its membership Charter was reduced from a document exceeding 300 pages to one comprising less than thirty pages, while drastically reducing membership requirements.[2] The need to modernize the organization to better achieve its missionary and evangelistic objectives was the impetus behind this reorganization, in light of the realization that TFI membership had not expanded beyond 10,000 members throughout its history or sustained large congregations (Chancellor 2005: 30–1). In 2008, a lengthy examination of the movement's culture and context had been undertaken to assess the kinds of adaptations that would be necessary to render the movement and its message more relevant to contemporary audiences. Leadership meetings were held with representatives from around the world, member surveys were conducted, and hundreds of letters from members were analyzed, culminating in the multiple changes introduced at the Reboot that touched virtually every aspect of TFI's belief system and lifestyle. Amsterdam concluded:

> Our approach to reaching the world, along with some of our longtime lifestyle customs, was no longer that relevant to today. We saw that we needed a new model for the world of today. The world has changed immensely, and we've had to acknowledge that the Family had not changed sufficiently to keep up with the needs of the people we're trying to reach, or even the needs of our own members.
>
> (Amsterdam 2010b)

Controversy and innovation

TFI has confronted an array of oppositional forces throughout its history in the form of hostile media, vocal apostates and anti-cult and counter-cult organizations. The first 'cult watch' organization, the Parents' Committee to Free Our Children from the Children of God (FREECOG), which would serve as the prototype for future anti-cult organizations, emerged in 1972 in response to the Children of God's early recruitment of young adults (Shupe and Bromley 1994: 5). The lobbying efforts of this coalition of disenchanted but relatively well-placed parents succeeded in galvanizing politicians, government agencies and journalists into action, resulting in the publishing of a condemnatory report in 1974 from New York's attorney general (Richardson 1999: 173). The report had little effect on the membership, as Berg had departed for Europe in 1971 to scout out new locations for the growing movement, in light of the increasing hostility the movement faced in the United States. Shortly thereafter, a mass exodus had been undertaken to Europe and Central and South America, eventuating in the establishment of TFI communities around the globe.

In 1978, in light of increasingly alarmist media coverage and heightened government scrutiny of unconventional new religions in the aftermath of the Jonestown murder/suicides, Berg directed the organization away from high-profile evangelistic outreach to less visible, clandestine forms of proselytization. Berg subsequently drafted numerous writings about the need for the movement to 'go underground' to avoid religious persecution and negative publicity (Berg 1979: 36–8). TFI's upper-end administrative infrastructure, known as World Services, had already gone into seclusion and lived in undisclosed locations, unknown even to the membership (Shepherd and Shepherd 2010: 16). Growing concerns of intrusive state intervention, stigmatization and religious persecution thus conspired to deepen TFI's separation from and suspicion of the System and institutional authorities, resulting in stronger boundaries being etched between members 'in the Family' and 'outsiders', and a greater concern for preserving TFI's 'otherness' (Barker 2005: 69).

In the early 1990s, anti-cult organizations and detractors on four continents collaborated to make claims of institutional child abuse, mobilizing authorities to take intrusive and draconian measures in the form of government raids and court cases, and the seizure of nearly 500 children by authorities, in some cases for several months. Members were vindicated in all cases; nonetheless, the human cost was formidable, and the battle to overcome stigmatizing media coverage demanded a new level of engagement in the public arena. Consequently, TFI began to adopt policies of greater transparency and openness: journalists, academics and government agencies were invited to visit TFI communities; numerous policy statements were drafted to articulate the movement's beliefs and respond to allegations and misconceptions; members were encouraged to develop charitable ministries to foster engagement in their local communities. Regional public relations representatives were designated to furnish a public presence for the organization, to interact with the media, and to lobby for religious freedom and tolerance.

By the early 2000s, the religious debate had been repositioned largely in the realm of cyberspace, which proved a contentious and unregulated frontier. The Web's characteristic culture of transparency obligated countercultural new religions such as TFI to rationalize their world view and to disclose previously private realms of religious belief and practice for public scrutiny. The Web afforded an accessible means of establishing religious identity, communicating with membership, attracting recruits and responding to critics and opposition; however, it equally provided space for counter-narratives that could be highly damaging due to the permanence of information on the Web (Barker 2005: 73). In this newest platform, an intense battle has been waged to dominate the defining narrative about the movement. TFI has faced cyber-obstacles from numerous sources, including hostile apostate forums; disaffected second-generation member narratives in media articles, blogs and self-published books; a stigmatizing profile on Wikipedia created by a counter-cult administrator with editorship authority; media centred around famous former second-generation actors, musicians and authors; and a battle for dominance of search engine results on the movement that has proved intractable. The permanence of negative profiles and counter-narratives on the Internet has hindered TFI's efforts to distance the movement from past controversies and successfully reinvent itself online. In its quest to achieve representation and a voice in cyberspace, TFI has struggled to navigate these often contested spaces of the Internet, a forum that has proved more amenable to countermovement propagation of (mis)information (Dawson and Cowan 2004:7).

In the early 2000s, three adversarial former member websites (exfamily. org, xfamily.org and movingon.org) gained prominence in the contest for dominance of the information disseminated about TFI, decisively repositioning TFI's engagement in the current-day online version of the 'cult wars'. A murder/suicide perpetrated by Karen Zerby's son, Ricky Rodriguez, placed the movement once again at the centre of stigmatizing media coverage, reviving old controversies long addressed, as well as providing a platform for new former member narratives (see ABC News 2007; The Family International 2005). TFI's online response featured the launch of a pro-TFI website by second-generation members (myconclusion.org), the issuance of statements and apologies from leadership to second-generation members and the initiation of attempts at reconciliation. TFI's engagement, however, in response to criticism and misrepresentation online or attempts to dominate search engine rankings, has been at best a secondary agenda, considering its primary agenda of evangelization. The movement lacks the resources to undertake costly marketing and web ad campaigns, a tactic Scientology has effectively adopted in the online information wars (Lee 2013). Nor can TFI afford to effectively employ 'search engine optimization' strategies to raise the rankings of its sites on search engines, a strategy successfully leveraged by the Latter-Day Saints (Chen 2011: 185). Cyberspace has unquestionably become a game-changing platform of religious negotiation, as it has provided a tremendous delivery system for the dissemination of countermovement information that is difficult for under-resourced minorities to effectively counter (Cowan 2004: 268).

TFI post-Reboot

The rationalization for the monumental changes introduced at the Reboot was mapped out in eighteen comprehensive documents, including a 'manifesto' articulating the ideological underpinnings of the Reboot (Amsterdam 2010c), a document revisiting TFI's history and Berg's impact and model (Amsterdam 2010a) and a four-part series addressing the multiple doctrinal revisions introduced (Fontaine 2010). The primary rationale given for theological modifications introduced at the Reboot was the alignment of TFI's doctrines more closely with orthodox Christian doctrine, and the affirmation of the supremacy of the Bible vis-à-vis TFI writings. Since the Reboot, a significant portion of Amsterdam's writings has focused on affirming standard Christian doctrine, as is the case with the 'Heart of it All' series, which summarizes the teachings of contemporary Protestant theologians without attempting to reconcile these with previous novel interpretations published in TFI Writings. (The Heart of it All series can be accessed at portal.tfionline.com/en/pages/getting-to-the-heart-of-it-all.) Considering TFI's long history of separation from mainstream Christianity and restrictions on exposure to literature or music produced by other Christians, this represents a significant step of accommodation.

The scope of change introduced at the Reboot proved overwhelming; many questions remained and life-altering adjustments had to be made to adapt to the rebooted version of TFI. In 2013, three years after the institution of the Reboot, Peter Amsterdam produced a series of videos in which he addressed questions from the membership such as: 'What is TFI today?' 'Why be a TFI member today?' 'Is TFI a dying movement?' The series sought to allay members' concerns surrounding the loss of collective identity and cohesion, requests that new agencies for community be developed, and the sense that the movement was in decline. Through informal videotaped talks, Amsterdam indicated that a new organizational structure would not be implemented in the foreseeable future (Amsterdam 2013a). He also affirmed that the coordination of fellowship and mission work would rest with individuals to mobilize and enact, in cooperation with other local members or through virtual media such as Skype and Facebook. He suggested that members join local churches if the online venues proved insufficient and members lacked TFI-based avenues for congregational activities:

> If you're in a situation where [you need personal fellowship] and you can't get it on-line, then go to church, find the right people, or find Christians who are unchurched and invite them over to your house and make your own church.
>
> (Amsterdam 2013a)

TFI's gradual transition to computer-mediated forms of communication from 2000 onwards was central to the implementation of the Reboot, enabling its exclusive adoption of Internet-based forums for communication since 2010. Numerous websites, accessible through TFI's community site,[3] were created in conjunction with the implementation of the Reboot to fully transition TFI writings and communications online, including sites for teens, children and parents. In the absence of organizational structure, the movement has organically morphed into a virtually networked community, with most of its interaction occurring on its websites, where members read posts from the directors, share prayer requests or news of their mission works, and read writings from a variety of TFI and mainstream Christian authors.

In the aftermath of the dissolution of the communal households that, in conjunction with the religious writings, were central to the construction of TFI's collective identity, the definition of what TFI is today has become somewhat nebulous. Its networked community model places few demands on its membership and commitment expectations are low. Its current emphasis on diversity, personal autonomy and individualized methods for evangelization, while empowering to individuals, has not served to foster a strong sense of collective cultural identity and community. Amsterdam acknowledged the dilemma this poses:

> It's difficult right now to define the Family. . . . I've come to the conclusion that there's probably 3568 different ways that the Family can be defined, and each of you are looking at it through your eyes, through your experience.
>
> (Amsterdam 2013b)

By and large, members have either embraced or adjusted to TFI's current model or discontinued their membership. Some members maintain vibrant mission works, while others have essentially reinserted themselves into society, taken on careers, enrolled children in public schools and developed new social networks, and their participation in TFI and its mission work is minimal. In other cases, the connection is purely cultural or nostalgic. Previous barriers separating members and former members have all but disappeared, and the informal gatherings organized locally often comprise committed members, former members and nominal members, with little distinction between participants.

Many of the controversial doctrines and practices that placed the movement at tension with society and engendered negative media coverage have been decisively toned down or discarded. This repositioning has resulted in a lessening of tension with former members, who have become virtually inactive in countermovement campaigns or chat rooms. Legacy issues tied to past controversies, however, have continued to trouble members due to the ease of access to negative information and previous controversies on the Internet. Consequently, at the Reboot it was announced that members need no longer affiliate their mission works with TFI or promote TFI or identify themselves with the movement. Many previously affiliated mission works have opted to disaffiliate in order to protect themselves from stigmatization and detractor campaigns.

TFI membership has been steadily declining since the Reboot; current statistics indicate that TFI's membership is hovering around 3,000 in comparison to 4,600 at the time of the Reboot (Table 10.1 and Figures 10.1 and 10.2, statistics courtesy of The Family International). Income to the organization through tithes and offerings has also diminished, necessitating the discontinuation of several services (Amsterdam 2014). The distribution of members of more than ninety nationalities in nearly ninety countries poses a unique set of challenges in rebuilding community and coordinating mission and evangelistic efforts. In an effort to compensate for the loss of pre-Reboot frameworks, TFI has taken steps towards strengthening its virtual community through the creation in 2013 of a community website (portal.tfionline.com), which also has a public interface to promote greater transparency and access. Most of its publications, previously restricted to internal membership, are publicly available on its community website, which offers subscription options to non-members.

Table 10.1 Membership Statistics

Year	Total Members	Countries of Residence
2010	4597	100
2011	4113	95
2012	3473	94
2013	3070	91

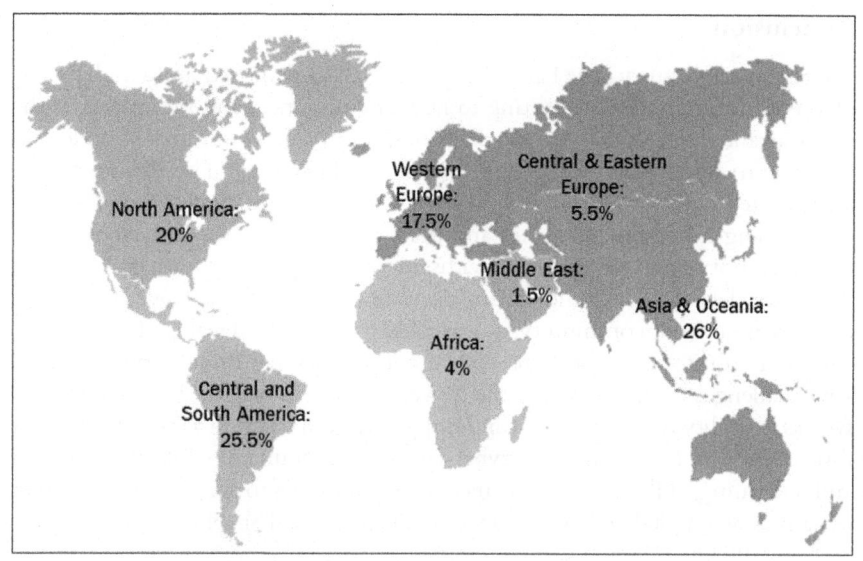

Figure 10.1 Location of membership by regions December 2013

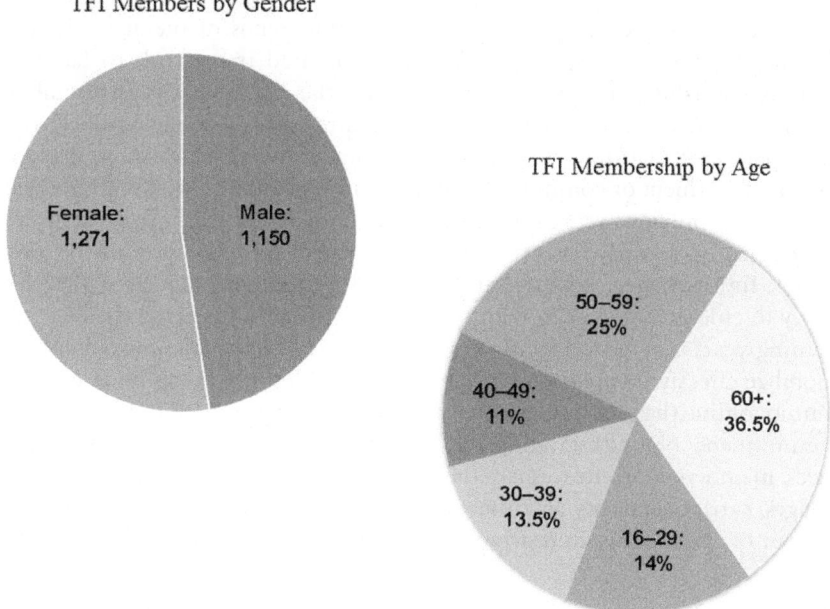

Figure 10.2 Analysis of membership as of December 2013 by gender and age

Conclusion

Throughout its history, The Family International has demonstrated a high degree of versatility in creatively adapting to new circumstances and innovating as the case warranted to retain its unique doctrines, preserve its communal lifestyle, and continue to disseminate its unique version of Christianity. The Reboot took a decisive step outside that tradition in dismantling its bedrock communal society and revising numerous doctrines and practices central to the movement's collective identity and cohesion. Notwithstanding the rich culture members have shared for decades, as the movement closes in on its sixth year since the Reboot cohesive models for community and worship have not yet developed organically. The transition to an amorphous virtual community has unquestionably posed new challenges to the vitality of the movement and its outlook for the future, as well as its ability to retain its cultural uniqueness and foster success in its evangelistic objectives. Navigating this cyber-landscape is bound to continue reshaping and redefining TFI's future, as the movement continues to adapt to the changing dynamics of a digitalized Web 2.0 world. Shepherd and Shepherd noted:

> Whether this radically individualized cyber form of guidance and support – which lacks a clear-cut organizational identity and does not issue rules and impose sanctions – will be sufficient to assure TFI's long-term survival as an organizational entity, however nebulous, remains, of course, to be seen.
> (Shepherd and Shepherd 2013: 93–4)

TFI's future vitality may ultimately depend on its ability to introduce innovative strategies and agencies to reverse current trends of membership loss, decline in financial support and lack of structured framework to facilitate congregation-building and community. As the life journeys of members continue to take them in new and diverse directions, it seems unlikely that attempts to restructure The Family International in ways that would demand greater investment or commitment of its members would be met with the type of response previous reorganizations elicited. In any case, the leadership has reaffirmed on a yearly basis that there is no intent to restructure in the foreseeable future; hence, it seems safe to conjecture that new models will be less likely to emerge organically with the passage of time. This being the case, the coming years may prove decisive in determining whether the movement can mobilize effective strategies to infuse vitality and foster a strong sense of community online that encapsulates the movement's signature zeal and evangelistic commitment. Notwithstanding the contemporary challenges the movement faces, members continue to share the Gospel message in more than twenty languages, carry out charity and humanitarian programmes, and add their unique flavour of Christianity in nearly ninety countries around the world.

Notes

1 This letter of apology can be accessed at www.myconclusion.com/category/letters-of-apology.

2 The Family International's current Charter can be viewed online at: http://tficharter.com.
3 http://portal.tfionline.com

References

ABC News 2007. Revenge against Religious Sect. http://abcnews.go.com/2020/Health/story?id=2838632&page=2.
Amsterdam, Peter 2010a. *Backtracking through TFI History*. The Family International.
—— 2010b. *Blueprint for the Future*. The Family International.
—— 2010c. *Change Journey Manifesto*. The Family International.
—— 2013a. Community and Structure. [Video file]. The Family International.
—— 2013b. What Is TFI Today? Part One. [Video file]. The Family International.
—— 2014. *The Second Quarter*. The Family International.
Bainbridge, William S. 2002. *The Endtime Family: Children of God*. Albany: State University of New York Press.
Barker, Eileen 2005. Crossing the boundary: New challenges to religious authority and control as a consequence of access to the Internet, in: Morten T. Hojsgaard and Margit Warburg (eds.) *Religion and Cyberspace*. London: Routledge, pp. 67–85.
Berg, David 1971. *Organisation 1*. ML #54. The Family International.
—— 1974. *The Law of Love*. ML #302C. The Family International.
—— 1979. *Coming of Age*. ML #771. The Family International.
Campbell, Heidi A. (ed.) 2013. *Digital Religion: Understanding Religious Practice in New Media Worlds*. New York: Routledge.
—— and Lovheim, Mia 2011. Rethinking the online-offline connection in the study of religion online. *Information, Communication & Society*, 14(8), 1083–96.
Chancellor, James D. 2005. A family for the twenty-first century, in: James R. Lewis and Jesper A. Petersen (eds.) *Controversial New Religions*. New York: Oxford University Press, pp. 19–42.
—— 2008. The Family International: A brief historical and theological overview. *Sacred Tribes Journal*, 3(1), 5–32.
Chen, Chiung H. 2011. Marketing religion online: The LDS church's SEO efforts. *Journal of Media and Religion*, 10(4), 185–205.
Cowan, Douglas E. 2004. Contested spaces: Movement, countermovement, and e-space propaganda, in: Lorne L. Dawson and Douglas E. Cowan (eds.) *Religion Online: Finding Faith on the Internet*. New York: Routledge, pp. 255–72.
Dawson, Lorne L. and Cowan, Douglas, E. (eds.) 2004. *Religion Online: Finding Faith on the Internet*. New York: Routledge.
Eskridge, Larry 2013. *God's Forever Family: The Jesus People Movement in America*. New York: Oxford University Press.
The Family International 2005. A Statement on the Deaths of Angela Smith and Ricky Rodriguez. www.rickyrodriguez.com/statement/index.html.
Fontaine, Maria 2010. *The Word of God – Yesterday, Today and Forever*. The Family International.
Lee, David 2013. How Scientology changed the Internet. *BBC*, 16 July. www.bbc.com/news/technology-23273109.
Melton, J. Gordon 2004. *The Children of God: 'The Family'*. Salt Lake City, UT: Signature Books.
Miller, Timothy 1999. *60s Communes: Hippies and Beyond*. Syracuse, NY: Syracuse University Press.

Richardson, James T. 1999. Social control of new religions: From 'brainwashing' claims to child sex abuse accusations, in: Susan J. Palmer and Charlotte E. Hardman (eds.) *Children in New Religions*, New Brunswick, NJ: Rutgers University Press, pp. 172–86.

Shepherd, Gary and Shepherd, Gordon 2005. Accommodation and reformation in the Family/Children of God. *Nova Religio*, 9(1), 67–92.

Shepherd, Gordon and Shepherd, Gary 2008. Evolution of The Family International/Children of God in the direction of a responsive communitarian religion. *Communal Societies*, 28(1), 27–53.

——— 2010. *Talking with the Children of God*. Urbana: University of Illinois Press.

——— 2013. Reboot of the Family International. *Nova Religio*, 17(2), 74–98.

Shupe, Anson and Bromley, David G. 1994. *Anti-cult Movements in Cross-cultural Perspectives*. New York: Garland Publishing.

Smith, Christian 1998. *American Evangelicalism: Embattled and Thriving*. Chicago, IL: University of Chicago Press.

Wellman, Barry 2001. Physical place and cyberplace: The rise of personalized networking. *International Journal of Urban and Regional Research*, 25(2), 227–52.

11 The Unification movement
Key issues in historical perspective

Richard Barlow

From its humble and somewhat obscure origins in post–World War II Korea, the new religious movement founded by the Reverend Sun Myung Moon had established a worldwide presence by the end of the twentieth century. Even if the core membership was never in the millions sometimes claimed by the movement itself, an exceptional level of dedication was demanded of most adherents, which acted as a force multiplier. The ability of their charismatic leader to draw upon the members' loyalty by mobilising them into a wide range of outreach programmes and parallel business activities has promoted a narrative of constant progress and growing acceptance within the wider community, after an initial period of misperception, hostility and outright persecution not uncommon in the early stages of many new religions.

The reality is more problematic: at least some of the reactions involved were generated by the Unification movement's opaque modus operandi and the personal lifestyle of the man who created it as a vehicle for his messianic ambitions, and who controlled its direction for more than six decades. Since Moon's passing on 3 September 2012 at the age of ninety-two, certain facts have emerged which reveal more of the hidden story behind the version of his life depicted in the official autobiography *As a Peace-Loving Global Citizen* (Moon 2010), which assiduously avoids all mention of the names of two sons, Hee Jin (born in Japan in August 1955) and Samuel (born in the United States in January 1966), whom he fathered with women outside marriage.

These facts and the issues they raise are the key to understanding why, as observed by the author of *Sun Myung Moon: The Early Years, 1920–53*, there would appear to have been 'two Sun Myung Moons, the widely-known disturber of society, and the man who doesn't want to hurt God's feelings' (Breen 1997). Further examination of such material may resolve the paradox of these contradictory accounts by presenting a third, more complex one, which takes note of recent revisions to the content of the church's central scripture, *Divine Principle*. In effect, the persistent, but always denied, rumours of Moon's sexual engagements outside marriage have now been conditionally admitted to core members, who have been advised to view them as part of his unique 'providential' mission. This content has not so far been approved for public discussion; in any published texts it has been 'coded'.

Korean roots: The sociocultural and religious background

Any attempt to place the Unification movement and its founder within a historical perspective must give due emphasis to its Korean roots. Knowledge of Korea's sociocultural and religious history provides insight into Unificationist practices.

Korea is said to have a 5,000-year history equal to anything seen in China or Japan. Factionalism was the bane of Korean history, and while this was by no means a uniquely Korean problem, it took on peculiarly damaging forms in that culture. As the 500-year-old Yi dynasty declined towards the end of the nineteenth century, Korea was no longer able to resist foreign interference and colonisation by Japan.

Korea's religious history presents a rich tapestry, ranging from indigenous shamanism, through absorbing the Chinese traditions of Taoism (seen today in the national flag of South Korea), to the missionary religions of Buddhism and Christianity. These imported religions became associated with state power – first Buddhism, and then neo-Confucianism – which led to a major cultural transformation under the Yi. The first Catholic missionaries and their converts experienced severe persecutions between 1801 and 1871. In the final attempts to wipe out Western influence, as many as 8,000 Catholic converts and nine French priests were executed. However, after the removal of the prince regent and the conservative faction of the Confucian bureaucracy, Christians were allowed to operate openly (Grayson 2002).

The priests and missionaries encountered a society influenced by folk shamanism and the more formal culture associated with Confucianism. The scholar Chong-sun Kim has observed that 'From antiquity to the present, the shaman has been a key figure in Korean life, and any study of Korean history warrants a close investigation of shamanism. In Korea the links between evangelical religions and shamanism are particularly strong because shamanistic beliefs have persisted down to contemporary times' (Kim 1978). Kim also notes that these two cultures have tended to exist in a state of tension, resulting in Koreans abandoning their Confucian propriety to indulge in folk rituals such as fertility rites and summoning spirits. Korean kings also played the role of shamans. For example, the gold crowns of the Silla dynasty kings (which Moon adopted in ceremonies) featured stylised deer antlers, an ancient shamanic icon.

Korea under Japanese colonial rule

In the early twentieth century, a period known as the 'Korean Revival', Koreans began to embrace Christianity in large numbers. Korean society was under pressure from the Japanese, who brought in laws replacing the Korean language with Japanese, and imported their own state religion, Shinto, with its worship of the Japanese emperor. The various churches Christian missionaries established were seen as representing Western democracy and education. Their Japanese overlords had modernised the country at a technical level, but the Koreans had become an underclass.

Soon after the end of the First World War, in the spring of 1919, a mass movement emerged to confront the Japanese. On 1 March adherents of the nationalistic indigenous religion of Chondo-kyo released a document which declared Korea's independence. The movement was violently put down, leaving a lasting trauma ('*han*') in the national psyche. However, this show of defiance also gave rise to a renewed hope of liberation. One of those who had played a significant role, leading a rally of 10,000 in Jeongju, was the Reverend Yoon-kook Moon, the youngest brother of Moon's grandfather Chi-kook. He had been a schoolteacher when he converted to Christianity in 1910, then he graduated from Pyongyang's Union Theological Seminary in 1918 at the age of forty. After the uprising the Japanese arrested and tortured him. He was sentenced to two years in prison (Breen 1997). His example, as a man of faith and a patriot, seems to have set a precedent which would serve to inspire the young Moon.

Sun Myung Moon's early years

Nine months after this historic event Sun Myung Moon was born, on 25 February 1920, according to the solar calendar (6 January, according to the traditional Korean lunar calendar), into a farming family in north-west Korea. Given the name Yong-myeong, he was the fifth child (out of twelve) and the second son. Michael Breen reports that

> In both character and appearance, Sun-myung took more after his mother than his father. A tall, handsome woman, Kim Kyung-gye was born in a nearby village in 1888, one of twelve children. She joined the household in a marriage arranged between the two families around 1905. . . . That she was sixteen and her husband only twelve when they married was not unusual.
> (Breen 1997)

In 1930, Moon's parents converted from their native Confucian ethos to the Christian faith. A series of strange events had taken place in their household. Two of Moon's sisters died before he was born, and some years on the family experienced apparent spiritual possession (by what was believed to be the spirit of a tiger), first of an older sister and then of Moon's elder brother. The family sought the services of a Christian healer and the protection of the Christian God. Soon afterwards, both his younger brother and youngest sister fell sick. 'They were given herbal medicines, but both died' (Breen 1997). These events were possibly the catalyst for Moon's search for a deeper meaning and purpose to his life.

> His own grief, and the pain of seeing his parents grieve for their children, underscored for the young Sun-myung Moon what was later to become his core teaching: that of God as the grieving parent of a lost mankind.
> (Breen 1997)

Breen believed that this painful experience 'would inform [Moon's] faith far more profoundly than the concerns for personal salvation or national liberation which fired the Christians with whom he later associated' (Breen 1997).

At the age of fifteen, during a period of intense spiritual questioning, he had what is said to have been a series of life-changing spiritual experiences on a mountainside near his home.

The Unification movement's controversial origins

Moon spent almost a decade attempting to associate with other groups whom some academics described as Korea's 'New Christians'. During this period he learned the contents of their teachings and began to proselytise on his own behalf. He also survived the ordeal of prison in North Korea, after coming to the attention of the 'Naemuso' (the communist authorities) for his controversial activities, and being charged with, among other things, 'destroying the family and institutions, and bringing disorder to society'. A female follower, Chong-hwa Kim, was charged with him. Moon received a sentence of five years, while Mrs Kim was sentenced to eighteen months.

When word of his imprisonment got back to his home village, his grandfather Chi-gook, who had marked him out as having an unusual nature from childhood, observed, 'He will either be very good or very evil' (Breen 1997). Chong-sun Kim has provided a more detailed account of this time from his own research:

> Some time in 1948, complaints were made against Moon, and he was charged with committing adultery. As a result, he was imprisoned for 100 days in Daedong detention house.
>
> (Kim 1978)

Kim is sceptical about Unificationist accounts of this event, which insist that members of the established churches reported Moon as a heretic to the communist authorities. For Moon's followers, the harrowing account of his time in Daedong, where he was said to have been extensively tortured, his broken body thrown into the snow, discovered by his disciples and revived over three days, is nothing less than a miracle. For Kim:

> the depiction of Sun Myung Moon as a religious martyr and a fervent opponent of communism in the 1950s is a cover-up for Moon's actual prison sentence as an adulterer. . . . [A]fter leaving prison, Moon resumed his activities and left his wife [Moon had abruptly left his wife and baby son in Seoul without any indication of his plans to go north] to marry his follower, [Chong-hwa] Kim. He referred to this marriage as 'God's wish'. On February 22, 1949, the North Korean police again arrested him on the grounds of bigamy and 'social disorder'.
>
> (Kim 1978)

Even in the labour camp at Heungnam, which he survived from February 1948 to the end of 1950, Moon continued to witness, and found a disciple, Chong-Hwa Pak, who advised him to change his name. His original birth name, Yong-Myeong, meant Shining Dragon. Christians might associate that name with the great dragon of the Book of Revelation. From then on he would be known as Sun Myung Moon, which means New Bright Word (the surname Moon stands for Character or Word, or can mean Education). The Unification Church translated the name as Word of God, Shining Light of the World.

When the prison compound came under bombardment during an advance by UN forces in October 1950, Moon and Pak both escaped and made their way back to the northern capital of Pyongyang, where Moon looked for his previous followers. Only one, a young man named Won-pil Kim, decided to follow him, so the three of them set out together for the south, making use of a bicycle to carry Pak, who had suffered an injury to his foot. The story of this epic journey, together with Moon's ordeal in the prison camp, forms key elements in the heroic narrative which can sustain the faith of Unification Church members. Pak is mentioned only once in Moon's autobiography, and tellingly only by his surname: 'We even took with us a man who could not walk properly. He had been among those who followed me in Heungnam Prison. His family name was Pak' (Moon 2010). However, in at least one officially sanctioned church publication, Pak was recognised as having been in a close and trusted relationship with Moon:

> True Father had been searching for the Word in silence. Around the time of Korean independence, he put in order the new Truth he had found during his stay in Japan and wrote a book entitled *Repentance*. He dictated the first draft of the *Divine Principle* to his disciple Mr. Jeong Hwa Park [*sic*] in Heungnam Prison; it was entitled *Ideal of the Circular Garden of Harmony*. These two books, unfortunately, were lost. Afterwards, beginning in May 1951 and continuing for one year, True Father wrote the *Divine Principle*.
> (Hwang 2010)

Chong-Hwa Pak's role as Moon's trusted disciple and confidant in the prison may well have been glossed over because he later turned against his 'master'. In 1993, forty years on, perhaps making use of the 'photographic' memory that Moon is said to have ascribed to him elsewhere, he published a book of his recollections in Japanese, under the strange title *The Tragedy of the Six Marys*, which painted an almost unbelievable picture of Moon's intimate relationships with women, and his 'providential reasons' for these.

When the book came out in Japan, it brought unwelcome media attention to the movement. Subsequently, under pressure (and financial inducement, as he later told friends), Pak agreed to allow a second book to be ghost-written in his name, which claimed that his previous apostasy had been motivated by jealousy at not receiving sufficient prominence among Moon's disciples.

However, several other early Korean ex-members corroborated his original story at the time in interviews with Japanese media.

The original book's contents were considered so potentially damaging to the innocent faith of Japanese members that Moon immediately called for a series of intensive workshops for 50,000 Japanese sisters to be held on the Korean island of Cheju.[1] The workshops were taught by Moon, Japanese church leader Hideo Oyamada and the Reverend Ken Sudo, the church's director of education. Sudo has subsequently translated some of this content into English, including the comment, 'At the later part of the workshops, Father began to mention that Japan would ruin if we failed to bring in the minimum of 50,000 sisters into this providential workshop.'[2]

The Unification Church begins: 1 May 1954

Together with five other associates, Moon founded the Holy Spirit Association for the Unification of World Christianity (Se-gye Kido-kyo Tong-il Shilyong Hyop-hae) officially in May 1954, in Seoul. A commemorative photograph shows a congregation of eighteen men and women. Moon later wrote that

> We chose this name to signify that we belonged to no denomination, and we certainly had no plans to create a new one. *World Christianity* refers to all of Christianity worldwide and both past and present. *Unification* reveals our purpose of oneness, and *Holy Spirit* is used to denote harmony between the spiritual and physical worlds built on the love of the father-son relationship at the center. Our name is meant to say, 'The spiritual world, centering on God, is with us.'
>
> (Moon 2010)

He commented also on the name by which the new group came to be known, the Unification Church (Tong-il Kyohoi):

> 'Unification Church' became our commonly known name later, but it was given to us by others. In the beginning, university students referred to us as 'the Seoul Church'. I do not like using the word *kyohoi* in its common usage to mean church. But I like its meaning from the original Chinese characters. *Kyo* means 'to teach', and *hoi* means 'gathering'. The Korean word means, literally, 'gathering for teaching'.
>
> (Moon 2010)

The role of the concubine in premodern Korea and ancient Israel

It was an acceptable and fairly common practice for men in traditional Korean society to take secondary wives, if they were wealthy enough to support them. This arrangement usually ensured they would produce sons, thereby fulfilling their primary duty to their ancestors of maintaining the lineage. It was also common to divorce wives who did not bear sons, leading to the wives' social exclusion and economic hardship. The Confucian social code was inflexibly patriarchal, setting out seven commandments for married women, including the obligation to bear sons and the injunction not to be jealous of their husbands' concubines (Palmer 1986). The Korean woman was expected to submit to three men during her life: her father, her husband and her son. This was called 'The Honour of the Three Submissions' (Yoon 2011). At the apex of the society, the kings of Korea maintained strings of concubines.

The widespread practice of taking concubines continued even under the Japanese. For Sun Myung Moon, born into these times, such arrangements would have been part of the social fabric, and even culturally acceptable.

After his family's conversion to Christianity, he would have become familiar with biblical history, including the custom of polygamy. There is no indication from within these texts that the God of Abraham, Isaac and Jacob deemed these practices immoral. As his theology and sense of mission began to develop, Moon's own words indicate a powerful sense of identification with the central figures in these tableaux. Like Abraham, his seed would number as the stars. Like Jacob, who gained victory over the angel, Moon would sire twelve sons, who would in turn create twelve clans to become twelve tribes. In the *Divine Principle*, Moon's descendants would become the 'third Israel', a new chosen people.[3]

This emphasis on the role of the biblical patriarchs as progenitors does, however, have its limitations and cautionary tales. The great lawgiver Moses did not follow this pattern, and the Ten Commandments could not have been more specific about the sins of fornication and adultery. However, the period of the judges was followed by the era of the kings, who are recorded as having taken wives and concubines at their pleasure. David's first six wives had all borne him sons, then he became so infatuated with Bathsheba that he conspired to place her loyal husband, Uriah, at the front of battle, his valiant death clearing the way for David. In his later years he is said to have sent away a group of sixty concubines. Solomon, his son by Bathsheba, is recorded as having 600 wives, many of whom were foreign. Solomon's God was not happy with this state of affairs, especially the foreign gods they imported, leading to the division of his realm into two separate kingdoms after his death.

The great progenitor and the new future of humankind

There would appear to be three levels or ranks to the new lineage Moon was intent on creating. The first comes from his own progeny (the 'fruit of his loins', in the biblical expression). The second is made up by the so-called royal couples (all Korean), whose wives received the *pikareum*, or blood-cleansing ceremony directly from Moon himself. He planned to select spouses for his own 'sinless' True Children from among the second generation of these families. The third and much larger group is formed by the families of all those couples who received the Holy Wine and The Blessing of the True Parents, then completed the three-day ceremony during which their marriage was consummated. It was explained by Hyo-Jin (Moon's first True Child) to the older blessed children that future generations of the ever-expanding True Family would share their bloodline with the descendants of the blessed families, engrafted into the Moon lineage through the marriage blessing. In this way, the Tree of Life first mentioned as an ideal in Genesis would become a substantial reality.

The Unification movement: court, church and 'chaebol'

Moon and his early followers established the various components of the Unification movement as an integrated platform from which to advance his aspirations. First, attending the Moon family with due reverence, is a carefully selected and trusted household staff or court, including a group of well-trained security personnel on twenty-four-hour alert. Staff members lived in close proximity to the Moons, to ensure the maintenance of their *kibun*, or sense of well-being. The key positions are held by Koreans. In America, where palatial mansions are kept in readiness for their visits to New York, Las Vegas and Hawaii, Japanese and American members are used in addition for secondary roles. Moon usually held meetings with senior church and business leaders over extended breakfast sessions, during which he would listen to reports, set goals and give directions on strategy.

The church secondly functions as a faith community, holding weekly worship services and conducting outreach programmes which bear witness to the 'new truth' of the *Divine Principle* and the coming of the Lord of the Second Advent and his bride as the True Parents of humankind. The church teaches that whereas in past ages the way to God was first through sacrifices and then through faith, in the Completed Testament Age it is by attendance as adopted members of the True Family, who are then prepared for The Blessing.

The movement's third component resembles a *chaebol*, or Korean-style business conglomerate, in most cases the product of the vision and drive of a lone entrepreneur, which is then handed on to one or more of Moon's sons. This business empire, now worth many billions of dollars, has played an essential role in supporting the Moon family's lifestyle, as well as funding organs of influence such as the *Washington Times* newspaper, and covering the cost of lawsuits, including recent ones between Moon's eldest living son, Hyun-jin (Preston) and his associates, who gained control of the board of the movement's major holding company in the United States, Unification Church International (UCI), and all its assets (Mickler 2013).

As a means of providing a 'providential' explanation for at least some of Moon's apparent violations of his own teachings, in 2009/10 the church's Korean leadership came out with a revised version of its core teaching, renamed the *Original Divine Principle* (in Korean, the same word translated as 'Original' is used for 'True'), including an explanation of the concept of the change of blood lineage which included the memorable phrase 'the journey of God's sperm'. Part of this content surfaced in an earlier version in Japan as far back as the early 1990s, when the movement there was faced with a series of magazine articles and television interviews with several of the earliest Korean members, including Moon's first wife, Sun-kil Choi, testifying to the existence of the hidden *pikareum* ritual (referred to as *'chiwake'* in Japanese).

The routinisation of charisma and other related developments

Abraham Lincoln once said: 'Nearly all men can stand adversity, but if you want to test a man's character, give him power.' Moon never achieved his oft-stated goal of sovereignty over one nation. It would have been interesting to see how he applied the heavenly laws he was so keen to promulgate. His pronouncements indicate that he intended them to be absolute and irrevocable, and that he expected nothing less than total compliance. Whether such a society would have delivered the 'kingdom of heaven' or something more Orwellian we will never know. But none of the potential successors to the leadership of his movement have such a hold on the members' undivided loyalty that they could feasibly consider that option. None of them can offer anything like Moon's unique heroic narrative, or his incredibly driven schedule. One Unificationist academic at the church's American theological seminary observed: 'Rev. Moon's presence has enabled the movement to survive infighting among the top leaders and factionalism between departments, as well as a climate of distrust between leaders and members. . . . The succession problem is further complicated by a multiplicity of candidates from the same charismatic family' (Mickler 1991). Nansook Hong, Moon's former daughter-in-law, presciently predicted a different future:

> The Reverend Moon has made no concrete plans for his succession. To do so would require him to relinquish some power while he is still alive, and that prospect is inconceivable to a man accustomed to being the central figure in a tightly controlled universe. The Unification Church is a classic example of what psychologists call a cult of personality. The failure to designate and groom a successor all but guarantees a familial bloodletting after the Reverend Moon's death. His sons are already locked in a battle for control of his business empire. That struggle will only intensify when the Unification Church itself is up for grabs.
>
> (Hong 1998)

It is self-evident that Moon saw himself as a dynast. His family has let him down in this regard by feuding, misbehaving and separating out. His oldest living son, Hyun-jin (Preston), while managing to avoid the dissolute lifestyle of the Moons' oldest son, Hyo-jin, is said to have had strong disagreements with his father about the way the movement was being run. He was ousted, according to his supporters, by a cabal which included two of his younger brothers and his older sister (Mickler 2013). Hyun-jin is a strategic thinker with a postgraduate degree from Harvard. Of Moon's sons, his character perhaps most resembles his father's. Arguably the most charismatic potential leader, Hyun-jin also appears to be the most schismatic, and after having been excluded from attending his father's funeral (his family was not mentioned in the official list of mourners), his *han* towards his mother and those siblings who engineered the situation runs deep. His potential for disrupting the movement's future course could be described in Shakespearian terms as the 'Coriolanus factor'. He and his camp, including his father-in-law, Rev. Chung-hwan Kwak (Moon's former trusted aide and representative), have been working on an alternative interpretation of the *Divine Principle* which incorporates a 'low' Christology, and which may ultimately prove more attractive to many members than the ever-increasing emphasis on the divinisation of the Moons by those Korean leaders who have remained in loyal attendance at the court of Moon's widow.

It is instructive to compare this mindset with that of the regime that has held power in North Korea since 1948. Although originally seen as communist, it has morphed over time into a dynastic succession unique in the communist world, as a solution to the leadership question. Brian Myers (2010) has described the regime's self-justification thus: 'The Korean people are too pure-blooded, and therefore too virtuous, to survive in this world without a great parental leader.'

Blind faith? Difficult questions and the issue of non-transparency

As a result of his interactions with members while researching the movement's religious aspect in the 1980s, George Chryssides (1991) advanced the thesis that many Unificationists, in common with many members of other faith traditions, may not fully understand their own religion. Others, such as James Beckford (1985), lend support to this contention. The majority of non-Korean members, not having visited Korea or been acculturated, remain unaware of the pervasive influence of the shamanistic indigenous elements within the religion. Even fewer 'foreign' members have learnt Korean, and are, therefore, generally unaware of the issues that gave rise to the movement's controversial reputation in its homeland.

The most potentially damaging accusations have been contextualised as part of a sustained campaign of falsehoods by the established churches in Korea. More recent scandals in the Moon family, such as Hyo-jin's affairs, drug and alcohol addiction and spousal abuse, evinced nothing more than a pained press release and privacy request by his parents. A scandal involving their daughter In-jin (Tatiana), who had a secret love-child with the lead guitarist of her Lovin' Life Ministries band while she was the senior pastor and CEO of the American church, could no longer be ignored after the baby's birth certificate appeared on the Internet. The unsigned announcement of her enforced resignation from the movement's international headquarters in Korea stated that it was 'for health reasons'.

The American members' reaction to this leaked information was so strong that the youngest son and putative heir-apparent, Hyung-jin, was reassigned from Korea to take charge of the American movement and head up a nationwide damage-limitation exercise. He was later removed as a result of a disagreement with his mother, and has begun holding services independently under the name of the 'Sanctuary Church' in Pennsylvania.

The Japanese movement is virtually leak-proof, and unofficial sources there reported that the members know nothing of the real reasons behind In-jin Moon's resignation. In America, her sudden departure triggered media interest and in-depth articles by the Washington, DC, journalist Mariah Blake (2013a, 2013b). These exposés contained details which appeared to have come from inside sources; this information shocked members unaware of True Family's life behind the scenes. The same cannot be said for the second-level leadership, some of whom had been forced to resign for their part in the cover-up of In-jin Moon's affairs.

The sole exception was the existence of Samuel Pak, who had grown up in the family of Moon's close aide and publisher of the *Washington Times*, Bo-hi Pak. Sam's true identity as Moon's son with Soon-hwa Choi had been acknowledged by both Nansook Hong and Moon's estranged daughter Un-jin, during interviews with Mike Wallace on *60 Minutes* on ABC News. Moon summoned all the members on the East Coast of America to his mansion in Westchester, where he reassured them, in a more cautious speech than usual, that he had 'never misused his member' (or 'love organ').

This statement was enough to maintain the faith and trust of most members, although it had an impact on both recruitment and retention at the time (1998). It takes a lot for members who have followed faithfully for decades, and raised families based on matchings arranged by their messiah, to walk away.

The influence of Daemonim and the 'Cheongpyeong providence'

Members have also been mentally 'cocooned' or conditioned by the intense and extended sessions of chanting and *ansu* (heavy and repeated slapping of various parts of the body, usually in large groups, to the rhythm of a large traditional drum), since a new 'providence' was announced in 1995. These almost constant workshops were initiated by a Mrs Hyo Nam Kim, who effectively assumed the role of a mediumistic *mudang* after she claimed that she was in regular communication with Mrs Moon's deceased mother, who was declared to have been elevated to a position of great honour in the spirit world and upon whom Moon had bestowed the title of 'Daemonim' ('Great Mother') in recognition for her life of faithful and obedient attendance. Mrs Kim has raised a phenomenal amount of money (especially from the Japanese) since beginning her ministry, by asking for 'special donations' to perform services including the liberation and blessing of 210 generations of their ancestors. This exercise, reminiscent to some of the practice of selling indulgences in the Catholic Church, has succeeded in raising sufficient funds to build a property portfolio including a magnificent marble palace in Cheongpyeong, a large training centre, a seminary, a hospital, a school and the largest indoor auditorium in Korea (Mickler 2013). The Cheongpyeong workshops also perform the function of a 'gateway test', whereby members who are dubious of their spiritual benefits have 'self-selected' to opt out, leaving a clearer atmosphere for the majority of members who have participated. Upon completion, these people are enjoined not to have 'give-and-take' with negative elements, including not only sexual impurity, but anything that might disturb their rededicated state of faith, such as ugly rumours or media scandals involving the Moons.

These injunctions have engendered a real fear among many members of 're-infestation' by evil spirits if they disobey, leading to avoidance of critical information, and thus a heightened sense of cognitive dissonance.

The possibility of another great disappointment (or a reality check)

How will history view Sun Myung Moon? As a truly messianic figure, one 'anointed' by heaven to usher in a golden age of peace and plenty, or as yet another Oriental 'mystagogue'?

Since coming to public attention, Moon has lived his life as though orchestrating a movie, and much of his later life, both public and private, was captured in photographs and recorded on video or audio by teams of technicians who, according to his wishes, have created a large archive for posterity. His many, many words have been transcribed into collected works in many languages, with the sense that they, as well as the *Divine Principle*, are sacred scripture.

Something else could be sensed at his strangely solemn *seonghwa* ('ascension and harmony') ceremony. It was the realisation that he had not in fact lived, as he had predicted, to usher in 'Foundation Day' on the date he had set, 22 February 2013.

Was Hyun-jin, correct when he issued a statement to the members at that time saying that there was not enough of a foundation to declare Foundation Day (the beginning of a new era, or heaven on earth)? According to the master of ceremonies at Moon's *seonghwa*, Moon said in his final prayer that he had 'completed, perfected and concluded' his mission although the reunification of the Korean peninsula which Moon predicted, prayed for and worked towards would remain an unrealised dream.

As more details have continued to come out which substantiate many of the long-standing rumours about Sun Myung Moon's hidden history, perhaps a different conclusion may be reached: that the Unification movement will serve as an example of the use of historical research to deconstruct a new religious myth while it is in the process of being formed.

Notes

1 Pak's book was scheduled for publication in October 1993. During twenty-five training sessions from 6 October to 22 December, a total of 51,800 sisters aged between sixteen and eighty were recorded as having attended the sessions, paying a substantial fee described as a 'national salvation donation', according to an entry in Japanese Wikipedia.
2 According to the Wikipedia entry, some attended twice in order to make up the numbers.
3 The first Israel (the vanquished angel gave this name to Jacob) being descendants of Jacob and the second Israel being the Christians, described as a new 'spiritual Israel' by Paul after he began witnessing to the Gentiles.

References

Beckford, James A. 1985. *Cult Controversies*. London: Tavistock.
Blake, Mariah 2013a. 'The Fall of the House of Moon'. *The New Republic*. 12 November.
―――― 2013b. 'Meet the Love Child Rev. Sun Myung Moon Desperately Tried to Hide'. *Mother Jones*. 9 December.
Breen, Michael 1997. *Sun Myung Moon: The Early Years, 1920–53*. Hurstpierpoint, W. Sussex: Refuge Books.
Chryssides, George D. 1991. *The Advent of Sun Myung Moon: The Origins, Beliefs and Practices of the Unification Church*. Basingstoke: Macmillan.
Grayson, James Huntley 2002. *Korea: A Religious History* (revised edition). Abingdon: RoutledgeCurzon.
Hong, Nansook 1998. *In the Shadow of the Moons: My Life in the Reverend Sun Myung Moon's Family*. Boston: Little, Brown.
Hwang, Sun Jo 2010. *Proclamation of the Substantial Word that Firmly Establishes the True Parents of Heaven, Earth, and Humankind and the Tribal Messiah*. Seoul, Korea: Tribal Messiahs' Federation for World Peace.
Kim, Chong-sun 1978. *Rev. Sun Myung Moon*. Lanham, MD: University Press of America.
Mickler, Michael L. 1991. 'When the prophet is yet living: A case study of the Unification Church', in: Timothy Miller (ed.) *When Prophets Die: The Postcharismatic Fate of New Religious Movements* (pp. 183–94). Albany: State University of New York Press.
―――― 2013. 'The post–Sun Myung Moon Unification Church', in: Eileen Barker (ed.) *Revisionism and Diversification in New Religious Movements* (pp. 47–64). Farnham: Ashgate.
Moon, Sun Myung 1973. *Divine Principle*. Thornton Heath: Holy Spirit Association for the Unification of World Christianity.
―――― 2010. *As a Peace-Loving Global Citizen*. Washington, DC: Washington Times Foundation.
Myers, B. R. 2010. *The Cleanest Race*. Brooklyn, NY: Melville House.
Nevalainen, Kirsti 2011. *Change of Blood Lineage through Ritual Sex in the Unification Church*. Self-published.
Pak, Chung Hwa 1993. *The Tragedy of the Six Marys*. Tokyo: Koyu Publishing.
Palmer, Spencer 1986. *Korea and Christianity: The Problem of Identification with Tradition*. Seoul: Royal Asiatic Society.
Sontag, Frederick 1977. *Sun Myung Moon and the Unification Church*. Nashville, TN: Abingdon.
Yoon, Insun 2011. *Civilizing Mission for Women: American Methodist Missionary Women and Social Change in Korea, 1885–1940*. Proquest, Ann Arbor, MI: UMI Dissertation Publishing.

12 The changing perception of ISKCON
Ancient faith or dangerous cult?

Anuttama Dasa

> The Hare Krishna Movement *"is historically very significant, for now, for the first time since the days of the Roman Empire, an Asian religion is being openly practised by people of Western origin in the streets of Western cities."*
>
> (Basham 2004: 497)

Introduction

The year was 1996. As the director of communications for the International Society for Krishna Consciousness (ISKCON), I was coordinating the first Vaishnava–Christian Dialogue in the United States.[1] Dr. Gordon Melton, one of two dozen participants, came as a person with deep knowledge of new religious movements (NRMs) and, more important, as a Christian minister.[2]

During the dialogue, the topic of ISKCON's historicity and its standing within Hinduism arose. Is ISKCON an ancient faith tradition, a new religious movement, or worse yet, a dangerous cult? Various perspectives were shared before Dr. Melton spoke, adding clarity via his personal example: "I am a member of a new religious movement," he proclaimed. "I am a United Methodist."

Dr. Melton explained to his somewhat stunned audience that the United Methodists a) are based on the 2,000-year-old biblical tradition and teachings of Jesus Christ; b) are an outgrowth of the Protestant Reformation and the eighteenth-century teachings of John Wesley; and c) were officially founded in 1968 in the United States when two older denominations merged to create the new United Methodist Church.

Hence, he belonged to an NRM.

Dr. Melton's clarity allows me to confirm that I too am a member of a new religious movement. The International Society for Krishna Consciousness (ISKCON) is a) solidly within the millenniums-old orthodoxy of Vaishnava Hinduism (and respected as such throughout India); b) an outgrowth of the later Bhakti movements in medieval India; and c) was officially founded as a religious institution in 1966, in New York.

Thus, within the context Dr. Melton described, I am a member of a new religious movement – one that has existed in its essential form for thousands of years. As such, I am honored to contribute to this volume.

The journey

> The founder of the Hare Krishna movement was 69 years old before he started the International Society for Krishna Consciousness. In his native India, Prabhupada had been a chemist and a Sanskrit scholar in Calcutta, but in 1965 he came to New York City with just fifty bucks, a pair of cymbals, and a desire to spread the teachings of Lord Krishna.
>
> (Trex 2010)

On August 13, 1965, an elderly Indian monk, A. C. Bhaktivedanta Swami, boarded the steamship *Jaladuta* in the harbor of Calcutta and began a journey across the sea to distant New York. He did so under the order of his spiritual preceptor, Srila Bhaktisiddhanta Sarasvati Goswami, with the specific mission of transporting the ancient devotional tradition of Vaishnavism to the world's Western shores.

The Swami left India with no institutional support. He carried only a few dollars' worth of rupees and several trunks of books – his translations and commentaries of India's classic spiritual text the *Bhagavata Purana or Srimad Bhagavatam*. Alone at seventy, undergoing two heart attacks at sea, and later finding no place to live but amid the dilapidation of the New York Bowery, A. C. Bhaktivedanta persevered and after one year of struggle began to attract followers among the youth of the city's avant-garde Lower East Side.

Bhaktivedanta Swami established a storefront temple in New York and in July 1966 incorporated his fledgling community as the International Society for Krishna Consciousness (ISKCON). Setting the tone for what he clearly saw as a global movement, the Swami listed in ISKCON's incorporation documents Seven Purposes including:

> To systematically propagate spiritual knowledge to society at large and to educate all people in the techniques of spiritual life in order to check the imbalance of values in life and to achieve real unity and peace in the world.[3]
>
> (Satsvarupa dasa Goswami 1980: 132–3)

Within a few months of ISKCON's founding, Bhaktivedanta Swami left New York for San Francisco to open a second temple, landing in the famed Haight-Ashbury district just as the 1960s counterculture came to full force. Soon he was traveling the world, including several tours of his native India, to continue his expansive mission.

Before his passing away in 1977, Srila Prabhupada, as he became known, or "the master at whose feet others sit," had circled the globe fourteen times, opened more than 100 temples and rural communities worldwide, initiated 5,000 disciples, and translated, commented on, and published more than sixty volumes of Vaishnava books via his Bhaktivedanta Book Trust.

Roots and identity

> ISKCON belongs to the Gaudiya Vaishnava sampradaya (denomination or tradition), a monotheistic tradition within Vedic or Hindu culture. Hindu culture is vast, and the term "Hinduism" encompasses numerous theologies, philosophies, religious traditions, and spiritual cultures. Thus, dialogue with Hindu traditions is often difficult. There are no official representatives of Hinduism, as the term Hinduism does not imply a single spiritual tradition.
>
> (Saunaka Rsi Dasa 1999)

The movement that Prabhupada founded, often simply known as the Hare Krishna movement, takes as primary scriptural sources the well-known Vedic, or Hindu Sanskrit texts, *Bhagavad-Gita* and *Srimad Bhagavatam*, as well as the more recent sixteenth-century Bengali text, the *Sri Caitanya Charitamrita*.

In the Western world the Advaita, or monistic schools (which advocate that ultimate reality is impersonal) are better known than the Dvaita, or dualistic schools of thought to which ISKCON adheres (and which advocate that ultimate reality is a personal God). However, scholars of Indian thought document that the Dvaita, or the devotional, monotheistic form of Hinduism known as Vaishnavism – of which ISKCON is perhaps the best-known global expression – is the largest of the various Hindu traditions in India.

The term "Hinduism" is a modern word that does not appear in any traditional texts. Thus ISKCON members, while acknowledging that they exist within the broad category of "Hinduism" or "Hindu culture," prefer the more accurate description of ISKCON as a Vaishnava tradition, specifically a Gaudiya, or Caitanya Vaishnava tradition (Rosen 2006: xvii).

Beliefs

> To help all people discern reality from illusion, spirit from matter, the eternal from the temporary. . . . To help every living being remember and serve Sri Krishna, the Personality of Godhead.
>
> (*Back to Godhead* 2013)

ISKCON members practice bhakti-yoga, the yoga of devotion, as outlined in the *Bhagavad-Gita* and *Srimad Bhagavatam*. In my brief summary, members of ISKCON believe that:

1 All living beings are individual, eternal, spiritual souls.
2 The source of all existence is Brahman, or spirit, which is ultimately realized to be the Supreme Personality of Godhead (God), Lord Krishna.

3   The goal of human life is to reawaken the soul's love for God.
4   The most effective process for awakening this love and returning to the Kingdom of God is practicing bhakti-yoga and chanting God's names.
5   The soul is separated from God by rebelliousness and clinging to materialistic desires that create one's karma, thus destining one to repeated birth and death.
6   The world's great religions share the same purpose – to reconnect the soul with God.
7   The primary values of spiritual practice are: cleanliness, truthfulness, mercy, and austerity (self-discipline).
8   Devotees of God should help to awaken knowledge of God within human society. Thus emphasis is given to public chanting of God's names, opening temples, and distributing religious literatures and sanctified vegetarian food.

Changing demographics

> There was no dispute that the [Hare Krishna Temple Bhaktivedanta] Manor meets the spiritual needs of large numbers of Hindus and that it is unique in the U.K. because there is no comparable establishment for teaching, worship, and meditation.
> (Gummer 1996: 10)

The face of ISKCON has changed since the 1960s and 1970s. While some may think of Hare Krishna members as living communally in temples across the globe, very few do so today. In their earliest years, ISKCON communities consisted of a tight-knit group of young converts living communally (although unmarried men and women did not associate intimately) and spending their days working for the society, most notably chanting in public venues, selling the society's literature, raising funds, engaging in temple worship, and expanding the number of temples. Today, however, the vast majority of ISKCON members live and work on their own and visit temples daily, weekly, or monthly depending on their level of interest and dedication.

For example, in Washington, DC, where I live, there are about twenty-five adults and six children living within the twelve-acre temple property in apartments owned by the temple. These are the primary priests and administrative heads of the temple. On any given Sunday, the main day of community worship in ISKCON, more than 400 members attend the two-hour services. Included are up to 100 devotees[4] who have taken vows within ISKCON, and thus are qualified to perform the rituals of Vaishnava worship. Yet these very committed Hare Krishna practitioners choose, and are almost always encouraged, to live outside the immediate community. On major holidays between 5,000 and 10,000 people flood the temple grounds and worship halls.

Some noting this change of demographics argue that the Hare Krishna movement has strayed from its original purpose. ISKCON was envisioned, they claim, to remain a communal structure, aloof from the mainstream and built on a core membership of temple residents and renunciates, that is, celibate *sannyasis* and *brahmacaris*. The growth of householder communities, they posture, was primarily a response to economic pressures on the movement in the 1980s (see Rochford 2007: 61–71).

With due respect, I beg to differ with such opinions. ISKCON's founder, Srila Prabhupada, was himself a family man. Before formally accepting the path of renunciation, or *sannyasa* at sixty-three, and leaving his family (a traditional function of pious Hindu men), he was faithfully married for forty years, lived at home, worked in the pharmaceutical business, and raised several children. At the same time he served his guru's mission by giving contributions, serving as a member of local temples, assisting as a part-time preacher, and so forth. His example was not an aberration. Historically the Vaishnava community, while strict in piety and practice, is a *grihastra* (householder) as well as a renunciate religious community. Vaishnavas do not hide from the world, but actively live and engage in the world, all the while trying to spiritualize it.

Other examples abound. They include nineteenth-century Vaishnava reformer Bhaktivinode Thakura, who happened to be the father of Prabhupada's guru. Thakura was an active Vaishnava preacher, author, and teacher, as well as a highly ranking magistrate within the British government in India (Sardella 2012: 56–63).

The demographics of the movement Prabhupada started, while in its earliest years filled with zealous young dropouts and hippies, was not so composed because that was Prabhupada's vision for the ideal ISKCON community, but because of the large numbers of soul-searching young people permeating the counterculture of the 1960s and 1970s.

Another major change in ISKCON demographics from its origins to today is the large number of Asian Indians now active in ISKCON temples.[5] In the West at least, ISKCON in the 1960s through 1980s, depending on which continent you study, was primarily attracting local Europeans, South and North Americans, and Australians.

Today, in countries hosting a large Indian diaspora, more often than not ISKCON attracts significant numbers of Asian Indians. Looking at the example of Washington, DC, again, on any given Sunday 80 percent of the participants are of South Asian origin. Some scholars and ISKCON members argue this augurs ill for ISKCON and point to the "Hinduization" of the society, a code word for watering down its strict allegiance to Chaitanya Vaishnavism and willingness to compromise to seek money and members from the broader Hindu community (see Rochford 2007: 181–200).

Again, I must offer a different analysis. Even a cursory study of the large numbers of South Asians – both first- and second-generation immigrants – that participate actively in ISKCON today reveals two facts:

1   ISKCON is accepted as a genuine expression of Hindu faith and a respected global manifestation – if not a source of pride – among many Indians due to its spreading of Vaishnava culture.

2   ISKCON does not just provide cultural comfort for those of Indian origin at the expense of its allegiance to Vaishnava *siddhanta*, or philosophical conclusion. ISKCON actively attracts and educates many in the global Hindu diaspora who left India to seek refuge in more affluent nations, and inspires them to become serious practitioners of their own indigenous religious culture. For instance, initiated members of ISKCON of whatever origin vow to avoid intoxication, gambling, and illicit sex; to refrain from eating meat, fish, and eggs; and to chant the Hare Krishna mantra two hours daily on their prayer beads.

Readers may find parallels in ISKCON's rapid global growth to that of early Christianity, as sociologist Rodney Stark outlined in *The Rise of Christianity* (Stark 1996). Stark argues that the Jewish diaspora played a historically significant role in quickening the spread of the young Christian sect by giving it a strong foundation outside its place of origin in Israel. I would argue that similar forces are at work – either divine or sociological – within ISKCON. Rather than being weakened by its burgeoning Hindu community, ISKCON is revitalizing the faith of both secular and religiously inclined Hindus around the world.

Indian roots and global presence

> I am a die-hard devotee of Lord Krishna and ISKCON. Be it in front of the camera or while performing on stage, I get very positive vibes from Krishna. . . . The basic teaching of ISKCON is the cleanliness of the soul. If your soul is clean then you will definitely look beautiful.
>
> (Hema Malini, film actress, member of the Indian parliament, in Jha 2014)

In 1970, Srila Prabhupada returned to India with a small group of Western disciples. He did so to introduce his students to India and to demonstrate to Indians that their ancestral religious practices, which many of them were abandoning in search of the promised rewards of Western materialism, were themselves in hot demand in the same places to which many Indians clamored to migrate.

Prabhupada's forays back to India with what he called his "dancing White Elephants" created a sensation, drawing packed crowds at major events across India, as well as helping to convince well-to-do pious Indians to support Srila Prabhupada's fledgling efforts to spread their culture around the world (see Satsvarupa dasa Goswami 1980: 121).

During Prabhupada's lifetime, ISKCON established only three major temples in India – one in the holy city of Vrindavana, on the main route between Agra and New Delhi; one in Bombay, now Mumbai; and one in Mayapura, West Bengal, ISKCON's "world headquarters" at the historic home of Chaitanya Vaishnavism.

Today ISKCON is a major presence with large, popular temples in dozens of cities across India. On Krishna's birthday, Janmastami, ISKCON's Juhu Beach

Mumbai temple alone attracts more than 300,000 worshipers over the two-day festival (see Jaisinghani 2011).

This growth and acceptance of ISKCON across India is a significant fact to consider when examining the growth, maturation, and global impact of the Hare Krishna movement.

Two recent stories shed light on this reality. In October 2014, I attended the traditional Diwali, the Hindu New Year celebration, in Tirupati, India. As ISKCON's governing body commission chairman, I was chief guest at the event alongside the managing director of the famous Balaji Temple, which sits nearby on the towering Tirumala Hills.

Tirumala is one of the primary centers of Hindu orthodoxy. Yet, here I was, a white American convert, sharing the stage with a leader of one of Hinduism's most ancient and popular temples. In fact, the multi-acre site on which the large ISKCON temple and guesthouse in Tirupati is located was donated by the Tirumala authorities. What's more, ISKCON and the Tirumala priests regularly contribute ritually to each other's ceremonies. And daily, ISKCON devotees drive thirty minutes to the top of the Tirumala Hills to staff four bookstalls within the spacious temple grounds provided by the Tirumala authorities. There, Prabhupada's books are sold to enthusiastic crowds of pilgrims.

A second recent example symptomatic of ISKCON's growth and acceptance in its historic home came in September 2014, when the governors of the Indian states of Uttar Pradesh, Mr. Ram Naik, and the governor of Nagaland, Mr. P. B. Acharya, joined tens of thousands of locals to inaugurate ISKCON's newest temple in Kanpur, India. The three-day event culminated in the ritual opening of the temple, speeches by government and other dignitaries, and two evenings of performances by singer, film star, and member of the Rajya Sabha, the upper house of India's parliament, Ms. Hema Malini. Dozens of favorable articles appeared in the local and state media.[6]

ISKCON is also active in providing social programs in India (and other nations). ISKCON's Food For Life program feeds 1.2 million schoolchildren daily in India alone in conjunction with the government's midday meal program. ISKCON has also established hospitals, medical clinics, and several schools across the subcontinent.

ISKCON has expanded since its inception into countries worldwide, with an estimated 600 major temples, and many thousands of less formal *namahattas*, groups of Krishna devotees who meet weekly for spiritual discourse and association.

Within this chapter, it is not possible to survey that growth and maturation other than to highlight a sampling of ISKCON's presence in a variety of countries. ISKCON's main impact on a global scale remains its book distribution with Prabhupada's books today translated into seventy-six languages and published in the hundreds of millions.

In addition, ISKCON now has numerous eco-villages, sustainable communities in North and South America, India, Europe, and Africa. In the UK

ISKCON runs the country's largest *ahimsa* (slaughter-free) milk production facility. ISKCON is also creating new educational institutions based on Vaishnava values. For example, an ISKCON affiliate is the official faith partner for the British government's network of Hindu Avanti schools. ISKCON members also conceived and are now active in the independent Oxford Centre for Hindu Studies.[7]

In Hungary, ISKCON maintains a large eco-village that shares in a variety of programs with university and government researchers, and a government-accredited Yoga College in Budapest. In South Africa, ISKCON once hosted a football stadium full of Rainbow Nation children to celebrate their newfound freedom with President Nelson Mandela. In Australia, ISKCON operates a nationwide chain of popular vegetarian restaurants. In Russia, ISKCON was the first new religious organization officially recognized in that country since World War II, yet still struggles with government officials and others who see ISKCON's growth as a threat to the traditional Russian Orthodox Church. In Belgium, ISKCON maintains an officially accredited theological college and its members were a founding force behind the respected Hindu Forum of Europe.[8]

Challenges

> Don't look now, but the Hare Krishnas have left the airport and entered the boardroom. The much-maligned Hindu sect has shed its freak-show status and, behind its yuppie-friendly pillars of yoga, meditation, and clean living, is transforming America into a postmodern ashram. Robes not required.
>
> (Blasengame 2014)

Despite ISKCON's growth and successes, it has faced many challenges, especially since the passing of Srila Prabhupada in November 1977. These include issues of succession after Prabhupada; child abuse in ISKCON's parochial schools in the 1970s and 1980s, especially in India and the United States; various leadership scandals; hermeneutical and sociological issues that threatened to divide the movement into East and West or conservative and liberal, and, of interest to this study, the pressure against ISKCON brought by anti-cult organizations.

Most pertinent to the focus of this volume is the history of ISKCON's interaction and challenges in regard to "anti-cult" leaders and organizations. Thus I will spend the balance of this chapter focusing on that discussion.

As outlined in other chapters of this book, fears about potential dangers of cults and new religious movements came to the fore in the late 1970s just as ISKCON was experiencing substantial global growth and high visibility, and was about to face the passing away of its founder.

During Prabhupada's time, charges of brainwashing and cultism had already been leveled against the Krishna movement (Bharata Shrestha Dasa 1998; Rochford and Heinlein 1998). These were inspired by a number of factors, including the society's advocacy of (what was at that time considered a questionable) a vegetarian diet, its promotion of ashram or communal lifestyles for young recruits, its core practice of two hours daily mantra meditation or the repetitive chanting of God's names on beads, its harsh (and often harshly delivered) critique of modern "materialistic" culture, the tendency of young converts to cut ties to their families, its questionable fundraising in public venues like airports, questions about women's roles, and the aforementioned cultural issues, including the visually different Hare Krishna dress, hairstyles, and public chanting.

Conversely, during that period many young ISKCON members concluded, somewhat naïvely but not without cause, that critics accused Hare Krishnas of brainwashing and other deviations due to the critics' own ignorance of Eastern religious practices and culture; or, perhaps because they simply couldn't imagine how young Western men and women could otherwise abandon their familial traditions as well as the worldly enticements of "sex, drugs, and rock and roll" to become monastics.

During this period, many ISKCON devotees were "deprogramed" by persons family members paid to remove loved ones at any cost from ISKCON. I don't know if a quantitative study was ever done of how often this occurred against ISKCON members. I do know of several Krishna devotees who were forcibly kidnapped, imprisoned by their captors in obscure places for days on end, and forced to recant their beliefs before they could be released.

I had personal experience of a case where one impetuous young man, after being kidnapped and deprogrammed, left the movement and publicly accused ISKCON of various abuses on national television. I also know of several cases where Krishnas either feigned a "reconversion" to their previous world view to gain their freedom, or, in one case, jumped through a pane glass window at great physical risk to escape.

Sadly, I also know of a situation where a young woman's family paid deprogrammers tens of thousands of dollars only to find their daughter refused to give up her faith in Vaishnavism. Later, humiliated and angry at the abuse caused by the family's errant desire to help her, she cut off all contact with her parents and other relatives for decades.

ISKCON and the anti-cult movement

> Some, for example, seem to presume that all groups labeled cults must be all bad and incapable of change. Messages on the Internet, for example, have asserted that this conference's program, "Can Cultic Groups Change: The Case of ISKCON," is a sign of naivety on AFF's part, or even a sign that "AFF has been taken over by cults." The underlying assumption of these criticisms seems to be that a group such as ISKCON is incapable of positive change; therefore, AFF must be wrong-headed or complicitous.
> (Langone 1999)

After two decades of on-and-off-again tension and attention between ISKCON and various anti-cult groups, often manifesting through TV debates, media battles, occasional deprogrammings, courtroom accusations and anecdotes,[9] and alternative reality narratives, ISKCON entered 1996 ready to celebrate its thirtieth anniversary credited with not only surviving but maturing into a responsible global minority faith.

That year, Gustav Niebuhr, religion reporter for the *New York Times*, wrote an article titled: "Hare Krishnas at 30: Real Changes or Just PR." In the article, Niebuhr quoted Marcia Rudin of the American Family Foundation (AFF), who said that although AFF had not received many complaints about the Hare Krishnas in recent years, often cult groups work to change their image but underneath the façade are still problematic (Niebuhr 1996).

As ISKCON's director of communications, I was disappointed to find that Niebuhr chose to quote an anti-cult critic of ISKCON, Marcia Rudin, in a story that had nothing directly to do with anti-cult accusations. It was our anniversary celebration, after all, and he had rained on our party by referencing these overgeneralized assumptions about ISKCON, based in part on experiences with groups entirely different and separate from us. The unfairness of it all was palpable, and I phoned Niebuhr to tell him so.

I had met Gus on several occasions, and I respected his work. My question was a simple one: Why did you find it necessary to quote an AFF spokesperson in this story? After all, I pointed out, it was a simple, happy thirtieth anniversary story. ISKCON hadn't done anything recently to warrant her criticism, or her being consulted. She almost said as much herself.

Gus's response was straightforward. He told me – regarding my concern that ISKCON was indirectly labeled a cult – "It's out there, Anuttama, you need to deal with it." It was an unpleasant pill to swallow, but I took Mr. Niebuhr's words as prophetic and practical. I contacted Ms. Rudin, told her I appreciated her mentioning that AFF had not fielded complaints about ISKCON recently, and asked if we could discuss whatever issues remained in AFF's dossier about ISKCON.

Marcia was courteous and directed me to Dr. Michael D. Langone, the executive director of AFF. That was the beginning of what has now been twenty years of dialogue between ISKCON and arguably our strongest, and occasionally misinformed, critics.

The first face-to-face meeting between Dr. Langone and me was a telling one, and it marked the path for a productive future. After attending a National Institute of Health seminar on cults conducted by AFF outside Washington, DC, Michael and two of his colleagues joined me, my wife, Rukmini, and a Krishna friend, Hari Dasa, who at the time was completing his master's degree in pastoral counseling, for dinner at a local vegetarian restaurant.

At dinner one of Michael's associates, David Clark, struck up a conversation by asking me, "What is Kirtanananda Swami Bhaktipada doing these days?" Kirtanananda Swami was an early disciple of Srila Prabhupada. He had been a senior leader of ISKCON and was one of the first of Prabhupada's students to himself become an initiating guru after Prabhupada's passing. He was also the first person officially expelled from ISKCON for deviating from ISKCON's principles and for attempting to set himself up as an authority outside the Governing Body Commission, which was established by Prabhupada and expressly appointed in his will to be the society's "Ultimate Managing Authority."

It was uncomfortable for me to be asked about Kirtanananda. Likely my face blushed and I remember having to clear my throat before speaking. Although expelled since 1986, I reported, Kirtanananda had continued to be a source of trouble and embarrassment for the society through ongoing media reports and government investigations into his alleged criminal activities. "Actually Kirtanananda was expelled from ISKCON in 1986 for a variety of personal and religious deviations," I explained. "He's had nothing to do with our society for over ten years. In fact, we cooperated with government investigations against him and he spent some time in federal prison."

David told me he wasn't aware of those facts and thanked me for sharing the information. After a few awkward moments I innocently continued the conversation.

"What is Ted Patrick up to these days?" I inquired. David seemed uncomfortable with my question, and oddly enough, echoed my earlier response to him: "Actually, Ted Patrick [the infamous deprogrammer] doesn't have anything to do with AFF anymore. We don't endorse him or his tactics in any way. He was found guilty of criminal behavior in connection to his deprograming activities, and spent time in prison."

I don't recall if we all chuckled at the mirrored effect of this exchange. One thing was clear. Both our communities had mixed histories. To make progress in addressing our differences as well as realizing any potential benefits in talking to one another would require openness, honesty, and a certain degree of trust.

The next year, I attended the AFF national convention and was invited to a private meeting with AFF leaders to discuss ISKCON's status and internal reforms and to see if there was potential for dialogue over our differences. As a result of that meeting, in 1999 at the AFF convention in St. Paul, Minnesota, I was invited to speak on a panel with my colleague Radha Dasi titled "Can Cultic Groups Change?: The Case of ISKCON."

The title itself was a stretch for both organizations. I wasn't comfortable to participate in something where ISKCON was being labeled a cult or a "cultic group." And, for the AFF leadership to even theorize that a cultic group could change from its documented deviancies was a radical departure from prior anti-cult orthodoxy. To my knowledge, Radha and I were the first active members of any group the AFF studied to be invited officially to speak at an AFF event.

The descriptive term "cultic groups" was and is an important one to consider. It denotes a thawing of the tension documented in this book. One factor of major importance in studying the "cult wars" is understanding how the perception of questionable groups evolved within the more open-minded cult-watching groups.

For a member of ISKCON there was no scope for dialogue, for example, with the former Cult Awareness Network (CAN) and its director, Cynthia

Kisser, although I tried. I phoned Kisser's office during a visit to Chicago, where CAN had its offices in the mid-1990s, to see if I could open up dialogue with that organization. She picked up the call and politely but firmly explained that members of her board would not tolerate her speaking with me, a Hare Krishna leader, in any kind of cooperative or even exploratory basis.

AFF, later known as ICSA, the International Cultic Studies Association, was different. From my first meetings and attendance at AFF/ICSA's events I learned that while some persons present held onto what I found to be a simplistic and indefensible belief in brainwashing – or the total loss of individual decision making at the hands of manipulative cult leaders – most of the people at ICSA spoke in more nuanced terms.[10]

The researchers I was most drawn to – and those who seemed to be gradually holding sway within the internal anti-cult debates – were more likely to speak in terms of "undue influence" and "cultic behaviors" rather than the less subtle, easily misconstrued paradigms of "brainwashing," "dangerous cults," and "mind control."

Many acknowledged, as did Langone, that despite the tendency of some anti-cult researchers and the sensationalist media to generalize and label a widely divergent group of organizations with the pejorative label "cults" and thus preemptively assign them to the category of dangerous groups,[11] that after years of research in the field, the only thing for certain was that some people, in some groups, abuse sometimes.

For my part, a more balanced study of the problems of abusive group dynamics made sense. I had lived through some of the excesses, abuses, and outright criminality of our own Kirtanananda Swami and others, and realized that *any* leadership was subject to abuse and extremism. I accepted that people *could* be led to do things harmful to themselves and others by charismatic leaders. The question in my mind was, and remains: What can thoughtful people do to minimize the risks of leaders – religious as well as military, political, social, or whatever – mistreating their followers, and to instead ensure and instill healthy group dynamics? In short, what can be done to ensure that what might start out as a healthy community, of whatever flavor or stripe, does not degrade into an abusive or "cultic" one?

Returning to the discussion of the panel on "Can Cultic Groups Change?: The Case of ISKCON," the session was a plenary one and was attended by several hundred "AFF-ers," former members of various groups, health care professionals, and scholars of cults and new religious movements. Radha and I shared the podium with Joe Kelly, an AFF member and professional exit counselor who had some expertise in Eastern traditions, and Dr. Steve Dubrow-Eichel, an AFF-affiliated psychotherapist who had studied the deprograming of a Hare Krishna member as part of his doctoral work (see Anuttama Dasa et al. 1999).

The session was a breakthrough in ISKCON/anti-cult relations. And, I think we forged the way for other organizations, whichever chose to do so, to open themselves up to AFF and its associates for scrutiny and perhaps a more informed and fair evaluation.

For my part, I explained to our audience how ISKCON had struggled since its founder passed away, offering brief examples of some of our leadership scandals and abuse. Some of these problems were known to the AFF audience; some were not. I explained what steps ISKCON had put in place to regulate and oversee the power of leaders.[12] I explained that ISKCON, unfortunately perhaps, is not a highly structured or top-down organization, and that despite our best efforts I couldn't vouch that ISKCON was fully successful in weeding out abusive practices by local leaders across its far-flung temple confederation. I also discussed our basic practices, some of which like mantra meditation had often been labeled as a manipulative mind control technique, and tried to explain such practices within the context of standard Hindu piety.

Radha Devi Dasi, a Harvard-educated attorney and professor of law, explained her personal issues with the traditional roles favored for women in ISKCON. She contrasted that with her deep appreciation for the tradition and the overall ISKCON community. She then told a story that energized the audience. Several years before, after asking why the girls and women must stand at the back of the temple behind the men (a rarity in ISKCON today), her three-year-old daughter had marched to the front of the temple and punched one of the men standing there. Radha commented that after this event she realized that the question of women's roles "wasn't just about me anymore" and that ISKCON had serious issues of socialization to address within its ranks.[13]

Since that time I have attended the AFF, now ICSA, annual conventions almost every year. More than a dozen of my ISKCON colleagues from North America and Europe also occasionally attend. Many of us have spoken on panels. I have done so several times, including a recent appearance on a panel with a former Catholic priest of the Legion of Christ order.[14]

I attend and speak at ICSA for several reasons. First, it is important for ISKCON to be able to answer its critics in a mature, reasoned manner based on facts and dialogue. Rather than hide behind claims and counter claims of authenticity versus aberrations, ISKCON needs to defend its values, actions, and contributions, while being ready to critique, reevaluate, and correct itself as needed. ISKCON's founder, Srila Prabhupada, did this often. He made measured choices how to lead his society, and when he found some of those decisions didn't work, he adapted and adjusted accordingly. I believe ISKCON is making positive contributions to the greater society and I must be ready to educate those who think otherwise, or who are misinformed about us.

Second, I believe that ICSA does address legitimate concerns about the potential for abuse within group dynamics and under religious authority. As a religious leader and the communications director for my own community, it is my duty to be aware of these dynamics so as to help avoid them. Who can doubt in this age of televangelical excesses and globally destructive forces like ISIS that religious fervor can exceed the range of healthy practices? As a leader of ISKCON it is important for me to understand the dangers of cultic dynamics – which have already caused havoc for my organization in too many places – in order to help weed out and uproot those tendencies.

Conclusion – being proactive

> Krishna Consciousness Movement is for training men to be independently thoughtful and competent in all types of departments of knowledge and action.
>
> (Prabhupada 1972)

In February 2014, as an executive officer of ISKCON's Governing Body Commission and its communications director, I made a presentation to a plenary session of more than 1,100 men and women who are international leaders of ISKCON at a global strategic planning meeting in India. My topic? "Leaders and Abuse: Manipulation, Harm and the Danger of Cultic Behaviors."

My talk was largely based on what I had assimilated from almost two decades of dialogue with AFF/ICSA. In my PowerPoint presentation I highlighted the fact that some ISKCON leaders had abused their positions, power, and influence to harm their followers, our communities, and our reputation. My goal was to educate the current leaders that such abuse and personal falls from our strict ideals are not inconsequential deviations from our norms. The potential problems are too great, and ISKCON needs to be proactive in guarding against "cultic" or abusive behavior.

The solution begins, I argued, with first recognizing that as a "high intensity" religious community[15] we are vulnerable to these types of excesses. Quoting from the famous Pogo cartoon, I told my audience that in this context, "We have met the enemy and he is us."

I explained that leaders need to be proactive and I listed warning signs of abusive leadership, including isolating oneself or his/her community, creating us versus them mentalities, refusing to be held accountable to higher authorities or the community, to think oneself above reproach or secular law, and thinking oneself to have special or unique authority. I ended by pointing out that, among other qualifications, healthy leaders seek peers to advise and correct them, do not surround themselves with "yes men," share power and delegate authority, are cautious in their dealings with the opposite sex, and are self-critical and open to critique from others.

I do not accept carte blanche the views members of ICSA put forward in their conferences or writings. I am even less inclined to agree with more hardline anti-cult organizations and activists. As I learned from my first visits to AFF/ICSA meetings in the late 1990s, the anti-cult movement – like ISKCON – has a wide spectrum of viewpoints and its own share of dogma, and perhaps, fanaticism.

That fact notwithstanding, I have learned that for any community to succeed, it needs to recognize its strengths as well as weaknesses and to correct its shortcomings. Within ISKCON, I believe that a culture of openness, integrity, and learning from the mistakes of the past must be the overriding cultural imperative. And I'm convinced that such values are part of our core historical Vaishnava ethics and beliefs.

Regarding ICSA, I have made many friends within the organization, although some no doubt still view me and my faith tradition with trepidation.

I believe that ISKCON and ICSA face shared challenges. That is, that all human beings are driven to seek meaning, yet some along the path will meet persons who may manipulate and attempt to abuse them. Nurturing the innate human quest and desire for meaning, and protecting us from those who may abuse that heartfelt yearning are, I believe, both noble and necessary tasks.

Notes

1 Vaishnava, or Gaudiya Vaishnava is the official disciplic succession (*parampara*) or monotheistic tradition within Hinduism to which ISKCON belongs; more on this topic later.
2 The Vaishnava–Christian Dialogues were started in Wales, UK, and later transferred to Boston and then Washington, DC, where they have continued annually since 1996. A volume of the scholarly *Journal of Vaishnava Studies* was dedicated to publishing some of the papers from those dialogues. It is available online at http://iskconcommunications.org/assets/jvs-se.pdf.
3 The other six purposes are:

    2) To propagate a consciousness of Krishna (God), as it is revealed in the great scriptures of India, Bhagavad-gita and Srimad-Bhagavatam.
    3) To bring the members of the Society together with each other and nearer to Krishna, the prime entity, thus developing the idea within the members, and humanity at large, that each soul is part and parcel of the quality of Godhead (Krishna).
    4) To teach and encourage the *sankirtan* movement, congregational chanting of the holy name of God, as revealed in the teachings of Lord Sri Caitanya Mahaprabhu.
    5) To erect for the members and for society at large a holy place of transcendental pastimes dedicated to the personality of Krishna.
    6) To bring the members closer together for the purpose of teaching a simpler, more natural way of life.
    7) With a view toward achieving the aforementioned purposes, to publish and distribute periodicals, magazines, books, and other writings.

4 "Devotee" is a common term of self-identification for ISKCON adherents.
5 Here I speak of ISKCON's membership outside of India. Within India, of course, ISKCON has attracted primarily the ethnic Indian Hindu population, although many "truth seekers" journeying to the East from abroad found their search ended within the Hare Krishna movement.
6 I personally saw many news articles in local languages. Also see "Thousands Flock to Opening of Second Largest ISKCON Temple in the World in Kanpur," by Madhava Smullen *ISKCON News*, Nov. 14, 2014. Available at http://iskconnews.org/thousands-flock-to-opening-of-second-largest-iskcon-temple-in-the-world-in-kanpur,4685/#gsc.tab=0. Accessed September 3, 2015.
7 See www.ochs.org.uk.
8 See http://hinduforum.eu and http://bhaktivedantacollege.com.
9 I attended a court case in Denver, Colorado, where a man I knew who had given up his practice and interaction with ISKCON years before used a brainwashing defense to try to excuse himself from criminal charges of smuggling. He blamed ISKCON for damaging his ability to take personal responsibility. More contrived yet was an "expert witness"

from a local university called to testify. Under oath the "expert" stated the only way to leave ISKCON was "with cement shoes on," in reference to the gruesome methods Mafia gangs employed to kill their enemies and hide the dead bodies by throwing them to the bottom of a river with their feet encaged in cement.

10 I will leave it to other more capable authors in this book to provide a scientific analysis of the term "brainwashing" and its evolution in meaning and application.

11 It is interesting to note that whole nations have been subject to an ill-informed and rather paranoid tendency to label nontraditional religious organizations as cults. Thus, within the list of possible sects, cults, and suspect groups composed by the French and Belgium governments we find such organizations as the Church of Jesus Christ of Latter-Day Saints (Mormons), Seventh-Day Adventists, the YWCA (Young Women's Christian Association), and ISKCON.

12 In the years prior to that meeting, and even more so in the past ten years, ISKCON has implemented more systematic training of leaders, including those serving as gurus. For example, today before a Krishna devotee can accept the role of spiritual teacher, or guru within the society, in addition to demonstrating deep understanding of Vaishnava philosophy and personal high standards of ethics and behavior, a potential candidate must undergo four days of training on the challenges and requirements of spiritual leadership, including the need for self-reflection, peer association, accountability, transparency, etc.

13 The role of women remains a point of contention within the global ISKCON society. ISKCON advocates the benefits of traditional roles for women as mothers and wives, and points to the loss of conservative family values as one of the main causes of social strife in the world. At the same time, unlike many great religious traditions, ISKCON empowers women as priests to perform all of the religious rituals men do. In some parts of India, though, ISKCON leaders restrict women priests from public worship functions, arguing that these are not the traditional norms for women in their area. However, this is not in keeping with a global ISKCON standard.

ISKCON also has women serving as temple presidents in some communities, including two of its most successful temples in the United States, namely Washington, DC, and the largest North American community in Alachua, Florida. Two women also serve on the international Governing Body Commission, ISKCON's ultimate authority. In October 2014, at its annual mid-term meeting in India, the Governing Body Commission spent three full days reviewing nearly 1,000 pages of scriptural references, historical evidence, and Prabhupada's writings and statements regarding "Vaishnavi Diksha Gurus," that is, whether women may serve as initiating spiritual masters within ISKCON. There is a history of women gurus in ISKCON's Gaudiya Vaishnava lineage and Prabhupada himself on several occasions mentioned that he wanted all his men and women disciples to become initiating spiritual masters. However, other statements by Prabhupada are less clear on the matter. The 2014 debate on the topic, while thought-provoking, did not produce a definitive conclusion. For more, see *ISKCON News* (news.iskcon.org); available at http://iskconnews.org/gbc-completes-three-day-special-session-on-vaishnavi-diksa-gurus,4648/. Accessed September 3, 2015.

14 For more on cultic abuse in the Catholic Church, see Paul Lennon, *Our Father, Maciel, Who Art in Bed: A Naive and Sentimental Dubliner in the Legion of Christ*. Lennon was a priest in the Legion of Christ order for twenty-four years before leaving to document the abuses, sexual and otherwise, of the Legion's charismatic founder, Father Marcial Maciel Degollado, long favored by the Vatican for his success in revitalizing the Church in Mexico and beyond.

15 High intensity in that ISKCON members are taught self-sacrifice and to dedicate several hours each day to study and prayer; that we are expected to give up common worldly

practices such as eating meat, gambling, and intoxication; that humility is a prized characteristic; and – most potentially problematic – that our scriptures teach us to see religious leaders as good as God because their role is to be a representative of God.

References

Anuttama Dasa, Radha-devi Dasi, Joseph Kelly, Michael Langone, and Steve Dubrow-Eichel. 1999. "Panel Discussion: Can Cultic Groups Change?: The Case of ISKCON." *ISKCON Communications Journal* 7:2. Available at http://content.iskcon.org/icj/7_2/72panel.html. Accessed September 3, 2015.

Back to Godhead. 2013. "Purposes." *Back to Godhead: The Magazine of the Hare Krishna Movement*, September/October, 3.

Basham, A. L. 2004. *The Wonder that Was India*. London: Picador.

Bharata Shrestha Dasa 1998. "ISKCON's Response to Child Abuse: 1990–1998." *ISKCON Communications Journal* 6:1: 71–80.

Blasengame, Bart 2014. "The Return of a Cult Classic – Hare Krishnas Are Back." *Details*, May 1. Available at www.details.com/culture-trends/critical-eye/201405/hare-krishna-returns-modern-religion-cult. Accessed September 3, 2015.

Gummer, John 1996. "Department of the Environment Report, May, 1996. From *Public Inquiry on Bhaktivedanta Manor Report*. Government Office for Eastern Region, Decision by Secretary of State for the Environment John Gummer and signed by Andrew N. Haynes, May 13. Bedford, UK. Regarding the appeal by International Society for Krishna Consciousness (ISKCON) Application No: 94/0014/TP. Available at www6.hertsmere.gov.uk/online-applications/files/1BDD1FB1AA5C4ECD3150B036FFC5663E/pdf/TP_94_0014-DNA1_1713.pdf-26903.pdf. Accessed September 3, 2015.

Jaisinghani, Bella 2011. "ISKCON Plans a Grand Janmashtami." *The Times of India*, August 20.

Jha, Sumit 2014. "Hema Malini: I Wonder Why Directors Don't Cast Married Actresses?" *The Times of India*, October 10.

Langone, Michael 1999. "Cults, Psychological Manipulation and Society: International Perspectives – An Overview." *ISKCON Communications Journal* 7:2. Available at http://content.iskcon.org/icj/7_2/72langone.html. Accessed September 3, 2015.

Lennon, J. Paul 2008. *Our Father, Marciel, Who Art in Bed: A Naive and Sentimental Dubliner in the Legion of Christ*. NP: J Paul Lennon.

Niebuhr, Gustave 1996. "Hare Krishnas at 30: Real Changes or Just PR." *New York Times*, May 11. Available at www.nytimes.com/1996/05/11/us/religion-journal-hare-krishnas-at-30-real-changes-or-just-pr.html. Accessed September 3, 2015.

Prabhupada, A. C. Bhaktivedanta Swami 1972. Letter to Karandhara Dasa, Bombay 12–22–72. From the Bhaktivedanta Book Trust Archives. Available at http://vaniquotes.org/wiki/Krishna_Consciousness_Movement_is_for_training_men_to_be_independently_thoughtful_and_competent_in_all_types_of_departments_of_knowledge_and_action,_not_for_making_bureaucracy. Accessed September 3, 2015.

Rochford, E. Burke Jr. 2007. *Hare Krishna Transformed*. New York: New York University Press.

——— and Jennifer Heinlein 1998. "Child Abuse within the Hare Krishna Movement, 1971–1986." *ISKCON Communications Journal* 6:1: 41–69. Available at http://content.iskcon.org/icj/6_1/6_1rochford.html. Accessed September 3, 2015.

Rosen, Steven J. 2006. *Essential Hinduism*. Santa Barbara, CA: Praeger Press.

Sardella, Ferdinando 2012. *Modern Hindu Personalism: The History Life and Thought of Bhaktisiddhanta Sarasvati*. Oxford: Oxford University Press.

Satsvarupa dasa Goswami 1980. *Srila Prabhupada-lilamrita*, Volume 2. Los Angeles, CA: Bhaktivedanta Book Trust.

Saunaka Rsi Dasa 1999. "ISKCON in Relation to People of Faith in God." *ISKCON Communications Journal* 7:1. Available at http://content.iskcon.org/icj/7_1/71srd.html. Accessed September 3, 2015.

Stark, Rodney 1996. *The Rise of Christianity: How the Obscure, Marginal Jesus Movement Became the Dominant Religious Force in the Western World in a Few Centuries*. Princeton, NJ: Princeton University Press.

Trex, Ethan 2010. "Famous Folks Launched Careers after 50." *CNN*, May 16, 2010. Available at www.cnn.com/2010/LIVING/worklife/05/16/mf.famous.career.after.50/index.html. Accessed September 3, 2015.

13 From the Church of Scientology to the Freezone

Terril Park

Many have heard of the Church of Scientology (COS); fewer have heard of Freezone, or Independent Scientology. Freezoners, or independents, are people who still practice Scientology but do not associate with COS. In fact, they can't. If one does Scientology outside COS, one is automatically considered a "suppressive person," or SP. According to COS policy, a suppressive person is an enemy of Scientology and an antisocial personality. But Freezoners and independents argue that "Scientology" can refer either to the subject itself or to a series of interconnected corporations known as the Church of Scientology. For a variety of reasons that will be reviewed in this chapter, they prefer to practice Scientology outside of COS.

In a sense, the forerunners of the Freezone were the Scientology Franchises, later renamed Missions. Franchises began in the early 1950s under the leadership of people with lots of auditor training and experience. Missions represented the greatest flowering of Scientology and spurred its greatest expansion. The Missions were very user-friendly and usually had very skilled counseling staff. A stellar example was Martin Samuels, who headed the Mission of Davis, a university town in California, and who expanded it to five Missions with a total of 500 staff members. Martin started the Delphian project in Oregon in 1973, which was to research alternative energy. He also started a school for the children of those on the project. The school became very popular with other Scientologists since it used Scientology study methods. After twelve years of work, he had five Missions and twelve schools. In one year, he had 3,000 people taking a Scientology communication course in his Missions.[1]

In October 1982, an international Mission Holders' conference took place in San Francisco. During the conference, the new management of COS, led by David Miscavige, stamped its authority on the Missions. All Mission Holders had to sign new contracts with COS. This gave COS control over the Missions, with the ability to enter Mission properties at any time and confiscate money from them for alleged infractions against COS.[2]

A few weeks after the conference, Martin Samuels lost his leadership role in all his Missions and was declared a suppressive person. A friend who lives in Davis, and was a member of the Mission in its heyday, says the Mission there in the mid-2000s only has one employee (personal communication, 2004).

Before the changes initiated at the conference, it was possible for Mission staff to earn enough to get mortgages and buy property. In comparison, at more or less the same time, I was on staff in the London COS and I earned about £5 per week.

The 1982 Mission Holders' conference resulted in the largest schism in the history of Scientology. Many thousands resisted Miscavige's efforts to exert more control over the Missions and left COS. Some Mission Holders took their Missions into the Freezone.

After the attempts to impose strict regulations on the Missions, Scientology field auditors, the individuals who trained as auditors but who operated independently of Scientology churches, were the next to experience greater attempts at regulation. Miscavige and the central leadership of COS formed a new organization in December 1982, the International Hubbard Ecclesiastical League of Pastors (or IHELP). Field auditors had to agree to be bound by IHELP's decisions. According to information in Jon Atack's *A Piece of Blue Sky*, this organization coerced and fined field auditors.[3] These actions against the Missions and field auditors were in large part what started the expansion of the Freezone.

My involvement in Freezone Scientology

I have been one of the most active advocates of Freezone Scientology since 2000, promoting it on Scientology Internet forums with "Success Stories" several times a week for more than fifteen years. With the success stories I also link to Freezone Yahoo! forums, two of which I own. For maybe twelve years, from around 2000 to 2012, I was averaging twenty to twenty-five new members to forums and/or people wishing to be directly connected to an auditor per month.

Although it seems counterintuitive, I had more success in getting people connected to the Freezone on forums that were primarily critical of Scientology/COS. In fact there are no open forums on the subject that are not primarily critical. For example, I'd post on Myspace, which one would expect to be neutral on the subject, and I'd be criticized as much there as I was on "alt.religion scientology," a notoriously hardcore critical forum. However, quite a few who were interested in Scientology would be on such forums.

The Internet has made it quite easy for Scientologists who no longer want to be connected to COS to meet likeminded people, and to find an auditor if they wish to get auditing. Freezone or independent Facebook groups are proliferating. As of this writing, there are few people joining Yahoo! Freezone forums, and Facebook forums are now the popular place to go. I serve as a moderator on one, "Free Scientology Chat," and about one new person joins a day.

In the earlier days of the Freezone, in the 2000s, I knew of only two places where one could go to train as an auditor in the United States, and I knew of most Freezone activities. Now there are at least fourteen that I know of, and it's harder to keep track nowadays.[4]

Defecting to the Freezone

In 2004, I traveled through the United States with the aim of meeting Freezoners who I knew from conversations over the Internet but had never met; I also met many I did not know. One of these was an old timer who worked with Hubbard and was a personal friend in the early 1950s, Phil Spickler. He has a Web site[5] and has put up quite a few videos of interviews with himself. He was either the first Mission Holder or one of the first; his Mission was in Palo Alto, California. The founder of Stanford University's remote viewing project was Hal Puthoff, who came from Phil's Mission. Phil also audited NFL quarterback John Brodie, then the most highly paid athlete in America. Brodie had hurt his arm in a car crash, and for an American football quarterback that was very bad and possibly career-destroying news. He consulted at least six doctors with no good results. A friend urged him to consult with Phil and, although reluctant, he eventually did. This is as good an example of the effectiveness of Dianetics and Scientology as you'll get. Brodie's book, *Open Field*, describes what he did in the auditing, which was so effective that Brodie went on to win an NFL MVP award. He gave Phil a Trans Am (an American muscle car) as a thank you present.

In 1975, Phil, on his own initiative, communicated with the IRS commissioner, a fellow Jew, and commented that they both had backgrounds in a religion that suffered from suppression, and that he would like to do something about the apparent suppression of his current religion, Scientology. The commissioner sent a special envoy to visit Phil, and the envoy said it would not be difficult to get religious status for COS again. The main problem was that most money went into a Hubbard account, not a COS one. The envoy left Phil with all the paperwork needed to regain religious recognition. So Phil sent it to top management. For his trouble, he received his final declaration of being a suppressive person! Phil then became a Freezone auditor around 1991. This was a very bad move by Scientology management because it squandered the goodwill Phil had developed with the IRS. The IRS later asked for back taxes of $1 billion. This would have bankrupted the Church of Scientology (Rathbun 2013: 151). So COS instituted more than 2,000 lawsuits against the IRS and some of the individuals working there and carried on fighting the IRS until 1993 when the IRS reversed its earlier position for reasons still not clear.

Ron's Orgs in the Freezone

The Ron's Orgs in Europe, Russia, and former Russian states have been very active in spreading Freezone Scientology. They originated in 1984 led by the former third in command after L. Ron Hubbard and Mary Sue Hubbard, Bill Robertson. When he found that he could no longer contact Hubbard, Robertson acted on instructions he claimed to have received from Hubbard himself. He said that Hubbard had told him that if Robertson could not contact him for a prolonged period, he was to start Scientology afresh. So Robertson went from the United States to Europe, where he had spent some time helping to build up Scientology, and did just that. In 1984, he formed Ron's Orgs [Ron's Organization and Network for Standard Technology] and coined the term *Freezone*. The Ron's Orgs flourished over the next decade.

Around 1995, when the Internet started expanding enormously, a group of Russians wrote to some of the senior people in Ron's Orgs and asked to meet with them. The meeting went extremely well, and they returned and delivered Scientology courses to around fifty Russian people. The Ron's Orgs have expanded enormously since and they now have somewhere between thirty and fifty organizations in Russia or former Russian states, as well as some in other countries. Ron's Orgs now have a total of some 2,000 active members (Hauri 2013). Ron's Orgs have been particularly strong in auditor training. They have between 50 and 100 class 4 auditors, who can deliver all the levels of the lower part of the Bridge to Total Freedom, and around twenty-five "L's" auditors. The L's offer the most powerful Scientology auditing available and require the highest level of technical training. At this time, there are probably more L's auditors in Ron's Orgs than in COS. In fact, one can observe Ron's Orgs auditor training in a production by the UK's channel 4, *The Beginner's Guide to L. Ron Hubbard*. It is just about the only TV program to ever comment positively on Scientology.[6]

Recent developments

COS gives yet another label to those who practice Scientology outside the Church. One is called a "squirrel," defined as someone who doesn't really understand Scientology and therefore messes people up. A good recent example of this negative labeling is its application to Marty Rathbun, former second in command of COS and leader of the Religious Technology Center from 1987 to 2004, when he left the Church. Rathbun previously was entrusted with auditing all COS celebrities, such as Tom Cruise and John Travolta, and also the top executives of COS.

Around 2009, Rathbun started a blog that was particularly scathing about the head of the Church, David Miscavige, claiming that he physically abused his juniors, destroyed most COS management functions, and imprisoned most of the top executives of the Church, including Rathbun. He also started to give auditing outside of the established COS structures to those who wanted it. Shortly afterward, COS sent a team of so-called squirrel busters to his residence. They wore cameras in their hats and harassed Rathbun and his wife, Monique, for 199 consecutive days (Childs and Tobin 2013b). Eventually, Marty and Monique moved to a secluded new property, but there again they found spy cameras trained on their house and a strange neighbor whose job seemed to be that of a spy. That neighbor, three separate Church organizations, and other individuals, including David Miscavige, have been named in a lawsuit by Monique alleging harassment (Childs 2013).

The Rathbun case shows how far COS is willing to go to squelch dissent and inhibit the practices of Freezoners and independents. In Marty Rathbun's latest book, *Memoirs of a Scientology Warrior*, he estimates that from 1981–6 COS spent $100,000,000 in litigation, at least some of it against Freezoners (Rathbun 2013: 313). In response, COS claims that it is acting within its rights. For example, in the ongoing lawsuit brought against COS by Monique Rathbun, one of COS's lawyers said:

> COS had the right to hire private eyes to determine whether Marty was delivering services in violation of copyright. The Rathbuns forfeited their privacy by conducting the business of delivering Scientology services in their home.
>
> (Childs 2014)

That statement also shows how COS moves back and forth between describing itself as a business (which, in this case, is defending its copyrighted materials) and a religion.

Rathbun has also endeavored to expose how COS has waged a battle against Freezone Scientologists. He has published a document from the Office of Special Affairs, a part of COS that handles investigations and dirty tricks, public relations, finance, and legal matters, that describes a long and detailed plan to destroy Ron's Orgs. It reads in part: "Program Purpose: To terminatedly handle the Freezone in Russia and CIS as a source of black PR on Scientology and as a travesty of standard tech that ruins people's spiritual future" (Rathbun 2010).

Like many other Freezoners and independents, I believe this type of activity runs counter to the assertion in the COS creed that assures that "all men have inalienable rights to their own religious practices and their performance" (see Church of Scientology 1998: vi). That sentiment is underscored in Hubbard's pamphlet *The Way to Happiness*, which, in its eighteenth precept, encourages its readers to "Respect the religious beliefs of others" (Hubbard 2015).

The Church of Scientology versus the Freezone

In 1992, COS wrote its enemies list, amounting to nearly 2,500 names and groups. In December 2013, another nearly 2,500 names had been sneaked out by someone on staff who hid a camera in an umbrella handle.[7] On the first half of the enemies list, 280 groups all seemed from their names to be Scientology Freezone groups. Most of them no longer exist.

David Mayo provides a vivid example of how COS deals with dissidents. Once the Senior Case Supervisor International, the senior Scientology Tech consultant, he apparently coauthored with Hubbard some of the confidential upper levels that can be delivered in the Scientology "Bridge." The "Bridge" is the series of counseling actions from beginning steps to higher steps up to the upper levels. These upper levels resulted from David's efforts to audit Hubbard when it was thought he may be dying in late 1978 (see Touretzky 2015).

David Mayo was declared a suppressive person in 1983. After that, he met up with other former associates, and they decided to start their own splinter group delivering Scientology. They called it "Advanced Ability Center," and by February 1983 some thirty associated organizations around the world formed.

The aggressive actions of COS to preserve the purity of COS doctrine and practice frequently led to expulsions of former members, and many of them become independent or Freezone practitioners. For example, in October 2013, eighteen of the most influential Scientologists in South Africa were declared suppressive persons. They are highly trained and have served Scientology for many years or even decades and it's looking like they are going to take the rest of the Scientologists in South Africa out of COS and into the Freezone.[8]

Many similar events can be quickly summarized. In 2012 an entire Israeli Mission, Dror, left COS en masse (Lewis 2014). One of its cofounders, Tami Lemberger, had twice won auditor of the year awards by COS. But she had received a copy of Debbie Cook's revelatory 2011 e-mail (see Cook 2011), which described in detail how asking for donations for internal church matters was against Hubbard's policies. Her husband, Dani, forwarded it to COS management asking for comment, but was treated as disloyal and subsequently decided to cut all ties with COS. Similarly, in Los Angeles in 2010, a Taiwanese Scientologist started her own organization and took all or most of the Taiwanese out of LA Scientology Orgs to study there. She also has an Org in Taiwan which has 100 staff members. It must have previously been a COS Mission since it has been in existence for twelve years (see Flasch 2010).

Developments like these lend credence to the comments of Jillian Schlesinger, who left the Sea Org, the paramilitary wing of COS composed of its most dedicated members, in February 2014. In an interview, she claimed that "I've been to orgs all over California, and they're empty. There are maybe five people there. And some of the fancy course rooms at the Ideal Orgs? They're being used for storage" (Ortega 2014a).

The perspectives Freezoners and independents offer raise substantial questions about COS's estimates of its own membership. Different sources from the Church suggest that the membership is between 10 and 15 million (see Rinder 2014b). But several official government statistics appear to be more accurate. The 2011 UK census estimated that fewer than 2,500 Scientologists lived in England and Wales.[9] Similarly, the 2011 Australian census identified fewer than 2,200 Scientologists there (see Cannane 2012). Further, the ARIS survey in the United States estimated that 25,000 Scientologists resided in the United States in 2008. Very roughly Scientologists in the United States are about 50 percent of the world total. Jefferson Hawkins, who headed the Scientology Central Marketing Unit, had access to all lists of members and other information; he estimates that at most COS has 40,000 members (Ortega 2011).

Other efforts by COS to inflate its impact on the world have been questioned as well. In the 2014 New Year's event at Flag in Clearwater, Florida, COS's largest organization and the only place where some of the upper levels of Scientology training are delivered, Miscavige showed videos that purportedly showed Scientologists being interviewed on two Irish radio programs, Ocean FM and BBC Radio Foyle, in Northern Ireland. As it turns out, they were both faked. When someone phoned up Ocean FM and asked about this program, the station's representatives said it was not their studio in the video and the person doing the interview is not known to them. On January 19, a spokeswoman for the BBC said about the video, "The BBC is an independent, impartial organisation. Any misuse of its brand is considered a serious matter and will be investigated" (see Martin 2014). In the video the front page of the *Donegal News* is shown with a story about COS's effort to campaign against drugs. Mr. Columba Gill, the editor of the *Donegal News*, described the front page depicted on the video as "bogus" (see Hickey 2014). There were also claims that COS's efforts had cut drug-related crime by 85 percent in Dublin. But the Irish government statistics show a drop of 7 percent. Although getting actual statistics of COS activity is difficult, Mike Rinder, former International Spokesperson for COS, gets information from all over from insiders and ex-scientologists and Freezoners who sometimes observe activity in COS and all reports are of greatly diminished activity. Clearly those inside COS and those outside it have very different perceptions of the health of the Church.

The Church of Scientology, the Freezone, and the future of Scientology

While COS confidently expects millions more to join in the future (Church of Scientology 2015), many of those who have left COS see an organization in substantial decline. They adduce a number of reasons, including monetary demands, the failure of COS to make good on its promises of self-betterment, the failure of programs like Narconon, and the dwindling number of qualified auditors.

Many critics have claimed that COS is mainly interested in raising money. They point to statements like this one from a write-up by a COS executive on raising funds for an ideal org: "So your 'Shills' [the technical term for someone who has agreed to donate in advance but appears to be doing it spontaneously] should be made aware they have a responsibility to use their donation to get others to donate as much as possible" (Childs and Tobin 2013a). Former members have expressed disillusionment with the pressures to give to the Church.

Others have criticized the Church for not delivering on the extraordinary personal advances it promises. For example, beyond even the powerful Operating Thetan levels comes "Cleared Theta Clear," a state Hubbard describes this way:

> A thetan who is completely rehabilitated and can do everything a thetan should do, such as move MEST [matter, energy, space, and time] and control others from a distance, or create his own universe; a person who is able to create his own universe, or living in the MEST universe is able to create illusions perceivable by others at will, to handle MEST universe objects without mechanical means and to have and feel no need of bodies or even the MEST universe to keep himself and his friends interested in existence.
> (Hubbard 1981: 114)

The state described above, however, has not been achieved in COS. Much as I have loved some of the gains in Scientology, even including some OT levels, which I did in the Freezone, I have not achieved this. I know of no one who has. It is the case that COS often oversells the benefits it provides. The highest level of auditing COS delivers is Operating Thetan level 8. In theory, COS should then deliver something which could achieve the above. However, after one has reached the highest part of the Bridge available, one is put instead . . . back to the beginning through the Purification Rundown and objective processing. The Purification Rundown is a detox program, and objective processing is simple processes to locate one in present time. One is also told that no one has ever done these levels properly before. This is in effect a Scientology version of blasphemy. It implies that the founder of Scientology, L. Ron Hubbard, couldn't do them and couldn't organize their delivery either.

Narconon is another area of COS that is rapidly unraveling via many lawsuits and criminal investigations into its practices. Narconon claims to get addicts off drugs for good, using basic Scientology techniques. The "purification rundown," for example, involves running and sweating in a sauna for up to five hours a day with increasing doses of vitamins, especially B3 and Niacin, at doses up to 5,000 mg per day. But, according to the U.S. National Institutes of Health, niacin at high levels can cause liver damage (see U.S. National Library of Medicine 2015). This applies much more to Narconon patients who as a result of heavy drug use can start with impaired livers. Narconon has falsely claimed that more than 70 percent of its graduates remain drug free. Narconon's actual success rates are below those of more established programs (see Touretzky 2015).

In June 2014, an Oklahoma State Grand Jury was empaneled to look into criminal insurance fraud allegations against Scientology's flagship drug rehab facility, Narconon Arrowhead. Three patients died in a nine-month period in 2011 and 2012, resulting in county and state investigations of the facility (Ortega 2014c).

Las Vegas attorney Ryan Hamilton has also filed twenty-nine federal lawsuits against Narconon, Scientology's drug rehab network, as of August 2015. He observed that "Most troublesome is the fact that there is no medical supervision of any kind for the patients." All but one of the suits were filed in federal court, and each of them names as defendants a local facility as well as Narconon International and Scientology's umbrella group, ABLE (Association for Better Living and Education). Narconon International and ABLE have already settled in seven of these lawsuits although the local Narconons have not, as of August 2015.

Narconon was started in 1966 in an Arizona prison by William Benitez, who had been an addict for many years. He was inspired by a Scientology book, *Fundamentals of Thought*. A well-known Scientology Mission Holder and later Freezoner, Alan Walter, went into Folsom Prison to teach the practices and principles Narconon then used. Although Narconon services were originally free, now participants in Narconon pay around $30,000. That's without the double billing sometimes given to clients' insurance companies (Ortega 2014c).

A new lawsuit was filed in May 2014 by the National Association of Forensic Counselors (NAFC), which named eighty-two defendants – again including Scientology leader David Miscavige. Although Narconon CEO Gary Smith was stripped of his NAFC certification when he failed to report three deaths at the facility, he has faced accusations that he has continued to advertise this certification online (Ortega 2014b).

Other serious problems loom in the future of COS. It seems COS doesn't want to train auditors. That alone could lead to its demise. Instead, it wishes to push for more straight donations. Mike Rinder, former international spokesperson for COS, posted on his blog (Rinder 2014a) that on April 25, 2014, there was not one student on the St. Hill Special Briefing Course in Los Angeles.[10] This is the largest and most comprehensive auditing course in COS. Mike's blog has many old-time Scientologists making comments, and quite a few commented on being on the SHSBC when there were hundreds of people on this course in the 1970s and 1980s.

The scene in Los Angeles is mirrored at St. Hill, UK, where the Briefing Course originated. However, as of February 2015, not only had there been no briefing course completions, there had been no auditor training completions of any sort (Rinder 2015). Not only is COS apparently doing minimal training, it is demanding that auditors be retrained from the beginning on its new training program.

It appears, then, that COS is losing auditors and the Freezone is gaining auditors. Most auditors in the Freezone, apart from Ron's Orgs, left COS or were kicked out. For example, in June 2014, Ronit and Yossi Charny set themselves up to deliver auditing in the Freezone. Previously they were delivering upper levels at Flag headquarters in Clearwater.

The current and future state of COS and its management structure is discussed by Chris Shelton in both video and written accounts on his Web site. He provides a simple and lucid overview of the very complex structure of COS. Read this and you will know more about the organization than almost all within COS. Chris was twenty-five years on staff, and left in December 2012 after seventeen years in the Sea Org and eight years as the executive in charge of auditing and training for the western United States. It's worth noting that prior to the 1982 Mission Holders' conference, the Missions were somewhat isolated from management interference; for example, the Sea Org could only enter Missions if invited, and this contributed to their expansion.

In 1996, Miscavige began to reposition himself as the actual source of Scientology with the release of what he called the Golden Age of Tech. This was basically a total rewrite of the entire subject of Scientology training. Miscavige's revisions have made it impossible for Scientology auditors ever to graduate. Thus began Scientology's steep decline as a service-oriented organization, with more and more attention going onto straight fundraising. The transformations of COS under Miscavige's leadership have led more people to practice Scientology independently or in the Freezone.

Mike Rinder has written as to why COS is concentrating its efforts on purchasing new buildings that it doesn't need. Tony Ortega and Mike have both posted several examples of the high-pressure selling to fundraise for these buildings.

In 2015 so far, there has been a lot of bad news for COS. The most important came with the showing of Academy Award–winning documentarian Alex Gibney's *Going Clear: Scientology and the Prison of Belief*, which premiered at the Sundance Film Festival and has shown at many arthouse cinemas worldwide. It premiered on HBO on March 29, 2015. HBO has 35 million viewers in the United States and outlets in 151 countries with a total of 114 million subscribers worldwide. In the United States, *Going Clear* was the second most-watched HBO documentary of the past ten years (Soriano 2015). The documentary is based on Laurence Wright's book of a similar name, and Wright came on board as a producer.

COS has taken out full-page advertisements in the *Los Angeles Times* and the *New York Times* and has put up Web sites attacking the filmmakers and their interviewees.[11] Alex Gibney has said that he is grateful for the publicity but wished "they'd put in showtimes."[12]

Ronald Miscavige, the father of David Miscavige, has had PIs following him for eighteen months at a cost of $10,000 per week. At one point, one PI thought Ronald was having a heart attack and phoned to ask instructions. David Miscavige rang back and said words to the effect that "If he dies, he dies." The senior Miscavige has decided to publish a book about his son and Scientology with David Miscavige's callous comment as the title. The PIs have made taped police confessions and have been found with many guns and an illegal silencer (Ortega 2015b).

Tony Ortega, journalist and former editor of *The Village Voice*, has been covering Scientology since around 1995. He published *The Unbreakable Miss Lovely* in May 2015, the story of COS's campaigns against Paulette Cooper, which included faking evidence of her making bomb threats. This attempt failed because the FBI found the documents of "Operation Freakout," the plan to get Paulette jailed or institutionalized, when its agents raided COS in 1977. Paulette's "crime" was writing *The Scandal of Scientology*, published in 1971. Tony and Paulette have been on a book tour since the publication of Tony's book, which is already going into its second printing.

In the summer of 2015, Tyndale University College and Seminary in Toronto hosted a five-day conference organized by Professor James Beverly and John Atack. It featured a who's who of critics and academics discussing Scientology. Lectures will be available after they are edited. By all accounts it was a great success (Ortega 2015a).

It is my opinion that the tide is also turning for academics in the field of new religious movements. Previously they had been in general uncritical about COS and Scientology. Now James Beverly has put on this conference. I had the pleasure of taking Dr. David Barrett and Professor Beverly to an "Anonymous" protest at COS in London. I've exchanged e-mails and conversed with

Professor James Lewis of the University of Tromsø and introduced him and one of his students to Ron's Org in Moscow. He and at least one of his students are writing papers about the Freezone (see Lewis 2013). COS would consider this enemy action. Also, I was invited to talk about the Freezone at INFORM's twenty-fifth anniversary conference – in the eyes of COS, more enemy action.

Conclusion

In this chapter, I have given details of how COS is shrinking and why. Debbie Cook's e-mail appears to have had a strong impact on COS (Cook 2011). For example, it inspired Freedom Medal winner Wendy Honnor to leave COS (Rathbun 2012). The exodus of many South Africans from COS was influenced by Cook, as was the breakaway Israeli Mission Dror. Her e-mail has most likely been seen by a large number of COS members because she asked that it be forwarded to others. In response, Miscavige initiated a lawsuit against Cook and her husband, but it backfired spectacularly, especially because Cook's testimony was filmed by ABC television in the United States. In her testimony, for example, she asserted that she "was put in a trash can, cold water poured over me, slapped, things like that. And it would – one time it went on for 12 hours" (Rathbun 2014). In addition to revealing what she went through, Cook detailed indignities and violence Miscavige visited upon others. The day after Cook testified, COS withdrew its lawsuit and a settlement was reached.

Taken together, the evidence from Cook, Rinder, Rathbun, and many others points to a dramatic contraction of COS. Course rooms that once used to have hundreds now have only a few. COS seems no longer to bother with training auditors. Instead, the public is relentlessly pursued by a multitude of high-pressure salespersons. In addition, almost every day media criticism of COS can be found somewhere in the world. Far from prospering, the Church of Scientology appears to be in significant decline.

Notes

1 www.instinct.org.bluesky/bs7–2.htm
2 Ibid.
3 Ibid.
4 See www.freeandable.com/business-listings/by-category/65-auditors.html.
5 http://community.freezone-tech.info/phil-spickler/
6 See www.youtube.com/watch?v=emKvMPGSc0s.
7 See http://xenu.net/archive/enemy_names/enemy_list.html.
8 See https://backincomm.wordpress.com/.
9 See https://scicrit.wordpress.com/2015/01/19/scientology-in-the-uk-what-does-the-2011-census-data-tell-us/.
10 See http://training.scientology.org/wis1_9.htm.
11 See www.freedommag.org/going-clear/.
12 See https://en.wikipedia.org/wiki/GoingClear(film).

References

Atack, Jon 1990. *A Piece of Blue Sky*. New York: Lyle Stuart.
Brodie, John, and James D. Brodie 1974. *Open Field*. New York: Houghton Mifflin.
Cannane, Steve 2012. "Scientology Membership in Drastic Decline." Available at www.abc.net.au/lateline/content/2012/s3536106.htm. Accessed August 19, 2015.
Childs, Joe 2013. "Wife of Scientology Critic Details Alleged Church Harassment," *Tampa Bay Times*, September 12, 2013. Available at www.tampabay.com/news/scientology/with-scientology-leader-as-a-defendant-church-legal-team-shows-up-in-force/2141406. Accessed July 10, 2015.
——— 2014. "Scientology Lawyer: Confrontations with Defector Were Peaceful Protests." Available at www.tampabay.com/news/scientology/scientology-lawyer-confrontations-with-defector-were-peaceful-protests/2160220. Accessed August 19, 2015.
———, and Thomas C. Tobin 2013a. "Couple's Lawsuit Accuses Church of Scientology of Fraud, Deception," *Tampa Bay Times*, January 23, 2013. Available at www.tampabay.com/news/scientology/couples-lawsuit-accuses-church-of-scientology-of-fraud-deception/1271893. Accessed July 10, 2015.
——— 2013b. "In Texas Lawsuit Judge Orders Scientology and Its Leader to Stop Harassment," *Tampa Bay Times*, August 21, 2013. Available at www.tampabay.com/news/scientology/in-texas-lawsuit-judge-orders-scientology-and-its-leader-to-stop-harassment/2137671. Accessed July 10, 2015.Church of Scientology 1998. *What Is Scientology?* Los Angeles, CA: Bridge Publications.
——— 2015. "What Is Scientology?" Available at www.scientology.org/what-is-scientology/scientology-background/the-growth-of-scientology.html. Accessed August 19, 2015.
Cook, Debbie 2011. "New Year's Email from Debbie Cook," December 31, 2011. Available at www.mikerindersblog.org/new-years-email-from-debbie-cook/. Accessed July 10, 2015.
Flasch, Helmut 2010. "David Miscavige Declared Suppressive." Available at www.scientology-cult.com/david-miscavige-declared-suppressive.html. Accessed August 19, 2015.
Hauri, Max 2013. Personal Communication via E-mail, October 9, 2013.
Hickey, Kate 2014. "Scientology's Dublin Mission Video Claims Slammed by the Irish (Video)." Available at www.irishcentral.com/news/Scientologys-Dublin-mission-video-claims-slammed-by-the-Irish-VIDEO.html. Accessed August 19, 2015.
Hubbard, L. Ron 2015 (1981). *The Way to Happiness*. Commerce City, CA: Bridge Publications. Available at www.thewaytohappiness.org/thewaytohappiness.html. Accessed August 19, 2015.
Lewis, James R. 2013. "Free Zone Scientology and Other Movement Milieus: A Preliminary Characterization," *Temenos* 49:2, 255–76.
——— 2014. "The Dwindling Spiral: The Dror Center Schism, the Cook Letter and Scientology's Legitimation Crisis," *Alternative Spirituality and Religion Review* 5:1, 55–77.
Martin, Ron 2014. "Ocean FM Investigates Scientology Video." Available at http://radiotoday.ie/2014/01/ocean-fm-investigates-scientology-video/. Accessed August 19, 2015.
Ortega, Tony 2011. "Scientologists: How Many of Them Are There, Anyway?" *The Village Voice*, July 4, 2011. Available at www.villagevoice.com/news/scientologists-how-many-of-them-are-there-anyway-6717701. Accessed August 19, 2015.
——— 2014a. "Jillian Schlesinger: How I Got into Scientology, and How I Got Out." Available at http://tonyortega.org/2014/03/26/jillian-schlesinger-how-i-got-into-scientology-and-how-i-got-out/#more-14022. Accessed July 10, 2015.

——— 2014b. "Scientology's Drug Rehab Network Sued for Conspiring to Misuse Counseling Credentials." Available at http://tonyortega.org/2014/05/19/scientologys-drug-rehab-network-sued-for-conspiring-to-misuse-counseling-credentials/. Accessed August 19, 2015.

——— 2014c. "Oklahoma Empanels Grand Jury to Investigate Scientology's Drug Rehab." Available at http://tonyortega.org/2014/06/11/oklahoma-empanels-grand-jury-to-investigate-scientologys-drug-rehab/#more-15274. Accessed July 10, 2015.

——— 2015a. "O Canada! All Eyes in the Scientology-Watching World Will Be Looking North Next Week." Available at http://tonyortega.org/2015/06/16/o-canada-all-eyes-in-the-scientology-watching-world-will-be-looking-north-next-week/#more-23330. Accessed August 19, 2015.

——— 2015b. "Scientology Leader's Father Signs a Book Deal for 'If He Dies, He Dies.'" Available at http://tonyortega.org/2015/06/30/scientology-leaders-father-signs-a-book-deal-for-if-he-dies-he-dies/#more-23751. Accessed August 19, 2015.

Rathbun, Marty 2010. "OSA's War against Independence." Available at https://markrathbun.wordpress.com/2010/03/18/osas-war-against-independence/. Accessed August 19, 2015.

——— 2012. "Wendy Honnor IAS Freedom Medal Winner Is Independent," June 24, 2012. Available at https://markrathbun.wordpress.com/tag/wendy-honnor/. Accessed July 10, 2015.

——— 2013. *Memoirs of a Scientology Warrior*. NP: Amazon Books.

——— 2014. "Scientology Inc. v. Debbie Cook – The End Game," April 24, 2014. Available at https://markrathbun.wordpress.com/2012/04/24/scientology-inc-v-debbie-cook-the-end-game/. Accessed July 10, 2015.

Rinder, Mike 2014a. "GAG II Killed Auditor Training Dead." Available at www.mikerindersblog.org/gag-ii-auditors-made/. Accessed August 19, 2015.

——— 2014b. "10 Million Scientologists – Where Are They?" Available at www.mikerindersblog.org/10-million-scientologists-where-are-they/. Accessed August 19, 2015.

——— 2015. "The SHSBC Is Dead." Available at www.mikerindersblog.org/the-shsbc-is-dead/. Accessed August 20, 2015.

Soriano, Mercy 2015. "HBO's 'Going Clear' Scientology Documentary: 5.5M Viewers; Film Slammed as John Travolta Stays Loyal." *The Christian Times*, April 18. Available at www.christiantimes.com/article/hbos.going.clear.scientology.documentary.5.5m.viewers.and.counting.film.slammed.as.john.travolta.stays.loyal/52118.htm. Accessed August 20, 2015.

Touretzky, David S. 2015. "The NOTs Scholars Homepage." Available at www.cs.cmu.edu/~dst/NOTs/index.html. Accessed July 10, 2015.

U.S. National Library of Medicine 2015. "Livertox: Clinical and Research Information on Drug-Induced Liver Injury." Available at http://livertox.nih.gov/Niacin.htm. Accessed August 19, 2015.

14 Scientology

From controversy to global expansion and recognition

Eric Roux

The story of Scientology, a religion relatively young at sixty years old, is quite a rich tale. This chapter focuses on the past twenty-five years, but with a prologue from the early 1980s, just before the death of Scientology's founder, L. Ron Hubbard, giving a broad overview.

The "struggling for survival" times

In 1984, L. Ron Hubbard was no longer involved in Church management affairs and had not been for years. His primary activity was to work on his research in order to complete his work regarding the Bridge to Total Freedom[1] that was the culmination of a life of research and that he left for all those who wished to travel it. At this time, the Church of Scientology, especially in the United States, was undergoing quite vicious attacks from personal injury lawyers attempting to obtain millions of dollars based on false allegations advanced by a handful of disaffected Scientologists, some of whom had a plan to close the Church down. Without entering too much into details, part of this plan was a tremendous number of civil trials instigated throughout America, on charges fabricated by Church detractors using former members to pretend they had been harmed by Scientology, and these false charges were repeated throughout every state in the United States.

Facing these attacks, Scientologists from all over the world decided to unite in order to guarantee that the Scientology religion could be practiced freely for all time and to defend the rights of man and the freedom of all religions. Scientologists from around the world gathered at Saint Hill Manor in East Grinstead, Sussex, England, in October 1984, recognizing the necessity to unite all Scientologists as one international body "to Unite, advance and protect the Scientology religion." They formed the International Association of Scientologists (IAS). They all signed what they called "The Pledge to Mankind," which starts with these words:

> Time and again, throughout the troubled history of civilization on this planet, new ideas, new religions and constructive thought have met with violent opposition. Such attacks come from those who would preserve the

status quo and particularly from those who seek to preserve and enhance their position through the domination, subjugation and even destruction of others. For this reason new religions have been born in blood at the cost of great sacrifice and suffering by adherents. It is only through a unity of purpose and unswerving commitment by a dedicated group that new ideas and new religions survive and expand.

Scientology has been in existence now for some thirty-four years. During that time it has suffered all manner of attacks from the forces of oppression in various countries. Yet Scientology has survived and expanded because of the dedication of its members and because it is a force for goodness and freedom which is easily recognized by men of goodwill.

(IAS 1984)

In Portland, Oregon, one particular trial turned bad for the Church in May 1985. The jury returned a civil verdict awarding $39 million in damages for a Scientology apostate, Julie Christofferson Titchbourne, who claimed to have been defrauded out of $3,000 in course fees in 1975 and reproached the Portland Church for not having improved her communication skills, intelligence, and creativity. The Church could not have afforded to pay the damages, even if it had used all of its reserves. Though more to the point, this trial was set up to serve as a precedent in the U.S. courts. With dozens of other similar trials ongoing, it represented the intention to bring about a complete bankruptcy of Churches of Scientology internationally. This was the purpose of the opponents of the Church, should the Portland trial decision have been upheld and the resulting precedent applied to other cases.

Then, through the work of the newly born IAS, 15,000 Scientologists from all over the world converged on Portland to protest this ruling, which they considered a denial of the protection guaranteed by the First Amendment of the U.S. Constitution. They called upon the presiding judge to overturn the ruling (Turner 1985). For some sixty days, they assembled for peaceful marches, concerts, and candlelight vigils, communicating with people to explain that Scientology really was far different from the misinformation spread by the media. The result was an unmitigated success. After having seen proof that the plaintiff had been held as a prisoner and "deprogrammed" by individuals hostile to new religious movements (Richardson 2004) before having filed her complaint, which the plaintiff herself acknowledged (Klunder 1985), the judge heard the testimony of a witness who was caught on tape bragging that he made up allegations he advanced against the Church to the government and who planned to plant false documents in Church files to "support" such allegations. Then the judge ruled that Scientology teachings were religious in nature, and overturned the judgment in July (Associated Press 1985). That decision took apart this particular strategy of the antagonists of the Church. The events surrounding the Christofferson case were the first in a long series of Scientology Religious Freedom Crusades and it was by no means the end of the battle in the United States. The Internal Revenue Service (IRS) had also started a determined campaign nationally against all the Churches of Scientology, refusing to allow them religious status, conducting fiscal harassment campaigns against every Church corporate entity, engaging in malicious rumor campaigns against Church leaders, harassing them by conducting fabricated charges and triggering bogus criminal investigations against them, as well as harassing 3,000 Scientologists individually through tax rulings simply because they were Scientologists.

In 1986, L. Ron Hubbard passed on. The Church not only had to deal with this, but also had to meet the challenge of finding its way through these extremely difficult legal and social circumstances, a critical test for any religious movement. As history has shown, this test was successfully passed, although few really knew what the Church had to endure during the following years. The battle with the IRS sometimes went to a point where the existence of the Church itself was endangered, and this continued to 1991. After the Department of Justice refused to bring a case based on the bogus claims advanced by the IRS and the IRS investigation was finally closed, the IRS agreed to conduct, at the insistence of the Church, a full and transparent examination (as opposed to biased) which lasted two years. This became what is likely the most thorough inquiry ever conducted of a religious movement, encompassing all of the Churches of Scientology's worldwide activities, including all financial records. Then, on October 1, 1993, the IRS issued a ruling recognizing the tax-exempt religious and charitable status of the Church of Scientology International – the church of the Scientology religion – and 150 affiliated churches, missions, and social betterment organizations.

The IRS rulings established that:

1 The Churches of Scientology and their related charitable and educational institutions are operated exclusively for recognized religious and charitable purposes.
2 The Churches of Scientology and their related charitable and educational institutions operate for the benefit of the public interest rather than the interests of private individuals.
3 No part of the net earnings of these Churches of Scientology and their related charitable and educational institutions inures to the benefit of any individual or non-charitable entity.
4 No part of the activities of the Churches of Scientology involve participation in any campaign for public office.
5 The purposes of these organizations do not violate fundamental public policy. (IRS letters, 1993, 1997)

Toward expansion and stressing the religious mission of the Church

This was of course a real turning point for Scientology not only in the United States, but worldwide. Indeed, even though Scientology had never ceased growing during these years (for example, Scientology centers could be found in fifty-two countries in 1980, and that number had expanded to seventy-four by 1992 [Melton, 2009]), this engagement with the IRS consumed a lot of attention from Scientology leaders and management, as well as many resources that would have otherwise been employed toward the growth of the religion were these attacks not carried out. So, when in 1993 the ecclesiastical leader of the Church, David Miscavige, announced to thousands of Scientologists in Los Angeles "The War is Over," he in fact announced (Newton 1993) that the real work of the Church could start. All the resources used to fight the battle with the IRS were now to be assigned to the fundamental mission of the Church: serving parishioners with Scientology spiritual technology all over the world, building new churches in every major city of the planet, conducting social betterment and humanitarian campaigns in every country or place where help was needed, and other programs dedicated to forwarding the aims of Scientology as laid out by its founder, L. Ron Hubbard: *A civilization without insanity, without criminals and without war, where the able can prosper and honest beings can have rights, and where Man is free to rise to greater heights* (Hubbard 1965).

The change was absolute. This was the start of a period of expansion for Scientology that has continued ever since. The United States became a "safe place" for Scientology, permitting Church management to focus on global expansion plans aimed at making Scientology available in its standard workable form according to the spiritual methodology laid out by its founder, all over the world.

The first thing to know about the way the Church of Scientology deals with any situation is that it is not done at random. An important part of the works written by L. Ron Hubbard is intended to give the policies and guidelines the Church must follow in order to keep growing and be able to fulfil its mission throughout the world and throughout the ages. These works are essentially what Scientologists call "the green volumes." The green volumes are a collection of very precise ecclesiastical administrative guidelines designed for giving Scientology a steady expansion, covering every function of the organization of the Church. These volumes represent more than 10,000 pages studied by Church staff members. (This body of knowledge is for the most part distinct from the religious technology that Hubbard wrote and that comprises the precise steps for attaining spiritual awareness and freedom.) While these volumes cover a wide range of activities, there is at least a basic principle on which all these policies are based: expansion. In his policy letter called "Expansion, Theory of Policy," published December 4, 1966, Hubbard wrote:

> It is an empirical (observed and proven by observation) fact that nothing remains exactly the same for ever. This condition is foreign to this universe. Things grow or they lessen. They cannot apparently maintain the same equilibrium or stability. Thus, things either expand or they contract. . . . This leaves expansion as the only positive action which tends to guarantee survival.
>
> (Hubbard 1966)

Most religions have understood at one point or another that in order to survive, they have to expand, and to organize themselves in one way or another. The various plans and programs the Church has undertaken for the past thirty years have been developed from L. Ron Hubbard's administrative and religious scriptures concerning expansion.

These programs have been originated and supervised by the Religious Technology Center (RTC), a nonprofit organization formed in 1982, during L. Ron Hubbard's lifetime, holding the ultimate ecclesiastical authority regarding the standard and pure application of L. Ron Hubbard's religious technology. It was Hubbard himself who entrusted that church with such a responsibility.

In 1983, Hubbard commented on RTC in a taped lecture called "Today and Tomorrow, the Proof":

> Recent surveys have been done on public and one of the main things that they are interested in is ensuring that the squirrels[2] get handled and off the lines. RTC is the organization that is effectively doing this. The response to RTC's handling of the squirrels has been excellent. . . .
>
> Scientology organizations were brought close to the brink and the new management salvaged them in grand style as you have heard. Very probably this team is the first truly competent independent management Scientology has ever had.
>
> BUT, can a power push against the Church happen again? Well, only if you fail to turn your back on squirrels and demand on-policy actions and HCOB[3] tech in all executives and if you support only those who work to keep Scientology working. My earnest advice is: only deal with or associate with those organizations licensed by RTC and auditors in good standing with the Church. Close your ears to false statements made by bad hats and thus really clear the planet.
>
> (Hubbard 1983)

So, while not being involved in the Church's day-to-day affairs, RTC inherited the duty to guarantee the purity and workability of Scientology far into the future. That is why it engaged in major plans and programs to restore, preserve, maintain, and keep uncorrupted the Scientology religious technology.

Delivering Scientology in its purest form

One of these major plans has been what Scientologists called the "Golden Age of Tech." "Tech" is a shortened form for "Technology," the whole body of Scientology religious techniques aimed at bringing total freedom to individuals as spiritual beings. The first stage of the Golden Age of Tech was implemented in May 1996, with the release of an entire body of training exercises aimed at enabling Scientology auditors (an auditor is a minister or minister-in-training of the Church of Scientology) to be trained far more effectively and efficiently in applying the religious procedures of Scientology technology. The goal of auditing is to restore the innate ability of oneself, the spiritual being. This is accomplished by: (1) helping individuals rid themselves of any spiritual disabilities; (2) increasing spiritual abilities. These Golden Age of Tech exercises had been compiled following instructions of the founder, L. Ron Hubbard, and their compilation had necessitated hundreds of thousands of hours of work, as thousands of exercises had to be developed to follow the instructions of Mr. Hubbard precisely regarding the large amount of technology contained in Scientology scriptures.

The 1996 launch of the Golden Age of Tech was followed by reviews of the way the "Bridge to Total Freedom" – the specific spiritual pathway within Scientology – was delivered to parishioners, in order to remove any unauthorized alterations which had crept in over time and slowed down the spiritual progress of Scientologists.

Then between 2005 and 2010, Scientologists experienced the completion of a twenty-five-year program to recover, verify, and restore the scripture of the Scientology religion. The quarter-century endeavor involved some 2 million man-hours to recover and make fully accessible all written and spoken words of L. Ron Hubbard. This completion has been called by Scientologists "The Golden Age of Knowledge." With the launch of The Golden Age of Knowledge in 2005 came the release of the recorded Congress Lectures, which were special events containing L. Ron Hubbard's announcements of each new milestone breakthrough in the research and development of Dianetics and Scientology. In 2007 came the release of the fully restored "Basics," Mr. Hubbard's eighteen books and 280 taped lectures comprising the core teachings of the Scientology religion. All these releases, which include the full audio restoration of all LRH lectures, were also translated, for many of them, into at least fifteen languages, although some of the basic materials have been translated into fifty languages. In the final days of 2009 came the release in English of L. Ron Hubbard's Advanced Clinical Course Lectures – another set of lectures on different spiritual subjects. In all, these materials comprise more than 1,000 lectures and 500 written publications chronicling the day-to-day record of L. Ron Hubbard's path of discovery in Dianetics and Scientology.

This review culminated in November 2013 when the Church announced the release of what is called the "Golden Age of Tech phase 2." All these projects were based on the original writings and lectures of the founder, amounting to tens of millions of words. They were studied in chronological order and then compared to existing manuscripts and other primary records, in order to find any departure from the originals. The final stage was to correct any departures from the original records and any impact it had on the delivery of Scientology to Scientologists. This has led to significant changes in the way the Bridge to Total Freedom is delivered to parishioners, both in regards to auditing and to the training of auditors, all of it now fully aligned with the intention and the writings of the founder. It has been the biggest and most important step of the history of Scientology regarding giving to Scientologists the purest technology possible, exactly as conceived by its founder. This project has been driven not so much by an ideological desire to have something in its original form but quite simply because, as Scientologists have experienced again and again, that when the technology is applied correctly, it works. Additions and subtractions by others are considered by Scientologists to do nothing but confuse and detract from the workability of Scientology religious technology.

In addition, a major auditing action never released previously, described by Ron Hubbard as able to put Scientologists into a new realm of ability enabling them to create a new world, was released for the first time. This auditing action can be now undergone by every Scientologist at a new building at the Scientology Headquarters in Clearwater, Florida (see below). This is called the Super Power Rundown (Freedom Magazine 2013), and since December 2013 thousands of Scientologists from all over the world have completed this.

Making Scientology religious services available to all through ideal churches

In parallel to these programs, another program has been run for some years in the world of Scientology. It's called the "Ideal Orgs" program ("Ideal Org" means ideal organization, a Scientology church that is established according to specific delineated "ideal" standards and is able to provide for its community as laid out in Scientology administrative and spiritual technologies). This program is aimed at making Scientology available to greater numbers of people and consists of opening new church buildings throughout the world, with each of these buildings being either newly built or purchased and fully renovated to meet the highest standards and full panoply of delivery of Scientology religious services. These buildings are designed to meet all the requirements as conceived by Hubbard, such requirements having been gleaned from the management and administrative methods outlined by him regarding how a Church of Scientology should be operated. An Ideal Org is configured to provide the full services of the Scientology religion to its parishioners, while also serving the community with social betterment and outreach programs. Each of these buildings is of adequate size to serve thousands of parishioners each week.

Actually, this program was based on an old wish and plan of Mr. Hubbard, when he started to speak about it in 1962 during a lecture called "Your Scientology orgs and what they do for you." He said:

> These are awfully good people in Central Organizations. These are terrific people. At a sacrifice of considerable income and a lot of other sacrifices, these fellows and girls stay on the job and get the job done. One could not render a high enough tribute to them, because it has not been easy and they have done it extremely well. And they're still there and they've still got the show on the road.
>
> And now we're thinking in terms of new buildings and designing new buildings all over the world. In other words, we've kept it there for a long time; now we're going to keep it there with exclamation points. We've even got the designs for these buildings.

Actually, it requires two types of building in one of these Central Organizations. It requires a city building, one that is downtown and rises straight up from the ground to some height. And it requires one out in the country which sprawls all over the place.

(Hubbard 1962)

To date, dozens of Ideal Orgs have opened their doors in major cities across four continents, and new ones are dedicated each month. For example, in December 2013, the first ideal org of Asia was opened in Taiwan before a gathering of 4,000 Scientologists, and blessed by a speech from the highest officials of the Taiwanese government, including the national policy advisor to the president of Taiwan, Liang-Chi Tan, who declared: "Your Church has carried a legacy of help in our land for more than two decades. As anyone would recall, when the mega 921 earthquake hit Taiwan, it was a disaster of immense magnitude. The Church of Scientology immediately dispatched volunteers to help handle the disaster. So it came as no surprise to me that you were presented by the President of Taiwan with the 'Good citizens, Good deeds' award for your work on that earthquake" (Tan 2013).

Since 2003, Ideal Orgs have opened their doors in Johannesburg, Madrid, San Francisco, New York City, London, Berlin, Malmo, Sweden, Dallas, Nashville, Rome, Washington, DC, Brussels, Quebec City, Las Vegas, a second one in Johannesburg, Los Angeles, Mexico City, Pasadena, Seattle, Melbourne, Moscow, Tampa, Florida, St. Paul, Minnesota, Inglewood in the Heart of the Afro-American community of Los Angeles, Hamburg, Sacramento, Cincinnati, San Jose, California, Orange County, California, Denver, Colorado, Phoenix, Arizona, Buffalo, New York, Los Gatos, California, Tel Aviv, Padova, Italy, Cambridge, Canada, Pretoria, South Africa, Portland, Oregon, and Sydney, Australia. And many more are lined up for the coming years (Scientology.org 2016). Furthermore, on November 17, 2013, after 2.5 million man-hours spent on its construction, a new building opened its doors at Scientology's spiritual headquarters in Clearwater, Florida. This building is 377,000 square feet, occupies a full city block, and has been called by Scientologists their twenty-first-century cathedral (Freedom Magazine 2013). It comprises sixty-two huge bronze sculptures describing the core tenets and beliefs of the Scientology religion. Moreover, and this is certainly the most important to Scientologists, this building allows a significant increase in the numbers of parishioners who can receive religious services at the spiritual headquarters every week – as well as providing the delivery for the first time of the L. Ron Hubbard auditing programs called Super Power Rundown and the Cause Resurgence Rundown, which Scientologists had anticipated for decades.

Humanitarian programs

After winning the "IRS battle," the Church engaged in far broader humanitarian programs, all of them supported by the IAS in one way or another. These international programs include anti-drug campaigns with the Foundation for a Drug-Free World; drug rehabilitation programs through Narconon; human rights education programs with the Youth for Human Rights International and United for Human Rights organizations and campaigns against illiteracy through Applied Scholastics. The Citizens Commission on Human Rights (cofounded by the Church and Thomas Szasz, Professor of Psychiatry Emeritus at the State University of New York Upstate Medical University in Syracuse) carries out watchdog and awareness programs to eradicate psychiatric abuses; criminal rehabilitation and restoration of human dignity projects are being done in prisons by Criminon; and moral values restoration campaigns are done by The Way to Happiness Foundation. All of these programs, supported by audiovisual productions, including public services announcements broadcast on TV all over the world, education kits, information booklets, and so forth, are nowadays reaching several million individuals every year, endorsed by governments, governmental agencies, partner NGOs, law enforcement agencies, and private sector companies all over the world (Scientology.org 2016).

In addition, the Volunteer Minister program was created in the 1970s by L. Ron Hubbard, and reached increased levels of activity over the past two decades. A Scientology volunteer minister is trained to bring spiritual assistance to anyone in any aspect of life, whether it is to increase his communication ability, his study skills, help raising children or save marriages, as well as dozens of other domains of intervention.

Moreover, volunteer ministers now form a global network of more than 200,000 trained ministers who can be mobilized in times of manmade or natural disasters. The mobilized teams work with governments, other relief organizations, and volunteer groups to help and provide material and spiritual aid on every continent. This "Volunteer Minister Disaster Response Team" was born out of the September 11, 2001, disaster in New York City, where more than 800 volunteer ministers worked with New York emergency teams for many weeks, seven days a week, day and night. They have intervened throughout the world, including in Southeast Asia after the 2004 tsunami, in Mississippi, Alabama, and Louisiana after Hurricanes Katrina and Rita, in Haiti after the 2010 earthquake, in Pakistan after the massive floods in 2010, in Fukushima after the earthquake and tsunami that destroyed the nuclear plant in March 2011, and in Bosnia helping rebuild entire villages after the May 2014 floods.

Conclusions

While this is just a rapid overview of these past thirty years of Scientology, it doesn't include many other developments that occurred within the Church during these years. There was a real turning point in Scientology's history in 1993 with the U.S. recognition. Internationally, after that turning point, the Church was able to concentrate on its real mission: to give Scientology to the world in its purest form, as well as serving the community with social betterment programs at an order of magnitude never reached before. Even if skirmishes still break out here and there, the recognition of Scientology as a bona fide religion has spread to many countries. To cover all the legal victories and government recognitions Scientology has had over the years would be another chapter, but it is worth mentioning the two last ones here. On October 17, 2013, in the Netherlands, the Appeal Court of Amsterdam, in addition to recognizing Scientology as an authentic religion, granted it public benefit status after having ruled that the purpose and objective of participating in Scientology religious services was no different than the purpose and objective of participating in the religious services of other religious institutions. In the United Kingdom, on December 11, 2013, the UK Supreme Court ruled that Scientology was a religion and that the London Church of Scientology chapel "is a place of meeting for religious worship within section 2 of the Places of Worship Registration Act" (UK Supreme Court 2013). The Supreme Court accordingly ordered that the Scientology chapel be registered as a place of worship and as a place for the solemnization of marriages, and in so doing brought the definition of religion, as viewed by the British courts, from the nineteenth to the twenty-first century. Here is part of the reasoning of the Court:

> 17. L Ron Hubbard identified eight human impulses which he termed dynamics of existence. In ascending order they are the urge of survival as an individual, the urge of survival through one's family, the urge of group survival, the urge of survival for all humankind, the urge of survival for all life forms, the urge of survival of the physical universe, the urge of survival for all spiritual beings and lastly the urge of existence as infinity. God is infinity but Scientologists do not describe God in anthropomorphic terms. All Scientology practices are aimed ultimately at complete affinity with the eighth dynamic or infinity. . . .
>
> 60. On the approach which I have taken to the meaning of religion, the evidence is amply sufficient to show that Scientology is within it.
>
> (UK Supreme Court 2013)

In conclusion, if one were to briefly summarize the changes that have occurred within the Church of Scientology over the past thirty years, a rather difficult exercise, it could be said that thirty years ago, the Church was struggling for its very existence because of the intensity of the attacks against it, but that since then, it has won a sufficient number of battles for this to no longer be the case and has reached the point where its existence is a foregone conclusion. It can now concentrate on the help it can bring to the peoples of the world, through its religious services delivered to a growing numbers of parishioners throughout 167 countries, and through its social betterment programs which now reach millions of people every year.

Notes

1 The Bridge to Total Freedom is the standard and exact route in Scientology that gradually leads an individual to spiritual freedom. It's comprised of many steps that help the individual attain a series of higher states of existence and spiritual skills on a gradient basis.

2 A squirrel in Scientology is the one who alters Scientology due to their non-comprehension of it and goes off into weird practices instead of applying standard technology. In a Professional Auditor Bulletin 90, written in June 1956, L. Ron Hubbard wrote: 'People such as our best-known squirrels are perfectly willing to snatch our hard won materials and misuse them, but they are not willing to support the effort which brought these materials into being. In other words, their existence is parasitic.' The word comes from the definition of 'to squirrel': Move in an inquisitive and restless manner (Oxford Dictionary).

3 HCOB means Hubbard Communications Office Bulletin. These are writings on different aspects of spiritual development, and much of Scientology's religious technology is contained in this form of communication, which was, for the most part, made freely available to Scientologists as the writings were released.

References

Associated Press, July 16, 1985. Judge Upsets $39-Million Award against Scientology: Lawsuit by Ex-member Cited Fraud. Available at: http://articles.latimes.com/1985–07–16/news/mn-6837_1_circuit-judge. Accessed August 25, 2015.

Freedom Magazine, December 2013. The FLAG Issue. CoS International.

Hubbard, L. Ron, 1962. Your Scientology Orgs and What They Do for You, Conference Given in Washington DC in September 1962. In the *Clearing Success Congress*, Golden Era Production.

――― September 1965. The Aims of Scientology. Available at: www.scientology.org/what-is-scientology/the-scientology-creeds-and-codes/the-aims-of-scientology.html. Accessed August 25, 2015.

――― 1966. Hubbard Communication Office Policy Letter: Expansion, Theory of Policy, Published December 4, 1966. In *Organization Executive Course, Volume 0*, New Era Publication International.

――― 1983. Today and Tomorrow, the Proof. Taped lecture in possession of the author.

International Association of Scientologists (IAS), October 7, 1984. The Pledge to Mankind, Saint Hill Manor. *Impact Magazine 120*, 75.

IRS letters, 1993. Issued on October 1, 1993. Reference: E:EO:R:2. Available at the IRS Public Information Reading Room in the National Office of the IRS. In possession of the author.

――― 1997. Issued on May 29, 1993. Written by Steven T Miller, Special Assistant for Exempt Organizations Matters of the IRS. In possession of the author.

Klunder, Jan, May 19, 1985. Scientologists Converge on Portland for Protest: Thousands to Assail Award of $39 Million to Ex-member in Suit. *LA Times*. Available at: http://articles.latimes.com/1985–05–19/news/mn-9212_1_church-member. Accessed August 25, 2015.

Melton, Gordon, 2009. Birth of a religion. In James R. Lewis, ed. *Scientology*. Oxford: Oxford University Press, 29.

Newton, Jim, October 13, 1993. Tax-Free Status OKd for Church of Scientology. *Los Angeles Times*. Available at: http://articles.latimes.com/1993–10–13/news/mn-45325_1_tax-exempt-status. Accessed August 25, 2015.

Richardson, James T., 2004. *Regulating Religion: Case Studies from Around the Globe*. Kluwer Norwell, MA, Academic/Plenum Publishers, 478–9.

Scientology.org 2016. David Miscavige: At the Helm in the Era of Expansion. Available at www.scientology.org/david-miscavige/meeting_the_global_demand_for_the_scientology_religion.html. Accessed April 11, 2016.

Tan, Liang-Chi, December 7, 2013. Speech at the Grand-Opening of the Kaohsiung Church of Scientology. Available at: www.scientologynews.org/press-releases/grand-opening-scientology-ideal-organization-kaohsiung-taiwan.html. Accessed August 25, 2015.

Turner, Wallace, June 13, 1985. Scientologists Scale Back Protests over Portland Jury Verdict. *New York Times*. Available at: www.nytimes.com/1985/06/13/us/scientologists-scale-back-protests-over-portland-jury-verdict.html. Accessed August 25, 2015.

UK Supreme Court, December 11, 2013. Hodkin and Another v Registrar General of Births, Deaths and Marriages. Available at: www.supremecourt.uk/decided-cases/docs/UKSC_2013_0030_Judgment.pdf. Accessed August 25, 2015.

Index

AFF (American Family Foundation) 12, 18, 142, 143, 144, 145, 146, 147, 148
AGPF (Aktion für Geistige und Psychische Freiheit) 13
anti-cult movement 4, 9, 81, 141, 147
apostates 11

Berg, David Brandt (aka "Mo" "Moses David") 95, 97, 98, 102, 103, 105, 109, 111
Bhagavad-Gita 136, 148n
Bhaktivedenta, A. C. (Swami Prabhupada) 135, 138, 139, 140, 141, 143, 146
bhakti-yoga 136, 137
Black Rose (Crna ruža) 83, 87, 88
blessing, the (Unification Church) 128
brainwashing 3, 4, 11, 12, 15, 16, 18, 25, 26, 27, 38, 47, 51, 57, 59, 71, 82, 88, 89, 141, 145, 148n, 149n
Branch Davidians 37, 41
Bridge to Total Freedom (Church of Scientology) 155, 156, 165, 170

CAM (Cult Awareness Movement) 9, 10, 11, 12, 13, 15, 18, 81, 82, 89
CAN (Cult Awareness Network) 12, 18, 38, 144
CESNUR (Center for Studies on New Religions) 2, 3, 14, 23–30, 76
CFF (Citizens Freedom Foundation) 36, 38
charisma 59
Children of God/The Family International 4, 15, 36, 95–106, 108–18
Christian Science 34, 35, 45
Church of Jesus Christ of Latter-day Saints (Mormons) 34, 35, 38, 43, 45, 47, 114, 149n
Church of Scientology 5, 9, 18, 70, 71, 83, 85, 86, 87, 88, 89, 114, 152–62, 165–74
CISK (The Center for Information on Sects and Cults) 81, 84, 85, 89

Completed Testament Age 128
Conversion 46, 56, 57
counter-cult movement 82
Christadelphians 3, 44
cult 10, 35
"cult apologists" 1, 16, 27, 37, 57, 88, 90
cultic milieu 56
"Cult wars" 2, 4, 33–41
cult watching groups 82

Danish Dialogue Center 13
deprogramming 14, 16, 20, 38, 57, 82, 142, 143, 144
deviance amplification 16
Divine Principle 121, 125, 127, 128, 130, 132
Dujmič-Delcourt, Branka 84

ECtHR (European Court of Human Rights) 69, 70, 71, 75, 83

FAIR (Family Action Information Rescue) 12
FBI (U.S. Federal Bureau of Investigation) 19
FECRIS (European Federation of Centers of Research and Information on Sectarianism) 84, 85, 86, 89
"Flirty Fishing" 97, 98, 99, 110
FREECOG (The Parents' Committee to Free Our Children from the Children of God) 12, 36, 112
Freezone Scientology 5, 152–62

Guardian Angels, the 81, 87, 88, 89

"Heaven's Gate" 3, 37, 46, 57
Holy Spirit Association for the Unification of World Christianity 126
Hubbard, L. Ron 5, 154, 156, 158, 165, 167, 168, 169, 170, 171

ICSA (International Cultic Studies Association) *see* AFF
Ideal Orgs (Church of Scientology) 171, 172
INFORM (Information Network Focus on Religious Movements) 4, 14, 18, 19, 26, 76
IRS (U.S. Internal Revenue Service) 5, 154, 166, 167, 168
ISAR (Institute for the Study of American Religions) 14, 26
ISKCON (International Society for Krishna Consciousness) 5, 11, 15, 36, 47, 71, 83, 134–48

Jehovah's Witnesses 3, 35, 43, 44, 45, 50, 51n, 70, 71, 72
Jonestown 37, 46, 58, 99, 108, 112

Kelly, Steve (aka "Peter Amsterdam") 95, 99, 101, 104, 105, 108, 115

Law of Love (Children of God) 110
legal cases about new religions 4, 69–76

Martin, Walter 46
Mind control 12
Miscavage, David 152, 155, 160, 161, 162, 168
Moon, Rev. Sun Myung 4, 121, 123, 124, 125, 127; as True Parent 4, 128
Moral panics 16, 19

Narconon (Church of Scientology) 158, 159, 160, 173
New CAN (new Cult Awareness Network) 18

Oneida Perfectionists 34

Patrick, Ted 12, 144
Peoples Temple 10, 36, 47
Pikareum ritual (Unification Church) 129

Rathbun, Marty 155, 156, 162
Reboot, the 4, 100, 101, 102, 103, 104, 105, 109, 111, 116, 118
Religious Communities Act (Croatia) 84
religious freedom 5, 69
RFRA (U.S. Religious Freedom Restoration Act) 69, 73, 75
RLUIPA (U.S. Religious Land Use and Institutionalized Persons Act) 69, 74
ROGs (Research Oriented Groups) 14
Ron's Orgs 154, 155, 160, 162
RTC (Religious Technology Center, Church of Scientology) 169

sect 10
secularization 57
Seventh-Day Adventists 45, 52n
Shakers, the 34
spiritualism 34, 35, 44, 45
"squirrel" 155, 169
"suppressive person" 152, 154, 156, 157
Swedenborgians 43, 44

Theosophy 29, 34, 35
Transcendental Meditation 83, 87

UNADFI (Union Nationale des Associations de Défense des Familes et d l'Individu) 13
Unification Church/movement 1, 3, 4, 5, 9, 15, 46, 47, 48, 71, 88, 121–32
U.S. Supreme Court 69, 73

Vaishnavism 134, 135, 136, 138, 139, 142, 148n, 149n
Van Baalen, J. K. 45

Zerby, Karen (aka "Maria Fontaine") 95, 98, 99, 101, 104, 105, 108